ALSO BY ADAM NICOLSON

WHY HOMER MATTERS

WHY HOMER MATTERS

Adam Nicolson

A JOHN MACRAE BOOK

Henry Holt and Company   New York

A John Macrae Book
Henry Holt and Company, LLC
Publishers since 1866
175 Fifth Avenue
New York, New York 10010
www.henryholt.com

Henry Holt® and 🐂® are registered trademarks of Henry Holt and Company, LLC.

Gary Beckman (ed.), excerpts from *Hittite Diplomatic Texts, Second Edition.* Reprinted with the permission of Society of Biblical Literature.

Jeremy Black, excerpt from the Sumerian poem from "Some Structural Features of Sumerian Narrative Poetry" in *Mesopotamian Epic Literature: Oral or Aural?,* edited by M. E. Vogelzang and H. L. J. Vanstiphout. Reprinted with the permission of The Edwin Mellen Press.

Edmond and Jules Goncourt, excerpt from *The Goncourt Journals,* edited and translated by Robert Baldick. Copyright © 1962 by the Estate of Robert Baldick. Used by permission of *The New York Review of Books.*

Excerpt from A. Heidel, trans., *The Gilgamesh Epic and Old Testament Parallels.* Copyright 1946, 1949 by The University of Chicago. Reprinted by permission of The University of Chicago Press.

Homer, excerpt from *The Iliad,* with parallel translation by A. T. Murray, revised by W. F. Wyatt. Copyright © 1999 by the President and Fellows of Harvard College. Reprinted by permission of Harvard University Press. Excerpts from *The Iliad of Homer,* translated by Richmond Lattimore. Copyright 1951, © 2011 by The University of Chicago. Reprinted with the permission of The University of Chicago Press. Excerpts from *The Iliad,* translated by Robert Fagles. Copyright © 1990 by Robert Fagles. Used by permission of Viking Penguin, a division of Penguin Group (USA) Inc. Excerpts from *The Odyssey,* with parallel translation by A. T. Murray, revised by G. E. Dimock. Copyright © 1999 by the President and Fellows of Harvard College. Reprinted with the permission of Harvard University Press. Excerpts from *The Odyssey,* translated by Richmond Lattimore. Copyright © 1965, 1967 by Richmond Lattimore. Reprinted by permission of HarperCollins Publishers Inc. Excerpts from *The Odyssey,* translated by Robert Fagles. Copyright © 1996 by Robert Fagles. Used by permission of Viking Penguin, a division of Penguin Group (USA) Inc.

Christopher Logue, excerpt from "The Iliad: Book XVI. An English Version" from *War Music.* Copyright © 1997 by Christopher Logue. Reprinted by permission of Farrar, Straus & Giroux, LLC, and Faber and Faber, Ltd.

Edwin Muir, excerpt from "The Horses" from *Collected Poems.* Copyright © 1960 by Willa Muir. Reprinted with the permission of Oxford University Press, Ltd., and Faber & Faber, Ltd.

R. B. Parkinson (ed. and trans.), excerpt from "The Tale of Sinuhe" from *The Tale of Sinuhe and Other Egyptian Poems 1940–1640 BC.* Copyright © 1997 by R. B. Parkinson. Reprinted by permission of Oxford University Press, Ltd.

Milman Parry, excerpts from *The Making of Homeric Verse: The Collected Papers of Milman Parry,* edited by Adam Parry. Copyright © 1971 by Oxford University Press, Inc. Reprinted by permission of Oxford University Press, Ltd.

Excerpt from Parry Conversation no. 6698 in *An eEdition of The Wedding of Mustajbey's Son Bećirbey,* as performed by Halil Bajgorić, edited and translated by John Miles Foley, www.oraltradition.org. Reprinted by permission.

George Seferis, excerpt from "Memory II" from Logbook III in *Complete Poems,* translated and edited by Edmund Keeley and Philip Sherrard. Copyright © 1995 by Princeton University Press. Reprinted by permission of Princeton University Press.

M. L. West, excerpt from *Lives of Homer* in *Homeric Hymns,* with parallel translation by M. L. West. Copyright © 2003 by the President and Fellows of Harvard College. Reprinted by permission of Harvard University Press.

William Butler Yeats, excerpt from "Among School Children" from *The Poems of W. B. Yeats: A New Edition,* edited by Richard J. Finneran. Copyright 1933 by Macmillan Publishing Company, renewed © 1961 by Georgie Yeats. Reprinted with the permission of Simon & Schuster, Inc.

The maps were done by HL Studios.

Library of Congress Cataloging-in-Publication Data

ISBN: 978-1-62779-179-3

Henry Holt books are available for special promotions and premiums. For details contact: Director, Special Markets.

First Edition 2014

Designed by Kelly Too

Printed in the United States of America
1   3   5   7   9   10   8   6   4   2

For
Sarah Raven
Molly Nicolson
Rosie Nicolson
Ben Nicolson
William Nicolson
Thomas Nicolson

CONTENTS

ILLUSTRATIONS

Minoan Kamares eggshell ware cup. *(Heraklion Archaeological Museum, Crete. Leemage/ UIG via Getty Images)*

Ivory cosmetics case in the form of a duck. *(© The Trustees of the British Museum. All rights reserved. Photo by Adam Nicolson)*

Minoan bath, mid-fourteenth century BC. *(© Carlos Collection of Ancient Art, Emory University)*

Dionysus on a boat, surrounded by dolphins, 530 BC. *(Staatliche Antikensammlung, Munich. Ann Ronan Pictures/Print Collector/Getty Images)*

TEXT ILLUSTRATIONS

Mural from Palace of Nestor at Pylos. *(Courtesy of the Department of Classics, University of Cincinnati)*

Rue Contrescarpe-Dauphine, ca. 1866, by Charles Marville. *(Courtesy of Philippe Mellot)*

Draft of Keats's sonnet "On First Looking Into Chapman's Homer," October 1816. *(Courtesy of the Houghton Library, Harvard University)*

The title page of the 1788 *Iliad* edited by Villoison. *(Courtesy of the Houghton Library, Harvard University)*

Detail from p. 111 of the Venetus A scholia. *(Center for Hellenic Studies. © 2007, Biblioteca Nazionale Marciana, Venice, Italy)*

Milman Parry. *(Courtesy of the Milman Parry Collection of Oral Literature, Harvard University)*

Bégan Lyútsa Nikshitch, photographed by Milman Parry. *(Courtesy of the Milman Parry Collection of Oral Literature, Harvard University)*

Bronze spearheads. *(Museo Archeologico Paolo Orsi, Syracuse. Photo by Adam Nicolson)*

The Uffington White Horse commands the site of a first-century BC Celtic fort, Uffington, Oxfordshire, England. *(James P. Blair/National Geographic/Getty Images)*

Back of a first-century BC gold Celtic stater of the Parisii or Quarisii (Paris region). *(Dea Picture Library/De Agostini/Getty Images)*

Sophia Schliemann, bedecked with diadem from Troy found by Heinrich Schliemann. *(Time Life Pictures/Mansell/Time Life Pictures/Getty Images)*

WHY HOMER MATTERS

The Bronze Age World

N

Faeroes

SWEDEN

Baltic
Sea

Orkney Is.

Stornoway
Hebrides

North Sea

DENMARK

Bernstorf

Berlin

BELARUS

County
Durham

Mayo
IRELAND   BRITAIN
Llandissilio   Oxford   Cambridge
Baltimore   London
            Wiltshire Kent
Cornwall
Falmouth

Leipzig

Bohemia

Pripiat
marshes
Karagod

Dniester

Heidelberg

Paris

Stuttgart
Munich

Vienna

HUNGARY

The Carpathians

Atlantic Ocean

The Alps

Milan

Venice

Florence

ROMANIA
TRANSYLVANIA

Danube

Massalia

Elba

Tuscany
Latium

ITALY

BOSNIA-
HERZEGOVINA

Bijelo Polje

MONTENEGRO

BULGARIA

Galicia

Porto

SPAIN
Madrid   El Pozuelo

Extremadura
Badajoz   Sierra de Aracena
Chinflón   Guadalquivir Córdoba
              Andalusia
Straits of
Gibraltar

Sardinia

Rome
Naples

Sicily

MACEDONIA

ALBANIA

Carthage

Mediterranean Sea

Troy
GREECE   Aegean
Athens   Sea
Mycenae
Izmir

Ionian Sea

Crete

FOREWORD

There is a pair of linked questions at the heart of this book: Where does Homer come from? And why does Homer matter? These ancient poems can be daunting and difficult, but I have no doubt that their account of war and suffering can still speak to us of the role of destiny in life, of cruelty, humanity, its frailty and the pains of existence. That they do is a mystery. Why is it that something conceived in the eastern Mediterranean Bronze Age, maybe four thousand years ago, as foreign as the Dayak, as distant as Vanuatu, can still exert its grip on us? How can we be so intimate with something so far away?

Perhaps it is a mistake to give the answer before the questions are properly asked, but this is complicated country, and an idea of the destination is worth having. Besides, it is a Homeric technique to tell the story before it begins. And so, if you ask why and how the Homeric poems emerged when they did, and why and how Homer can mean so much now, the answer to both questions is the same: because Homer tells us how we became who we are.

That is not the usual modern answer. The current orthodoxy is that the *Iliad* and the *Odyssey* are both products of the eighth century BC, or thereabouts, early Iron Age Greece, a time that has been called the Greek Renaissance. In the preceding half millennium, Greek civilization had largely sunk into isolated pockets of poverty. Many of the islands in the Aegean were deserted. One or two had remained rich and kept up links with the Near East, but the great palaces of an earlier Greece had fallen into ruin. But for reasons that have yet to be explained, the eighth century saw a widespread revival. The population of Greece and the islands began to grow. The tempo of life quickened. The art of making bronze, dependent on imported tin, was revived for the first time in four centuries. Colonies, trade, improved ships, gymnasiums, coinage, temples, cities, pan-Hellenic competitions at Olympia (the first, traditionally, in 776 BC), the art of writing, of depicting the human figure on pottery and in the round, the first written law codes, the dating of history, the first tentative moves toward the formation of city-states—every one of these aspects of a renewed civilization quite suddenly appeared all over the eighth-century Aegean. Homer, in this view, was the product of a new, dynamic, politically inventive and culturally burgeoning moment in Greek history. Homer was the poet of a boom.

I see it differently: my Homer is a thousand years older. His power and poetry derive not from the situation of a few emergent states in the eighth-century Aegean, but from a far bigger and more fundamental historic moment, in the centuries around 2000 BC, when early Greek civilization crystallized from the fusion of two very different worlds: the semi-nomadic, hero-based culture of the Eurasian steppes to the north and west of the Black Sea, and the sophisticated, authoritarian and literate cities and palaces of the eastern Mediterranean. Greekness—and eventually Europeanness—emerged from the meeting and melding of those worlds. Homer is the trace of that encounter—in war, despair and eventual reconciliation at Troy in the *Iliad*, in flexibility and mutual absorption in the *Odyssey*. Homer's urgency comes from the pain associated with that clash of worlds and his immediacy from the eternal principles at stake: what matters more, the individual or the community, the city or the hero? What is life, something of everlasting value or a transient and hopeless irrelevance?

The idea I have pursued is that the Homeric poems are legends shaped around the arrival of a people—the people who through this very process would grow to be the Greeks—in what became their Mediterranean homeland. The poems are the myths of the origin of Greek consciousness, not as a perfect but as a complex, uneasy thing. As a civilization, what emerged in Greece was distinct from both the northern steppelands of the Bronze Age and the autocratic bureaucracies of the Near East, and fused qualities of both. Homer is a foundation myth, not of man nor of the natural world, but of the way of thinking by which the Greeks defined themselves, the frame of mind which made them who they were, one which, in many ways, we have inherited. The troubled world described by Homer remains strangely familiar.

This is also a book about epic poetry, and the value of epic in our lives. Epic is not an act of memory, not merely the account of what people are able to recall, since human memory only lasts three generations: we know something of our grandparents but almost nothing, emotionally, viscerally, of what happened in the generations before them. Nor is it a kind of history, an objective laying out of what occurred in a past to which we have little or no access. Epic, which was invented after memory and before history, occupies a third space in the human desire to connect the present to the past: it is the attempt to extend the qualities of memory over the reach of time embraced by history. Epic's purpose is to make the distant past as immediate to us as our own lives, to make the great stories of long ago beautiful and painful now.

A wonderful painting of epic itself survives from Mycenaean Greece. In the summer of 1939, the University of Cincinnati archaeologist Carl Blegen, along with a Greek team, began excavating the Mycenaean palace of Pylos, in the southwestern Peloponnese. In the great columned room at the center of the palace, Blegen discovered, in pieces on the floor, where it had been dumped by the fire that brought the Mycenaean world to an end around 1200 BC, a revelatory fresco.

Against a ragged background, perhaps a rough, mountainous horizon, a poet—call him Homer—sits on a luminous, polychromed rock, a nightclub idea of a rock, dressed in a long striped robe with the sleeves of his overshirt coming almost halfway down his bare brown arms. His hair is braided, tendrils of it running down his neck and onto his back. He looks washed. Everything about him is alert, his eye bright and open, his body poised and taut, upright, ready. In his arms he holds a large five-stringed lyre, the fingers of his right hand plucking at those strings, which bend to his touch.

Against the florid red of the wall behind him—the color of living, not dried, blood, the red of life—is the most astonishing part of this image: an enormous pale bird, the color of the bard's robe, the feathers of its wings half delineated in the red that surrounds it, its eye as bright and open as Homer's, its body larger than his, its presence in the room huge and buoyant, nothing insubstantial about it, making its way out into the world, leaving Homer's own static singing figure behind.

The bird is poetry itself taking wing, so big, so much stronger than little Homer with his hairdo and his fingers on the lyre. It is the bird of eloquence, the "winged words," *epea pteroenta*, which the Homeric heroes speak to each other, *epea* having the same root as "epic," *pteroenta* meaning "feathered": light, mobile, airy, communicative. Meaning and beauty take flight from Homer's song.

It is one of the most extraordinary visualizations of poetry ever created, its life entirely self-sufficient as it makes its way out across that ragged horizon. There is nothing whimsical or misty about it; it has an undeniable other reality in flight in the room. There is a deep paradox here, one that is central to the whole experience of Homer's epics. Nothing is more insubstantial than poetry. It has no body, and yet it persists with its subtleties whole and its sense of the reality of the human heart uneroded while the palace of which this fresco was a part lies under the thick layer of ash from its burning in 1200 BC. Nothing with less substance than epic, nothing more lasting. Homer, in a miracle of transmission from one end of human civilization to the other, continues to be as alive as anything that has ever lived.

Homer is no wild, gothic figure. He is shown supremely controlled, as organized and calmly present as anything in this civilized place, with its great storerooms, its archive center and its beautifully dressed and fragrant inhabitants. He is civility itself. By the time this fresco was painted, the Greeks had been able to write for about 250 years, running sophisticated palace-based economies, with record-keeping bureaucracies to organize tax and military service, and to administer complex commercial and quasi-imperial relations across the eastern Mediterranean.

If that is the world in which Homer sang, it is not the world he sang about, which was much older, rougher, more elemental. He sang of the past that the occupants of this palace had left behind. That time gap allows one to see the Homeric poems as I think they should be seen: as the violence and sense of strangeness of about 1800 BC recollected in the tranquillity of about 1300 BC, preserved through the Greek Dark Ages and written down (if not in a final form) in about 700 BC. Homer reeks of long use. His wisdom, his presiding, godlike presence over the tales he tells, is the product of deep retrospect, not immediate reportage. His poetry embodies the air of incorporated time, as rounded as something that for centuries has rolled back and forth on the stony beaches of Greece. But it is also driven by the demands of grief, a clamoring and desperate anxiety about the nature of existence and the pains of mortality. This is the story of beginnings, and that feeling for trouble is the engine at the heart of it.

This book will make its way back toward that fresco, looking for Homer anywhere he might be found, in my own and many others' reactions to the poems, in life experiences, in archaeology and in the landscapes where the Homeric ghosts can still be heard. It is a passionate pursuit, because these epics are a description, through a particular set of lenses, of what it is like to be alive on earth, its griefs, triumphs, sufferings and glories. These are poems that address life's moments of revelation. Here you will find "the neon edges of the sea," as Christopher Logue described the waves on the Trojan beach; the horror of existence, where "Warm'd in the brain the smoking weapon lies," as Pope translated one murder in the *Iliad*; and its transfixing strangeness—the corona-light in the scarcely opened helmet slits of Achilles's owl-like eyes, which Logue saw burning "like furnace doors ajar."

In all the walking and thinking this book has given me, no moment remains more lasting in my mind than an evening on a small rocky peninsula near Tolo on the southeastern coast of the Peloponnese. I had been thinking about George Seferis, the Greek poet and diplomat who won the Nobel Prize in 1963, and who had come here before the Second World War, when archaeologists were discovering that this little stony protuberance into the Aegean was the acropolis of Asinē, a place entirely forgotten, except that it had survived in the *Iliad* as a name, one of the cities from which Greek warriors had set out for the siege at Troy.

The sea in the bay that evening was a mild milk-gray. The puttering of the little diesel-driven fans that keep the air moving through the orchards on a frosty night came from the orange groves inland. The sky promised rain. Sitting by the sea squills and the dry grasses blowing in the wind off the Gulf of Argolis, I read what Seferis had said about our relationship to the past. "The poem is everywhere," he wrote. Our own imaginative life

> sometimes travels beside it
> Like a dolphin keeping company for a while

With a golden sloop in the sunlight,
then vanishing again.

That glowing, if passing, connection is also what this book is about, the moment when the dolphin is alongside you, unsummoned and as transient, as Seferis also said,

"as the wings of the wind moved by the wind."

1 · MEETING HOMER

One evening ten years ago I started to read Homer in English. With an old friend, George Fairhurst, I had just sailed from Falmouth to Baltimore in southwest Ireland, 250 miles across the Celtic Sea. We had set off three days earlier in our wooden ketch, the *Auk*, forty-two feet from stem to stern, a vessel which had felt big enough in Falmouth, not so big out in the Atlantic.

It had been a ruinous journey. A mile or so out from the shelter of Falmouth we realized our instruments were broken, but we had been preparing for too long, were hungry to go, and neither of us felt like turning back. A big storm came through that night, force 8 gusting 9 to 10, west of Scilly, and we sailed by the stars when it was clear, by the compass in the storm, four hours on, four hours off, for that night, the next day and the following night. The seas at times had been huge, the whole of the bow plunging into them, burying the bowsprit up to its socket, solid water coming over the foredeck and driving back toward the wheel, so that the side-decks were like mill-sluices, running with the Atlantic.

After forty hours we arrived. George's face looked as if he had been in a fight, flushed and bruised, his eyes sunk and hollow in it. We dropped anchor in the middle of Baltimore harbor, its still water reflecting the quayside lights, only our small wake disturbing them, and I slept for sixteen hours straight. Now, the following evening, I was lying in my bunk, the *Auk* tied up alongside the Irish quay, with the *Odyssey*, translated by the great American poet-scholar Robert Fagles, in my hand.

I had never understood Homer as a boy. At school his poems were taught to us in Greek, as if they were a branch of math. The master drew the symbols on the green chalkboard, and we ferreted out the sense line by line, picking bones from fish. The archaic nature of Homer's vocabulary, the pattern of long and short syllables in the verse, the remote and uninteresting nature of the gods, like someone else's lunchtime account of a dream from the night before—what was that to any of us? Where was the life in it? How could this remoteness compare to the urgent realities of our own lives, our own lusts and anxieties? The difficulties and strangeness of the Greek were little more than a prison of obscurity to me, happily abandoned once the exam was done. Homer stayed irrelevant.

Now I had Fagles's words in front of me. Half idly, I had brought his translation of the *Odyssey* with me on the *Auk*, as something I thought I might look at on my own sailing journey in the North Atlantic. But as I read, a man in the middle of his life, I suddenly saw that this is not a poem about *then* and *there*, but *now* and *here*. The poem describes the inner geography of those who hear it. Every aspect of it is grand metaphor. Odysseus is not sailing on the Mediterranean but through the fears and desires of a man's life. The gods are not distant creators but elements within us: their careless pitilessness, their flaky and transient interests, their indifference, their casual selfishness, their deceit, their earth-shaking footfalls.

I read Fagles that evening, and again as we sailed up the west coast of Ireland. I began to see Homer as a guide to life, even as a kind of scripture. The sea in the *Odyssey* is out to kill you—at one point Hermes, the presiding genius of Odysseus's life, says, "Who would want to cross the unspeakable vastness of the sea? There are not even any cities there"—but hidden within it are all kinds of delicious islands, filled with undreamed-of delights, lovely girls and beautiful fruits, beautiful landscapes where you don't have to work, fantasy lands, each in their different way seducing and threatening the man who chances on them. But every one is bad for him. Calypso, a goddess, unbelievably beautiful, makes him sleep with her night after night, for seven years; Circe feeds him delicious dinners for a whole year, until finally one of his men asks him what he thinks he is doing. If he goes on like this, none of them will ever see their homes again. And is that what he wants?

In part I saw the *Odyssey* as the story of a man who is sailing through his own death: the sea is deathly, the islands are deathly, he visits Hades at the very center of the poem and he is thought dead by the people who love him at home, a pile of white bones rotting on some distant shore. He longs for life, and yet he cannot find it. When he hears stories told of his own past, he cannot bear it, wraps his head in his "sea-blue" cloak and weeps for everything he has lost.

It was Odysseus I fell in love with that summer as we sailed north to the Hebrides, Orkney and the Faroes: the many-wayed, flickering, crafty man, "the man of twists and turns," as Fagles calls him, translating the Greek word *polytropos*, the man driven off course, the man who suffers many pains, the man who is heartsick on the open sea. His life itself is a twisting, and maybe, I thought, that is his destiny: he can never emerge into the plain calm of a resolution. The islands in his journey are his own failings. Home, Ithaca, is the longed-for moment when those failings will at last be overcome. Odysseus's muddle is his beauty.

He is no victim. He suffers, but he does not buckle. His virtue is his elasticity, his rubber vigor. If he is pushed, he bends, but he bends back, and that half-giving strength was to me a beautiful model for a man. He is all navigation, subtlety, invention, dodging the rocks, storytelling, cheating and survival. He can be resolute, fierce and destructive when need be, and clever, funny and loving when need be. There is no requirement to choose between these qualities; Odysseus makes them all available.

Like Shakespeare and the Bible, we all know his stories in advance, but one in particular struck me that summer sailing on the *Auk*. We had left the Arans late the evening before, and George had taken her all night up the dark of the Galway coast. We changed places at dawn, and in that early morning, with a cup of tea in my hand and the sun rising over the Irish mainland, I took her north, heading for the Inishkeas and the corner of County Mayo, before turning there and making for Scotland.

The wind was a big easterly, coming in gusts over the Mayo hills, the sun white and heatless. George and my son Ben, who had joined us, were asleep below. There were shearwaters cruising the swells beside us, black, liquid, effortless birds, like the sea turned aerial, and a fulmar now and then hung in the slot between the headsail and the main, flying with us on the current of air. The *Auk* surged on the wind that morning, heeling out into the Atlantic, churning her way north, horselike in her strength. I don't know when I have felt so happy.

Steering across the swells, holding the wheel against them as they came through, releasing it as they fell away, I tied the great Robert Fagles translation of the *Odyssey* on the compass binnacle, holding it open with a bungee cord against the wind. That morning I read the story of the Sirens. Just as we do, Odysseus knows he will be exposed to the songs that the strange, birdlike creatures sing to mariners and with which they lure passing ships onto the shore, wrecking them there and then leaving the men to linger until they die. The only way Odysseus can get past the Sirens is to cut up a round cake of beeswax, knead it in his hands, softening the wax in the heat of the sun, and then press plugs of it into the ears of the sailors. Once they are deafened, he has himself lashed to the mainmast, so that any desire he may have to steer toward the delicious honeyed voices can have no effect on his men. Only if he is powerless can he listen to them singing from their meadow, as Robert Fagles described it, "starred with flowers."

That meadow of death is the most desirable place any man could imagine. It is yet another island into which a man might long to sink and die. A dead calm falls on the sea. The men brail up the sail and then sit to their oars. The Sirens, just within shouting distance of the ship, taunt Odysseus as he passes. They can give him wisdom if he will come to them and listen. If he will let them, they will make him understand. They press on him the comfort and beauty of what they have to offer. They sing to him, and Odysseus longs for them, his heart *throbbing* for them, as Fagles says, and with his eyebrows gestures to the crew to set him free. But the crew won't respond. Deaf to all persuasion, they bind him tighter and row the ship through and past.

Never is Homer more rapid. Like Odysseus's "sea-swift" ship, the whole scene sweeps past in forty lines. Rarely can something so brief have spread its ripples so wide. But the point is this: the song the Sirens sing is not any old crooning seduction tune. It is the story of the *Iliad* itself.

"We know all the pains that the Greeks and Trojans once endured
On the spreading plain of Troy when the gods willed it so—
All that comes to pass on the fertile earth, we know it all."

The Sirens sing the song of the heroic past. That is the meadow of death. They want to draw Odysseus in with tempting stories of what he once was. And Odysseus, after his years of suffering and journeying, of frustration in the beautiful arms of Calypso, whose name means "the hidden one," the goddess of oblivion, longs to return to the active world, the world of simplicity and straightforwardness he had known at Troy. The Sirens are wise to that; they know the longing in his heart. The prospect of clear-cut heroism summons him, and he struggles to escape his bindings. But his men, like the poem itself, know better, and they tie him tighter to his ship. They won't be wrecked on the illusions of nostalgia, the longing for that heroized, antique world, because, as the *Odyssey* knows, to live well in the world, nostalgia must be resisted; you must stay with your ship, stay tied to the present, remain mobile, keep adjusting the rig, work with the swells, watch for a wind-shift, watch as the boom swings over, engage, in other words, with the muddle and duplicity and difficulty of life. Don't be tempted into the lovely simplicities that the heroic past seems to offer. That is what Homer and the Sirens and Robert Fagles all said to me that day.

I can still see the sunlight coming sheening off the backs of the swells that morning, as they made their way past and under me, combed and slicked with the sea-froth running down them, every swell the memory of storms in the Atlantic far to the west, steepening to the east and then ruining themselves ashore. The *Auk* sailed north with the shearwaters, and the morning became unforgettable. It was when this book began.

I thank God I met Homer again that summer. He was suddenly alongside me, a companion and an ally, the most truly reliable voice I had ever known. It was like discovering poetry itself, or the dead speaking. As I read and reread the *Odyssey* in translation, I suddenly felt that here was the unaffected truth, here was someone speaking about fate and the human condition in ways that other people only seem to approach obliquely; and that directness, that sense of nothing between me and the source, is what gripped me. I felt like asking, "Why has no one told me about this before?"

The more I looked at the poems in different translations, and the more I tried to piece bits of them together in the Greek with a dictionary, the more I felt Homer was a guidebook to life. Here was a form of consciousness that understood fallibility and self-indulgence and vanity, and despite that knowledge didn't surrender hope of nobility and integrity and doing the right thing. Before I read Pope's Preface to the *Iliad*, or Matthew

Arnold's famous lectures on translating Homer, I knew that this was the human spirit on fire, rapidity itself, endlessly able to throw off little sidelights like the sparks thrown off by the wheels of an engine hammering through the night. Speed, scale, violence, threat; but every spark with humanity in it.

2 · GRASPING HOMER

Paris, 11 May 1863, Le Repas Magny, a small restaurant up a cobbled street on the Left Bank in the Sixième. Brilliant, literary, skeptical Paris had gathered, as usual, for its fortnightly dinner. The stars were there: the critic and historian Charles Sainte-Beuve; the multitalented and widely admired playwright and novelist Théophile Gautier; the unconscionably fat Breton philosopher, the most brilliant cultural analyst of the nineteenth century, Ernest Renan; the idealistic and rather intense Comte de Saint-Victor, a minor poet and upholder of traditional values; and observing them all the supremely waspish Jules de Goncourt, with his brother Edmond.

The Magny dinners, every other Monday, were ten francs a head, the food "mediocre" apparently, everyone shouting their heads off, smoking for France, coming and going as they felt like it, the only place in Paris, it was said, where there was freedom to speak and think. Jules de Goncourt transcribed it all.

"Beauty is always simple," the Comte de Saint-Victor said as the waiters brought in the wine. He had a way, when saying something he thought important, of putting his face in the air like an ostrich laying an egg. "There is nothing more beautiful than the feelings of Homer's characters. They are still fresh and youthful. Their beauty is their simplicity."

Magny's restaurant, in the rue Contrescarpe-Dauphine, Paris.

"Oh for Christ's sake," Edmond groaned, looking over at his brother. "Must we? Homer, *again*?"

Saint-Victor paused a moment, went white and then very deep red like some kind of mechanical toy.

"Are you feeling well?" Goncourt said to him across the table. "It looks as if Homer might be playing havoc with your circulation."

"How can you say that? Homer, how can I put it . . . Homer . . . Homer is . . . so *bottomless*!"

Everyone laughed.

"Most people read Homer in those stupid eighteenth-century translations," Gautier said calmly. "They make him sound like Marie-Antoinette nibbling biscuits in the Tuileries. But if you read him in Greek you can see he's a monster, his people are monsters. The whole thing is like a dinner party for barbarians. They eat with their fingers. They put mud in their hair when they are upset. They spend half the time painting themselves."

"Any modern novel," Edmond said, "is more moving than Homer."

"*What*?" Saint-Victor screamed at him across the table, banging his little fist against his head so that his curls shook.

"Yes, *Adolphe*, that lovely sentimental love story by Benjamin Constant, the sweet way they all behave to each other, his charming little obsession with her, the way she doesn't admit she wants to go bed with him, the lust boiling away between her thighs, all of that is more moving than Homer, actually more *interesting* than anything in Homer."

"Dear God alive," Saint-Victor shrieked. "It's enough to make a man want to throw himself out of the window." His eyes were standing out of his head like a pair of toffee-apples.

"That would be original," Edmond said. "I can see it now: 'Poet skewers himself on street-lamp because someone said something horrid about Homer.' Do go on. It would be more diverting than anything that has happened for weeks."

Chairs were shoved back from the table, somebody knocked over a bottle of wine, the waiter was standing ghoul-faced at the door, Saint-Victor was stamping and roaring like a baby bull in his own toy bullring, as red in the face as if somebody had said his father was a butcher and his mother a tart. Everyone was bellowing.

"I wouldn't care if all the Greeks were dead!"

"If only they were!"

"But Homer is divine."

"He has got nothing to teach us!"

"He's just a novelist who never learned how to write a novel."

"He says the same thing over and over again."

"But isn't it deeply moving," Saint-Victor said imploringly, "when Odysseus's dog wags the last sad final wag of his tail?"

"You can always tell a bully," Edmond said quietly to his brother. "He loves dogs more than their owners."

"Homer, Homer," Sainte-Beuve was murmuring through the uproar.

"Isn't it strange," Jules said to Renan afterward. "You can argue about the Pope, say that God doesn't exist, question anything, attack heaven, the Church, the Holy Sacrament, anything except Homer."

"Yes," Renan said. "Literary religions are where you find the real fanatics."

Homer loomed up again at another Magny dinner the following October. They were talking about God, whether God was definable or even knowable. Renan ended up by comparing God, his particular God, in all possible piety and seriousness, to an oyster. Uniquely itself, beautifully self-sufficient, not entirely to be understood, mysteriously attractive, mysteriously unattractive, wholly wonderful—what was not godlike about the oyster? Rolling laughter swept up and down the table.

That was when Homer emerged. To the Goncourts' horror, these modern, skeptical destroyers of faith, the most fearless critics of God that France had ever known, burst into a song of Homeric praise which made the brothers retch. The diners at le Repas Magny might have been partisans of progress, but all agreed that there was a time and a country, at the beginning of humanity, when a work was written in which everything was divine, above all discussion and even all examination. They began to swoon with admiration over individual phrases.

"*The long-tailed birds!*" [Hippolyte] Taine [the philosopher and historian] cried out enthusiastically.

"*The unharvestable sea!*" exclaimed Sainte-Beuve, raising his little voice. "A sea where there are no grapes! What could be more beautiful than that?"

"*Unharvestable sea*"? What on earth did that mean? Renan thought some Germans had discovered a hidden significance in it. "And what is that?" asked Sainte-Beuve.

"I can't remember," Renan replied, "but it's wonderful."

The Goncourt brothers sat back, regarding this mass expression of Homer-love with their habitual, jaundiced eye.

"Well, what do you have to say, you over there," Taine called out, addressing them, "you who wrote that antiquity was created to be the daily bread of schoolmasters?"

So far the brothers had said nothing and had let the Homer-hosannas go swirling around the dining room without comment, but now Jules said, "Oh, you know, we think [Victor] Hugo has more talent than Homer."

It was blasphemy. Saint-Victor sat as upright as a fence post and then went wild with rage, shouting like a madman and shrieking in his tinny voice, saying that remarks like that were impossible to stomach, they were too much, insulting the religion of all intelligent people, that everybody admired Homer and that without him Hugo would not even exist. Hugo greater than Homer! What did the Goncourts know? What idiot novels had they been producing recently? He shouted and screamed, dancing up and down the room like an electrified marionette. The Goncourts shouted back, increasingly loudly, raging at the supercilious poet, who for some reason thought he was more in touch with the meaning of things than they ever could be, sneering at them down his peaky red nose, while they could feel nothing but contempt for the man they would think of forever after as the nasty, little self-congratulatory Homer-lover.

These conversations seem as distant as the Bronze Age. Where now is our violence on behalf of a poet? Who feels this much about Homer? The Goncourts, with their skepticism and their modernism, their contempt for antiquity, have won the day. Their prediction has come more than true: the ancient world is now the daily bread not of schoolmasters but of academics. Everyone has heard of Homer, probably of the two poems, and many have read some passages; but no one today ends up shouting at dinner about him. Mention Homer across a table and a kind of anxiety comes into the face you are looking at, a sort of shame, perhaps a fear of seeming stupid and ignorant. Almost no one loves the poems he wrote or the phrases that recur in them.

Why should they? The place of Homer in our culture has largely withered away. I can only say that, for me, the growing experience of knowing Homer, of living with him in my life, has provided a kind of ballast. He is like a beautiful stone, monumentally present, a paternal foundation, large, slightly ill-defined, male and reliable. He is not a friend, a lover or a wife; far more of an underlayer than that, a form of reassurance that in the end there is some kind of understanding in the world. Goethe thought that if only Europe had considered Homer and not the books of the Bible as its holy scripture, the whole of history would have been different, and better.

That quality does not exist in some floating metaphysical outer sphere.

It is precisely in the words he uses, and on that level something like "the unharvestable sea" is a beautiful expression. It is the twin and opposite of another of Homer's repeated, metrically convenient, perfect and formulaic phrases, "the grain-giving earth." And why is it beautiful? Because it encapsulates the sensation of standing on a beach and looking out at the breaking surf, and seeing in it the unforgiving brutality of the salt desert before you. Everything you are not stares back at what you are. It is a phrase which knows that, as you are looking out at that hostility, behind you, at your back, are all the riches that the earth might give, the olive and the grape, the security of home, the smell of cut hay, the barn filled with the harvested wheat and barley, the threshed grains, the sacks tight with them in the granaries, the ground flour, the bread at breakfast, the honey and oil. "The unharvestable sea"—two words in Greek, *pontos atrygetos*—is a form of concentrated wisdom about the condition of life on earth. It states the obvious but also provides a kind of access to reality, both painful and revelatory. All Homer is in the phrase.

Those words occur many times in both the *Iliad* and the *Odyssey*, often poignantly. Almost at the beginning of the *Odyssey*, Odysseus's son Telemachus, at the end of almost twenty years' waiting for his father to return, first from the war against Troy and then from his vastly extended and troubled journey home across the sea, has decided to go in search of him, to ask in the mainland of Greece, in Pylos and Sparta, if there is any news of the man most people now consider dead.

Homer, over the course of thirty-five lines, prepares the ground for the climactic words. Telemachus needs to get ready for his journey, and to do so he goes down into his father's treasure chamber in the palace in Ithaca, his *thalamos*. Upstairs, all is anarchy and chaos. The young men who are living in the palace, clamoring to marry Telemachus's mother, Penelope, are eating up the goods of the household. But down here, like a treasury of the past, of how things were before Odysseus left for the wars half a lifetime ago, all is order and richness. Clothes, gold and bronze are piled in the chamber, but also sweet-smelling oils, wine, which is also old and sweet, all lined up in order against the walls. All the accumulated goodness of the land is in there. Telemachus, whose name means "far from battle," meets an old woman, Eurycleia, down here. She was his nurse as a child, feeding and raising him. Now that he is a man, she tends and protects these precious fruits of the earth. He asks her for the best wine to be poured out for him into small traveling jars, and for milled barley to be put into leather sacks. He must take the earth's goods out onto the sea.

But Eurycleia—the name of this private nurse, this tender of things, means "wide-fame"—dreads Telemachus going where his father has gone to die. A wail of grief breaks from her when he tells her his plans, and she suddenly addresses him as she had years before:

> Ah dear child, how has this thought come into your mind?
> Where do you intend to go over the wide earth,
> you who are an only son and so deeply loved?
> Odysseus is dead, has died far from home in a strange land.
> No, stay here, in charge of what is yours.
> You have no need to suffer pain
> or go wandering on *the unharvestable sea*.

Nothing could be clearer: the unharvestable sea is not to be visited. It is the realm of death. When Odysseus does finally come home (and Eurycleia plays a key role in that return), Homer has a one-word synonym for the sea: "evil." The word she uses here for wandering is also dense with implication: *alaomai* is used of seamen, but also of beggars and the unhomed dead. The unharvestable sea is where life and goodness will never be found. Everything Eurycleia has devoted her life to, the nurturing and cherishing of the goodness of home, has been the harvest of an unwandering life. The man standing in front of her is one of those fruits. The unharvestable sea is a kind of hell, and in that phrase the drama of his life, her life, Odysseus's life, the life and death of those Ithacans who have not returned from Troy, of Penelope weaving and unweaving the cloth that will not be woven until Odysseus returns—all of it is bound up in *pontos atrygetos*.

For all the Goncourts' wit and skepticism, I am on the side of Renan, and Hippolyte Taine, and Sainte-Beuve, and even the ludicrous Comte de Saint-Victor. Homer, the most miraculous and ancient of survivals in our culture, comes from a time of unadorned encounter with the realities of existence. It is absurd now to call the sea "unharvestable," but it is also beautiful and moving. For all of Saint-Victor's despised sententiousness, he was right in this. Homer's simplicity, its undeniably straight look, is a form of revelation. Its nakedness is its poetry. There is nothing here of ornamentation or prettiness, and that is its value. "Each time I put down the *Iliad*," the American poet Kenneth Rexroth wrote toward the end of his life,

> after reading it again in some new translation, or after reading once more the somber splendor of the Greek, I am convinced, as one is convinced by the experiences of a lifetime, that somehow, in a way beyond the visions of artistry, I have been face to face with the meaning of existence. Other works of literature give this insight, but none so powerfully, so uncontaminated by evasion or subterfuge.

This book is driven by a desire to find the source of that directness and that understanding.

In the early autumn of 1816, John Keats was not yet twenty-one. He had been writing poetry for two years, living with other medical students in "a jumbled heap of murky buildings" just off the southern end of London Bridge, working as a "dresser"—a surgeon's assistant—in Guy's Hospital. He was miserable, good at his job but hating it, out of sorts with "the barbarous age" in which he lived, filled with a hunger for life on a greater scale and of a deeper intensity than the ordinariness surrounding him could provide.

At school in Enfield, his headmaster's son Charles Cowden Clarke, who had ambitions himself as a poet and litterateur, had introduced him to history and poetry, immersing him in Shakespeare, Milton and Wordsworth. Clarke gave him the first volume of the great Elizabethan English epic, Edmund Spenser's *Faerie Queene*, and, as Clarke remembered later in life, Keats took to it

> as a young horse would through a spring meadow—ramping! Like a true poet, too—a poet "born, not manufactured," a poet in grain, he especially singled out epithets, for that felicity and power in which Spenser is so eminent. He hoisted himself up, and looked burly and dominant, as he said, "what an image that is—'sea-shouldering whales'!"

When Keats at this age saw the wind blowing across a field of barley still in the green, he jumped on a stile and shouted down at Clarke, "The tide! The tide!" Here was a boy, born the son of a London ostler, hungry for depth, for a kind of surging reality, for largeness and otherness which only epic poetry could provide. Poetry for him, as Andrew Motion said, was "both a lovely escape from the world and a form of engagement with it." It was not about prettiness, elegance or decoration but, in Motion's phrase, "a parallel universe," whose reality was truer and deeper than anything in the world more immediately to hand. Poetry gave access to a kind of Platonic grandeur, an underlying reality that everyday material life obscured and concealed. It is as if Keats's sensibility was ready for Homer to enter it, a womb prepared for conception. All that was needed was for Homer to flood into him.

Perhaps at Clarke's suggestion, he had already looked into the great translation of Homer made by the young Alexander Pope between about 1713 and 1726, the medium through which most eighteenth- and early-nineteenth-century Englishmen encountered Homer. But this translation came to be despised by the romantics as embodying everything that was wrong in the culture of the preceding age: interested more in style than in substance, ridiculously pretty when the Homeric medium was truth, a kind of drawing-room Homer which had left the battlefield and the storm at sea too far behind.

Where, for example, Homer had said simply "the shepherd's heart is glad," Pope had written, "The conscious swains, rejoicing in the sight/Eye the blue vault, and bless the useful light." From the point of view of the 1780s, Pope's Homer was about as Homeric as a Meissen shepherdess with a lamb in her lap.

This wasn't entirely fair to Pope. His preface to the *Iliad*, published in 1715, is one of the most plangent descriptions ever written in English of the power of the Homeric poems. Northern European culture had been dominated for too long by what they considered the processed and stable maturity of Virgil's *Aeneid*, the Latin epic par excellence, written in about 20 BC. Homer represented an earlier stage in human civilization, a greater closeness to nature, to the potency of the sublime, a form of poetry which was not to be admired from afar but which would bind up its reader or listener in a kind of overwhelming absorption in its world. "No man of true Poetical

Spirit," the young Pope had written, "is Master of himself while he reads him; so forcible is the poet's Fire and Rapture." Translation was not a calm carrying over of the meaning in Greek into the meaning in English, but a vision of the processes of the mind as a flaming crucible in which the sensibilities of translator and translated were fused into a new, radiant alloy.

Pope may have been the darling of the establishment. In his preface, he thanks a roll call of the eighteenth-century British great—Addison, Steele, Swift, Congreve, a string of dukes, earls, lords and other politicians—but for all that, his entrancement with Homeric power is not in doubt. Homer is like nature itself. He is a kind of wildness, "a wild paradise" in which, as the theory then was, the great stories and figures he describes came into being.

> What he writes is of the most animated Nature imaginable; every thing moves, every thing lives, and is put in Action . . . The Course of his Verses resembles that of the Army he describes,

> *They pour along like a Fire that sweeps the whole Earth before it.*

This inseparability of Homer and his world is what excited Pope. It seemed to him like a voice from the condition of mankind when it was still simple, quite different from "the luxury of succeeding ages." Poetic fire was the essential ingredient. "In *Homer*, and in him only, it burns every where clearly, and every where irresistibly."

Pope grasped the essential point: unlike Virgil, Homer is no part of the classical age, has no truck with judicious distinction or the calm management of life and society. He precedes that order, is a *preclassic*, immoderate, uncompromising, never sacrificing truth for grace. "*Virgil* bestows with a careful Magnificence: *Homer* scatters with a generous Profusion. *Virgil* is like a River in its Banks, with a gentle and constant Stream: *Homer* like the *Nile*, pours out his Riches with a sudden Overflow."

In this preface to the *Iliad*, Pope can lay claim to being the greatest critic of Homer in English. But what of his translation? Was he able to embody this deep understanding of Homer's "unaffected and equal Majesty" in the translation he made? Perhaps not. Take, for example, a moment of passionate horror toward the end of the *Iliad*. For most of the poem Achilles has been in his tent, nursing his grievance and loathing against Agamemnon, but now that Patroclus, the man he loved, has been killed by Hector, Achilles is out to exact revenge. He is on his blood-run, gut-driven, pitiless, the force of destiny. Among his enemies on the field, he encounters a young Trojan and looks down on him with the vacancy of fate. The young warrior stares back up.

> In vain his youth, in vain his beauty pleads:
> In vain he begs thee, with a suppliant's moan
> To spare a form and age so like thy own!
> Unhappy boy! no prayer, no moving art
> E'er bent that fierce inexorable heart!
> While yet he trembled at his knees, and cried,
> The ruthless falchion [a single-edged sword] [oped] his tender side;
> The panting liver pours a flood of gore,
> That drowns his bosom till he pants no more.

"It is not to be doubted," Pope writes in his own preface, "that the *Fire* of the Poem is what a Translator should principally regard, as it is most likely to expire in his managing." But that is what has happened here. Apart from what Leigh Hunt, the great liberal editor of the *Examiner*, called Pope's trivializing, "cuckoo-song" regularity, he has lost something else: Homer's neck-gripping physical urgency. In the Greek everything is about the body. The boy crawls toward Achilles and holds him by the knees. It is Achilles's ears that are deaf to him, his heart that remains unapproachably fierce. The boy puts his hands on Achilles's knees to make his prayer, and then the sword goes into the liver, the liver slipping out of the slit wound, the black blood drenching the boy's lap and "the darkness of death clouding his eyes." Nothing mediates the physical reality. Homer's nakedness is his power, but Pope has dressed it. "The panting liver . . . pants no more"; that is so neat it is almost disgusting, as if Pope were adjusting his cuffs while observing an atrocity. Dr. Johnson called the translation "a treasure of poetical elegances." That was the problem.

Keats had undoubtedly read Homer in Pope's translation; there are echoes of Pope's words in what Keats would write himself. But he was ready for something else. His life was constrained in the crowded and meager streets of south London, filled with the "money-mongering pitiable brood" of other Londoners. He had been to Margate with his brothers and had seen "the ocean" there in the pale shallows of the North Sea, but nowhere farther. In early October 1816 he went for the evening to see his old friend Charles Cowden Clarke, who was living with his brother-in-law in Clerkenwell. Cowden Clarke had been lent a beautiful big early folio edition of the translation of the *Iliad* and the *Odyssey* made by the poet and playwright George Chapman.

The two men began to look through its seventeenth-century pages. Clarke's friend Leigh Hunt, who had just published in the *Examiner* the first of Shelley's poems to be printed, had already praised Chapman in the August issue, for bottling "the fine rough old wine" of the original. In the next few days Keats was about to meet Hunt himself, with the possibility in the air that he too might swim out into the world of published poetry and fame. The evening was pregnant with the hope of enlargement, of a dignifying difference from the mundane conditions of his everyday life. To meet Homer through Chapman might be an encounter with the source.

It is touching to imagine the hunger with which Keats must have approached this book, searching its two-hundred-year-old pages for something undeniable, the juice of antiquity. The two of them sat side by side in Clarke's house, "turning to some of the 'famousest' passages, as they had scrappily known them in Pope's version." Chapman had produced his translations—almost certainly not from the Greek but with the help of Latin and French versions—between 1598 and 1616. Homer often seems to haunt the present, and Chapman himself had met him one day in Hertfordshire, not far from Hitchin, where Chapman had been born, Homer masquerading as "a sweet gale" as Chapman walked on the hills outside the town. It was a moment of revelation and life-purpose for him, so that later he could say, "There did shine, /A beam of Homer's freer soul in mine." The eighteenth century had not admired what Chapman had done. Pope had called it "loose and rambling," and Chapman himself "an Enthusiast" with a "daring fiery Spirit that animates his Translation, which is something like what one might imagine *Homer* himself would have writ before he arriv'd to Years of Discretion." Dr. Johnson had dismissed it as "now totally neglected." But Coleridge had rediscovered it. In 1808 he sent a copy of Chapman's Homer to Sara Hutchinson, Wordsworth's sister-in-law, the woman he loved. "Chapman writes & feels as a Poet," he wrote, "—as Homer might have written had he lived in England

in the reign of Queen Elizabeth . . . In the main it is an English Heroic
Poem, the *tale* of which is borrowed from the Greek."

Chapman's distance, his rough-cut unaffectedness, stood beyond the
refinements of the Enlightenment, as if he were the last part of the old
world that Homer had also inhabited, before politeness had polluted it.
Here the romantics found Achilles as the "fear-master," and horses after
battle which liked to "cool their hooves." Cowden Clarke and Keats were
hunched together over pages that were drenched in antiquity. Ghosts must
have come seeping out of them.

Something that had seemed quaint to the eighteenth century now
seemed true to the two young men. They pored over Chapman together.
"One scene I could not fail to introduce to him," Cowden Clarke wrote
later,

> the shipwreck of Ulysses, in the fifth book of the "Odysseis" [Chapman's
> transliteration of the Greek word for *Odyssey*], and I had the reward of
> one of his delighted stares, upon reading the following lines:

> Then forth he came, his both knees falt'ring, both
> His strong hands hanging down, and all with froth
> His cheeks and nostrils flowing, voice and breath
> Spent to all use, and down he sank to death.
> *The sea had soak'd his heart through.*

It is the most famous meeting between Homer and an English poet.
Keats had read and stared in delight, shocked into a moment of recognition, of what the Greeks called *anagnōrisis*, when a clogging surface
is stripped away and the essence for which you have been hungering is
revealed.

At this stage Odysseus has been at sea for twenty days. For nearly two
hundred lines he is churned through the pain Poseidon has wished on
him: "Just as when, in the autumn, the North Wind drives the thistle
tufts over the plain and they cling close to each other, so the gales drive
the raft this way and that across the sea." The sea is never more vengeful
in these poems, never more maniacally driven by violence and rage. The
raft is overturned and broken, the giant surf hammers on flesh-shredding
rock. It is one of Odysseus's great tests. His name itself in Greek embeds

the word *odysato*, meaning "to be hated," and that adjective appears twice in this storm. He is the hated man on the hateful sea. This is his moment of suffering, and the sea he sails on is loathing itself.

Throughout the *Odyssey* he is the man of many parts, inventive, ingenious, with many skills and many gifts, but here is merely *polytlas*, the man who dares many things, suffers many things and endures many things. Only when a goddess-bird and then Athene herself come to his aid can he finally drag himself to the shore.

Here in a virtually literal translation is what Homer says as Odysseus emerges from the surf.

> he then bends both knees
> and his strong hands-and-arms; for sea has killed his heart.
> Swollen all his flesh, while sea oozes much
> up through mouth and nostrils, he then breathless and speechless
> lies scarcely-capable, terrible weariness comes to him.

The Greek word Chapman translated in "*The sea had soak'd his heart through*"—the phrase which Keats loved so much—is *dedmēto*, which means "overpowered" or "tamed." It comes from a verb, *damazo*, of immensely ancient lineage, its roots spoken in the steppelands of Eurasia at least six thousand years ago, used to describe the breaking-in of animals and later the bending of metal to your desires and needs. It is essentially the same word as "tame" in English, or *domo* in Latin, the word for reduction, to kill in a fight, to domesticate and dominate. But in the *Iliad* it also appears as a word for seduction, or more likely the rape of girls. Young girls, enemies, heifers and wives are referred to in Homer by words that come from the same stem. So Odysseus here is tamed and unmanned by the sea. The sea defeated him. As a hero reduced to the condition of a heifer, his heroic willpower temporarily overcome, he is no better than a corpse, bloated, destroyed, owned, possessed and dominated.

Pope, encased in the language of politesse, fell short when faced with this challenge.

> his knees no more
> Perform'd their office, or his weight upheld:

His swoln heart heaved; his bloated body swell'd:
   From mouth and nose the briny torrent ran;
     And lost in lassitude lay all the man.

On a sofa? you might ask.

Others have tried and failed: "For the heart within him was crushed by the sea," wrote Professor A. T. Murray in 1919; "Odysseus bent his knees and sturdy arms, exhausted by his struggle with the sea," was E. V. Rieu's prose version, in the bestseller published by Penguin in 1946; "his very heart was sick with salt water," wrote the great American scholar-poet Richmond Lattimore in 1967; "The sea had beaten down his striving heart," Lattimore's successor, Robert Fagles, in 1996.

Keats was right. None approaches "*The sea had soak'd his heart through*" perhaps because Chapman's English has absorbed the vengeful nature of the sea Odysseus has just experienced; has understood that his soul is as good as drowned; has not lost the governing physicality of the Homeric world, so that Odysseus's heart appears as the organ of pain; and is able to summon a visual image of a marinated corpse, blanched and shriveled from exposure to the water, as white as tripe. Chapman had understood *dedmēto*: Odysseus's sea-soaked heart is a heart with the heart drained out of it.

Clarke and Keats read Chapman together all night, and at six in the morning Keats returned to his Dean Street lodgings—his "beastly place in dirt, turnings, and windings"—with Chapman looming in his mind. On the journey home across London he had begun to frame the sonnet which on arrival he wrote down. The manuscript, which he paid a boy to take over to Cowden Clarke that morning, so that it was on his breakfast table by ten o'clock, survives. The big, loopingly written words of that first morning text are not quite the same as what is usually printed.

On the first looking into Chapman's Homer

Much have I travell'd in the Realms of Gold
   And many goodly States and Kingdoms seen;
    Round many Western islands have I been,
Which Bards in Fealty to Apollo hold.

On the first looking into Chapman's Homer

Much have I travelld in the Realms of Gold,
  And many goodly States, and Kingdoms seen;
  Round many Western islands have I been,
Which Bards in featly to Apollo hold.
Of one wide expanse had I been told,
  Which deep brow'd Homer ruled as his Demesne;
  Yet could I never judge what Men could mean,
Till I heard Chapman speak out loud and bold.—
Then felt I like some Watcher of the Skies
  When a new Planet swims into his Ken,
Or like stout Cortez, when with wond'ring eyes
  He star'd at the Pacific, and all his Men
Look'd at each other with a wild surmise—
  Silent upon a Peak in Darien—

Keats's draft of his Homer Sonnet, written in October 1816.

Oft of one wide expanse had I been told,
  Which ~~low~~ deep brow'd Homer ruled as his Demesne:
  Yet could I never judge what Men could mean,
Till I heard Chapman speak out loud, and bold.
  Then felt I like some Watcher of the Skies
When a new Planet swims into his Ken,
Or like stout Cortez, when with wond'ring eyes
  He star'd at the Pacific, and all his Men
Look'd at each other with a wild surmise—
  Silent upon a Peak in Darien—

It was the first great poem he wrote. And it is a poem about greatness, not about first reading Homer; nor even about first reading Chapman's Homer; it's about first looking into Chapman's Homer and, from one or two fragments and passages, understanding for the first time what Homer meant. It is as if that big 1616 folio were a sort of aquarium into which he and Clarke had peered in amazement, looking up at each other as they found the beauties and rarities swimming in its depths. No other version had given Keats this plunging perspective into the ancient. Politeness had dressed Homer in felicity, when his underlying qualities are more like this: martial, huge, struggling through jungle, dense, disturbing and then providing that moment of revelatory release, of a calm pacific vision emerging onto what had been fields of storm or battle. Men had assured Keats that Homer possessed such a realm, but he had been unable to see it in the translations he knew. Here at last, though, was the moment when, cresting a rise, a new and deeper, ineffably broad landscape had opened in front of him. Homer might be dressed up as a cultural convenience, a classic, but in truth he is not like that. He is otherness itself: impolite, manly, cosmic, wild, enormous.

Keats made a mistake: it was Vasco Núñez de Balboa, not Cortés, who first sighted the Pacific Ocean. He didn't correct that, but when he came to revise this poem for publication he did change a word or two, most importantly the seventh line. In the first early-October-morning version, after his night of revelation, it had been

Yet could I never judge what Men could mean,

which acts as the core of the poem, the rejection of the instruction and learning he had received, substituting it with the vast scale of the new understanding that Chapman had given him. For publication, he replaced that with

Yet did I never breathe its pure serene

which is politer and not entirely concordant with what the rest of the poem aims to mean. More than that, he had borrowed the verb and the key adjectival noun from Pope's *Iliad*.

The troops exulting sat in order round,
And beaming fires illumined all the ground.
As when the moon, refulgent lamp of night,

O'er heaven's pure azure spreads her sacred light,
When not a breath disturbs the deep serene . . .

Keats, on the verge of his twenty-first birthday, even as this sonnet was announcing his new discovery of Homeric depth and presence, had not shrugged off that eighteenth-century inheritance.

For all that, coursing through the sonnet is a sense of arrival in the world of riches, a sudden shift in Keats's cosmic geometry, moving beyond the drabness and tawdriness by which he felt besieged. Keats had become everybody in the sonnet's fourteen lines: the astronomer, himself, Chapman, Homer, Cortés and "all his Men." All coexist in the heightened and expanded moment of revelation. Pope had found fire in Homer; Keats discovered scale. And scale is what then entered his poetry, as a kind of private and tender sublime, the often agonized heroics of the heart, in which, just as in Homer, love and death engage in an inseparable dance.

Homer, or at least the idea of Homer, pools into Keats's poetry. Hostile Tory reviewers in *Blackwood's Magazine* started to call him "the cockney Homer," but in *Endymion*, the long poem he had been contemplating when he wrote the Chapman sonnet, and which he began the following spring, his experience of that night with Cowden Clarke shapes the core phrases. People remember the poem's beginnings.

A thing of beauty is a joy for ever:
Its loveliness increases; it will never
Pass into nothingness; but still will keep
A bower quiet for us, and a sleep
Full of sweet dreams, and health, and quiet breathing.

That is poetry as balm, even, as Andrew Motion has said, as medicine, the discipline which Keats was now abandoning for life as a poet. Keats went on to describe the ways in which beauty manifests itself in the world, the consolations it provides in "Trees old and young," "daffodils/With the green world they live in," streams and shady woods, "rich with a sprinkling of fair musk-rose blooms." But then, at the center of this first part of the poem, drenched in memories of Shakespeare's sweetest lyrics, comes this, the bass note of a Homeric presence, a sudden manliness, a scale of imagined beauty that encompasses the depths of the past: "And such too is the grandeur of the dooms/We have imagined for the mighty dead."

Homer is the foundation of truth and beauty, and Keats was happy to say that "we" had imagined his poetry. Homer will enlarge your life. Homer is on a scale that stretches across human time and the full width of the human heart. Homer is alive in anyone who is prepared to attend. Homerity is humanity. Richmond Lattimore, making his great version of the *Iliad* in the late 1940s, when asked "Why do another translation of Homer?" replied, "That question has no answer for those who do not know the answer already." Why another book about Homer? Why go for a walk? Why set sail? Why dance? Why exist?

3 · LOVING HOMER

Homer-love can feel like a disease. If you catch it, you're in danger of having it for life. He starts to infiltrate every nook of your consciousness. What would Homer have had for breakfast? (Oil, honey, yogurt and delicious bread. One of the things that is wrong with the Cyclopes is that they don't eat bread.) Or a picnic? (Grapes, figs, plums, beans.) How did he feed his heroes? (Grilled meat and thoroughly cooked sausages.) What did he think of parties? (He loved them; no moment was happier for a man than sitting down to a table loaded with wine and surrounded by his friends.)

These were questions the Greeks asked. In fifth-century Athens, Socrates was impressed by Homer's decision, for example, that no hero should ever eat iced cakes: "all professional athletes are well aware that a man who is to be in good condition should take nothing of the kind." Protein—well salted, not boiled—was the stuff for heroes. And it had to be red meat; fish was the last resort, and chickens had yet to arrive from the Far East: they reached the Aegean in about 500 BC, known to the Greeks as "the Persian Bird."

I have a way now of finding Homer wherever I look for him. No encounter, no landscape is without its Homeric dimension. In a way, Homer has become a kind of scripture for me, an ancient book, full of urgent imperatives and ancient meanings, most of them half discerned, to be puzzled over. It is a source of wisdom. There must be a name for this colonization of the mind by an imaginative presence from the past. Possession, maybe?

Mindjack? In one of his Socratic dialogues, Plato has a wonderful image for the secret and powerful hold that Homer has on his listeners. Socrates is talking to Ion, a mildly ridiculous rhapsode, a man who made his living by reciting and speaking about Homer. "I am conscious in my own self," Ion tells Socrates in phrases which even two and a half millennia later have a whiff of the stage, "and the world agrees with me in thinking that I do speak better and have more to say about Homer than any other man." If Greeks had mustaches, Ion would be twirling his.

The Socratic eyebrow rises a little, but he then tells Ion the truth, a little slyly, the Socratic wisdom masquerading as flattery. "The gift which you possess of speaking excellently about Homer," Socrates says,

> is not an art, but an inspiration; there is a divinity moving you, like that contained in the stone which Euripides calls a magnet . . . This stone not only attracts iron rings, but also imparts to them a similar power of attracting other rings; and sometimes you may see a number of pieces of iron and rings suspended from one another so as to form quite a long chain: and all of them derive their power of suspension from the original stone. In like manner the Muse first of all inspires men herself; and from these inspired persons a chain of other persons is suspended, who take the inspiration.

The poet, Socrates tells him, is "a light and winged and holy thing"— Homer not as great bearded mage, but like the bird Blegen found, or a mosquito, a flitting bug—of no substance, swept here and there on the winds of poetry. "There is no invention in him until he has been inspired and is out of his senses, and the mind is no longer in him."

Plato affects to despise poetry, for the way it interferes with the rational mind, but it is clear that he was in love with it, moved by it as much as Ion could ever hope to be. And he identified the mechanism: there is no act of will in loving Homer. You don't acquire Homer; Homer acquires you. And so, like Ion, you hang as a curtain ring from him, who hangs from the Muse, who hangs from her father Greatness and her mother Memory.

I cannot go for a walk in the English chalklands without imagining the cold damp *Iliad*s that must have been sung there. Every burial in an English Bronze Age round barrow must have had a version of these heroic songs sung at its making. But Homer is also in the Hebrides and off the coast of Ireland. Traditions of heroic song have endured there. One eighteenth-century bard was given a lovely estate in Harris by his MacLeod chief, for which he had to pay "1 panegyrick poem every year." That is Homeric rent. Wild unadorned landscapes or places of great antiquity summon his archetypes and their stories. Pope thought that for Virgil, Homer and nature were indistinguishable, and for me Homer is also everywhere: from the North Atlantic to the plain of Troy, in the mountains of Extremadura, on the beaches of Ischia.

No shore now is without its Homeric echoes. It is one of the realms of the heroes, the great zone of liminality between land and sea, the sphere of chance-in-play. Outcomes are never certain there. It is the governing metaphor for the position of the Greeks in the *Iliad*. The Trojans are never seen on the beach, unless battling there, but that is where the Greeks are at home. It is a place of ritual and longing: in book 3 of the *Odyssey*, the people of Pylos are making a giant sacrifice to the gods on the beach; in book 5 Odysseus weeps on the beaches of Calypso's island for his sorrows and his distance from home. It is also the place of promise: in book 6, his eyes rimmed red with sea salt, he finds Nausicaa and her girls and their assurance of life, colored by the hint of sex. It is the realm of threat, where Odysseus and his men on their descent to Hades draw up their ships in the cold and dark, in terror at the experiences they know await them. It is above all the field of ambiguity, where at the very center of the *Odyssey*, Odysseus lands, this time still asleep, on Ithaca, fails to understand he has reached home at last, or to acknowledge that trouble awaits him, and sets off, uncertain, into the island he would like to call home.

In the *Iliad*, when Odysseus and Ajax go to Achilles in book 9 to urge him to rejoin the fight against the Trojans, they walk there by a seashore that is roaring with the violence and scale of Poseidon's terror.

> The way they take is along the strand of the deep sea,
> Where the battle lines of breakers crash and drag,
> Uttering many prayers to the holder and shaker of earth
> That they might persuade the proud heart of great Achilles.

It is also the place of grief, where later in the *Iliad*, in the restlessness of his despair over the death of his beloved friend Patroclus and when sleep will not come, Achilles goes in the night

To wander in anguish, aimless along the surf,
where one morning after another,
Flaming over the sea and shore, dawn would find him pacing there.

As so often in Homer, the single moment encapsulates the enormous story. Man and landscape interfuse. The dawn-lit Achilles in the agony of sorrow wanders by the aimless surf; no place for Homer is more filled with tragedy than the beach. It is on the beach that Achilles builds the great funeral pyre for Patroclus, the man he loved, now dead, as Achilles will soon be.

As an extension of the beach itself, nothing is more potent in Homer than the first moments of a vessel leaving it. Leaving a beach is moving off from indecision. The setup for departure, like the arming for battle or the preparation of dinner, is repeated time and again. These scenes contain the oldest form of Greek and are at the deepest level of these many-layered poems. They are as old as Homer gets.

And so today a friend—Martin Thomas—stands in the shallows, his trousers rolled up, his calves in the water, hands on hips, saying, not shouting, the good-bye from the beach. Homeric departures are full of verbal formulas, repeated every time a boat puts to sea, describing the necessary actions. The repetitiveness is often concealed in translations, as if it were an embarrassment and some variation were needed in the saying of these words, but their formulaic nature is important, as if the poem were an incantation, a ritual departure-charm, a way of getting ready for sea, an arming of the ship, getting the words right in the way that things on the boat must be got right.

So Martin asks, like a hero, if I am all right. Am I prepared? Have I stepped the mast properly? Is the running rigging free? Are the sheets through the fairleads? Is the rudder secured on its pintles? Is the mainsheet caught on the rudderstock? Do I have water, something to eat, my phone?

Homeric crews almost never sail away. From the shelter of their bay or quayside, they nearly always row out into the seaway to catch the wind. So today at home in Scotland, there has been a turn in the wind, and the water in the bay is lying still, in its own calm. If I could walk on it, I would walk on it this morning. It looks more like oil than water. A blackbird half a mile away is singing in the arms of a Scots pine. A curlew I can hear but not see moans somewhere over there beside the rocks. The seawater itself is green with the reflected woods, an ink of molten leaves and boughs.

But beyond the bay, beyond its two headlands, I can see out into the sound, where there is a suggestion of wind. I must row out there and follow the Homeric pattern. As I drift away from the shore, Martin walks up the beach, looks back once or twice and the sand goes blue beneath me with the depth.

Homeric departures are often at dawn, in the calm before the wind gets up. As the day begins, the voyage begins. Everyone knows that Homeric dawn is "rosy-fingered"—not rayed with her outspread fingers, but touching the tips of trees and rocks with her fingers. She also sometimes sits "on her golden throne" as if she were the goddess of the glowing sky; or, beautifully, she can wear "her veil the colour of saffron," *krokopeplos*, the crocus-cloth, the warmest color in the world, from the stigmas of the Cretan crocus, the flush of well-being and luxury. And as she rises over the water in those beautiful clothes, the color is spread across the whole of the sea beneath her, a drenching and staining of the world with the beauty of dawn. She presides over the launching, to sponsor it, but the hero of the ship must lead his men. The voyage cannot happen without human will. And so under his command but with his goddess alongside him, the hero and crew embark, loosen the stern lines that hold the ship to the shore, sit on the benches and "strike the sea with their oars."

That is how it is here now too. Martin is back in the house, and I settle on the bench in my small boat, the main thwart, put the oars in the rowlocks and ease the blades into the green sea. I can't help but feel the ancientness of it, my own life woven into the fabric of the past. The boat slips forward in a dream of liquidity, released from ploddingness into a kind of flight. With each stroke—a pull, the bending of the shaft of the oar as it is drawn against the water, the sucking puddle as the blades exit and then their dripping onto the perfect skin of the sea—I join the continuous past. Whoever first made a boat, even a simple punt driven forward with a pole, or a dugout with a basic paddle, must have seen and felt this fluency as a kind of magic, a suspension of the earthbound rules of existence.

But you long for wind. You imagine wind before it comes. You look for it on the water. None of this is far from praying for wind or even sacrificing for it. Part of the Homeric ritual is to make a libation to the goddess as you leave. And the goddess you choose summons her own kind of wind. So Athene, never moderate, owl-eyed, all-seeing, sharp beyond all human understanding, sends a fierce wind for Telemachus as he heads out from Ithaca to find his father, a wind from the west "that bellows roaring over the wine-coloured sea." His voyage is anxious, uncertain, driven by that demanding mentor.

At the same time, somewhere else in the realms of fantasy and loss, his father is being given a wind by the amorous goddess Calypso, who has imprisoned him on her island of deliciousness for the last seven years. He has been sitting weeping on the shore, longing for home. Now at last she will release him, and her wind is like her, all-embracing, warm and seductive, a sleep-with-me- wind sending him on his way. He spreads his sail gladly to it, a bosom of wind, wafting him away from her comforts to the world of truth and reality.

As the wind comes, they hoist "the white sail," the sail fills "and the wind and the helmsman guide the ship together." It is an act of cooperation between man and the world, a folding in of human intention with what the world can offer. The ship is a beautifully made thing, as closely fitted as a poem, as much a mark of civilization as any woven cloth, and the wind in the *Odyssey*, when it is a kind wind, is a "shipmate," another member of the crew. It is not the element in which you sail but a "companion" on board. The human and divine dimensions of reality meet in it.

And now, when I am out in the sound, and the right wind comes, I think of it like that, as something else to be welcomed aboard. That coming of the wind is a moment when you can't help but smile, when the world turns in your favor. It is also a moment of extraordinary potency in Homer, never more than when in the *Iliad* the Trojans find themselves in a terrifying and difficult phase of the battle and things are against them, until they see Hector and his brother Paris coming out of the gates of the city, armed, ready to help. It is, the poem says, like that moment when the crew has been struggling for too long with the oars, and their arms are weary, and they have been praying for wind, and then, as a blessing, the wind seems to come and the weariness drops from their bodies and they can rest in its strength and power: "So these two appear to the Trojans, who have longed for them."

Matching that instant of relief and triumph is another, almost at the other end of the *Iliad*, when the winds become the indispensable companions of the heroes. Achilles has made the great funeral pyre on the beach for Patroclus. Timber has been cut and carried, and the pyre is now a hundred feet in each direction. Animals have been slaughtered and the fat laid on the pyre. But it will not light, and Achilles realizes he has failed to do one thing: he must pray to the two winds, the west wind and the north wind. And they come, sweeping in from their distant dwelling places, driving the clouds before them. A vast, inhuman blaze erupts in the pyre, and under the winds' fierce encouragement, one shrieking blast after another, it burns all night long, incinerating everything but the bones. Only then do the winds retire "Back towards home again, over the Thracian sea, And it heaves with a long, groaning swell as they cross it."

The wind never comes unsummoned, or in a solid block. All you feel at first is a finger or two, the faint chilling of the skin on the cheek, or stroking the nape of your neck. But then it builds a little, one finger becomes five, the canvas stirs, like a dog in a bed, begins to acquire a form, and the boat gains a sense of purpose, a coherence it had lacked as it slopped in the chop or swell. The wake slowly starts to bubble behind you, "the gleaming wake" that runs behind Homeric ships as a sign of life and excellence, the cockpit drains gurgle with the air sucked through them, and with tiller and sheet in hand you sit up and pick your course across the sea. That is the Odyssean moment; everything liquid but directed, everything mobile but related: the sea itself, your boat in it, the air and its winds, all the possibilities. The ritual is done, the routines have been followed and your chances are now set fair.

Of all Homeric departures, none is more poignant than when Odysseus and his men, right in the center of the *Odyssey*, set off for Hades, to hear from the blind seer Tiresias the way home to Ithaca. Circe, "the trim-coifed goddess," as Ezra Pound described her, set them on their way. They have no choice. Only Tiresias can tell them the way home. They have made all their tackle secure and provided themselves with food and drink. The wind has joined the crew and is now there alongside the helmsman, guiding "the black ship in the bright sea" as their companion. But neither Odysseus nor any of his men is making this voyage with any hint of delight. This is a journey down and under the world, into the dark places, into themselves as much as to the edge of the physical universe. As the wind holds fair for them, they sit on their benches and grieve. Big, heart-wrenching tears fall on the pale timbers of the deck. The wind is taking them toward a terrifying destination, the place of death which

Odysseus has so far exercised all his wit and skill to avoid. The wind knows nothing of that and propels their ship onward, its red-painted bows plunging and rising with each oncoming sea, the swells breaking and surging around the stempost, while above that foam of life the wind never falters or wavers.

> The wind catches the sail, bellying it out, and the blue-shadowed waves
>   resound under the fore-foot of the running ship as she lies over on
>   her course and races out to sea.
> Thus with stretched sail, we go over sea till day's end.
> Sun to his slumber, shadows over ocean.

4 · SEEKING HOMER

All modern versions of Homer are descendants of the edition made by a French nobleman, Jean-Baptiste Gaspard d'Ansse de Villoison. In 1788, in Paris, he published the most important Greek text of the *Iliad* ever printed. Ten years earlier he had arrived in Venice, sent there by the enlightened instincts of the French crown, to trawl through the holdings of the great St. Mark's library on the Piazzetta. Villoison was agog at what he found, and soon began writing ecstatic letters to his friends all over Europe. He had made the great discovery: a Byzantine edition of the *Iliad* that seemed to derive from the scholars who had worked on it in Alexandria in the second century BC, sifting the true text from the mass of alternative readings they had gathered in the great Ptolemaic library in the city. It was, Villoison wrote, the *"germana et sincera lectio,"* the real and uncorrupted reading.

Villoison thought he had discovered the essence of a work by a single poet called Homer. But he had sown the seeds of his own demise. The idea was already in the air in the eighteenth century that Homer was not one poet but many, and that the poems were the product of a whole culture, not an individual genius. Villoison's discovery turned out to be the Copernican moment. The mass of alternative readings rejected by the Alexandrian scholars itself threw doubt on the idea of a single great original text. They had chosen to make a single Homer, but farther back in time it seemed as if there were multiple Homers to choose from. William Cowper, the English lover and translator of Homer, read Villoison and

The title page of the 1788 *Iliad* edited by
Jean-Baptiste Gaspard d'Ansse de Villoison.

stood aghast at the fragmentation of his hero. As he wrote to his friend the
Reverend Walter Bagot in the winter of 1790, "I will send you some pretty
stories from [Villoison] which will make your hair stand on end, as mine
has stood on end already, they so horribly affect, in point of authenticity,
the credit of the works of the immortal Homer."

Homer now was not one but many, and most of them were obscure. In
1795 Villoison was challenged by the young, highly analytical German
scholar Friedrich August Wolf. How could Villoison tell if the decisions
made by the Alexandrian editors were the right ones? Surely what Villoison had published was evidence that the *Iliad*, as they all knew it, was
a set of late, corrupt and unreliable texts, brought together in one poem

but with their origins in bardic songs which had been radically altered by every hand they had passed through. The originals were unrecoverable. Homer, whoever that was, could never now be known.

The scene was set for the long struggle over the so-called Homeric Question raised by Wolf which has lasted ever since. "Some say, 'There never was such a person as Homer,'" the English essayist Thomas De Quincey joked in 1841. "'No such person as Homer! On the contrary,' say others, 'there were scores.'" Nevertheless, the text of the *Iliad* over which the battles were fought between the lumpers and splitters, the one-Homer advocates and the scores-of-Homer advocates, the Homerophiles and Homerophobes, continued to be almost precisely the one published by Villoison in 1788.

He was not the first in the field. The first printed Greek Homer had appeared in 1488, in Florence, published by an Athenian, Demetrius Chalcondyles, who had come to Italy to teach Greek to the humanists of the Italian Renaissance. Soon other copies were being printed in Milan, Heidelberg, Leipzig, Paris and London. And behind those first printed books stands a long manuscript history. Many of the medieval manuscripts of Homer migrated late to the European libraries, because in the early Middle Ages Homer was unread in Europe. Dante had Virgil call him the "sovereign poet," but Europeans had lost the ability to read Greek, and even though the great fourteenth-century humanist Petrarch was said to have owned a copy of the *Iliad*—he was used to kiss it in reverence—he could not understand a word it said. Homer, he wrote, "was dumb to me and I am deaf to it."

Nevertheless, Homer continued to lurk in the European mind; pervasively there but rarely seen. Medieval *Odyssey*s are scattered through scholarly Europe, in Cambridge and London, Milan and Munich, Naples and Moscow, in Paris, Venice, Stuttgart and Vienna. There are *Iliad*s in the Bodleian in Oxford (from the twelfth century), the Bibliothèque Nationale in Paris (a copy which probably came from Mount Athos), in the Escorial and in Florence. Through these few precious manuscript books, Homer survived in medieval Christendom.

All of them derive in the end, but through routes that are now forever hidden, from the tradition of scholarship that was maintained far to the east in Greek-speaking Byzantium. The earliest complete *Odyssey* to have survived is from the late tenth century, now in Michelangelo's Laurentian

Library in Florence, held as one of the greatest of treasures in those beautiful, treasure-rich halls. But slightly earlier than that, and the earliest
complete manuscript of Homer anywhere, is the *Iliad* which Villoison
thrillingly rediscovered in 1788 in the Biblioteca Marciana in Venice. It is
an extraordinary and beautiful manuscript, 654 large goatskin vellum
pages, decorated with Byzantine imaginings of the great heroes and notes
enclosed within giant lyres. This manuscript, known as Venetus A, was
written out in the middle of the tenth century AD in Constantinople, by a
scribe who took immense pains with the work, adding in the wide margins a mass of notes and references from earlier scholars there in Byzantium, in Rome and Alexandria. It had been brought to Italy in the first
years of the fifteenth century, and in 1468 deposited in the doge's palace,
until it was transferred to Sansovino's library in 1554. There are other
still earlier manuscripts from the same Greek tradition surviving in the
Vatican and in St. Catherine's Monastery in the Sinai Desert, but none of
them can match the completeness of Venetus A.

From the time Villoison discovered it, that manuscript takes Homer
back a thousand years to the scholarly libraries of Byzantium. A series of
beautiful discoveries made in the nineteenth century by Europeans traveling in Egypt took Homer farther back still. In the early years of the century, Egyptians who had dug rolls of papyrus out of ancient tombs began
to offer them for sale. Pieces found their way into gentlemen's libraries
across Europe. From the mid-nineteenth century onward, Egyptologists
began a more systematic search for these ancient documents, none more
assiduous than the thoroughly unkempt, restlessly energetic and no-
sock-wearing Englishman William Flinders Petrie. He was a man who
since boyhood had understood that the careful unraveling of historic
deposits layer by layer, an exfoliation of the past, was the only way to
approach them. In the winter of 1887 he began to dig in the large necropolis at Hawara, in the Fayum Depression to the west of the valley of the
Nile.

Almost every mummy was accompanied by an image of the person,
their unwavering gaze, their necklaces and earrings and carefully braided,
gathered hair. With them were other artifacts, beads and vials, mirrors
and, tucked in by the dead children, rag dolls with carved heads and real
hair. The dolls had changes of clothes, dresses, little tables and wooden

William Flinders Petrie in Abydos, Egypt, 1922.

bedsteads with which the girls played. Their coffins were made of a kind of papyrus-based papier-mâché, and Flinders Petrie found within their fabric the remains of many ancient texts.

To help with those documents he had with him his old friend, an Oxford Assyriologist, the Reverend Professor Archibald Sayce. "The floating sand of the desert," Sayce wrote the next year, "was found to be full of shreds of papyrus inscribed with Greek characters . . . They seem to have formed the contents of the office of some public scribe, which have been dispersed and scattered by the wind over the adjoining desert." It's an image from Shelley, the world after Ozymandias: ancient texts blowing in tatters and fragments across the Egyptian desert.

But then Flinders Petrie came across the greatest of all his treasures. On the morning of 21 February 1888, under the head of a woman who was not named on her coffin and was buried in an otherwise unmarked stretch of the necropolis, he found a large roll of papyrus, a papyrus pillow. This was no chance leftover. "The roll had belonged to a lady with whom it had been buried in death," Sayce wrote. "The skull of the mummy showed that its possessor had been young and attractive-looking, with features at once small, intellectual, and finely chiseled, and belonging distinctively to the Greek type."

The papyrus had been damaged in its outer leaves, but Petrie began to unfold it, as if he were looking into the innards of a wasp's nest, and peering beyond the outer covering found himself reading the Greek numbers twelve and eighty, and the names Agamemnon, Achaeans, Corinth. The roll with which the young woman had been buried was the first two books of the *Iliad* and, here from book 2, Flinders Petrie, with the sand of the Sahara blowing around him, was reading lines from the Catalogue of Ships, Homer's enumeration of the Greeks who sailed to Troy.

This Hawara Homer, written on papyrus in about AD 150, is now in the Bodleian Library in Oxford, its lines numbered by Flinders Petrie in August 1888. It is one of the most time-vertigo-inducing objects I know. In columns aligned left, the clear Greek capitals are spooled out across the reedy, vegetal surface of the papyrus sheets. There are no gaps between the words, but they are entirely legible, the relaxed and masterful calligraphy rolling on for line after line like a wave that will not break. This is a text to travel to the next world with, the strokes in each letter just curved away from straightness, so that in its combination of open *o*'s and *u*'s and the *w*'s of its omegas, and the slight flexing in the pen strokes of its *k*'s and *n*'s and *t*'s, this is one of the greatest images of the generous and beautiful word ever made. Other contemporary manuscripts found by Flinders Petrie are far more sketchy and scratchy, less steady in their progress across the page; but this is Homer as monument, as scripture, as "the grandeur of the dooms/We have imagined for the mighty dead."

The most intriguing aspect of the Hawara Homer, and other papyri of the same era, is how close they are to the text of Homer as it was transmitted to the Byzantine scholars who were assembling the Venetus A manuscript eight hundred years later. By the time the unnamed woman was buried with this precious pillow in the Hawara necropolis, Homer had already become the Homer we now have.

The key phase in this creation of the Homer that Roman, Byzantine, late medieval, Renaissance and early modern Europe all thought of as the undeniable text was in the halls of the Ptolemaic library in Alexandria. Between the third and second centuries BC, a sequence of great Alexandrian editor-scholars, enormously funded by the wealth of the Ptolemies, the rulers of Egypt, created the monumental Homer that is visible in the Hawara grave, the Byzantine codex Venetus A and in the

minds of Alexander Pope and John Keats. That Alexandrian era is the narrow neck through which an earlier and rather different Homer passed.

The famous library of Alexandria was not just a gathering of texts but
far more energetic and dynamic than that, a massive multidisciplinary
research institute, an engine for establishing Alexandria as the center of
the civilized world. By royal edict from the Graeco-Egyptian dynasty of
pharaohs, no ship could call at the port of Alexandria without being
searched for the books it carried. Every one would be copied with unforgiving exactness and marked in the catalog as "from the ships." Occasionally the librarians held on to the original and returned the copy.

The Alexandrian library was the repository for Greek culture, the place
in which the plays of the Athenian tragedians and the works of Plato and
Aristotle were preserved, but it was devised and run on a Near Eastern
model. For thousands of years it had been the practice of great Near Eastern kings to establish libraries and archives on a scale that individual Greek
city-states had never come anywhere near. Alexandria fused Babylon and
Nineveh with Athens and Sparta.

With thirty to fifty state-funded scholars at work in the library, the
head librarian also the royal tutor, and the agents of the Ptolemies scouring the Mediterranean for copies of all books—magic, music, metaphysics,
zoology, geography, cosmology, Babylonian, Jewish, Greek and Egyptian
thought—the Alexandrian library was a grand central knowledge machine.
It was an exercise in cultural dominance, tyranny through control of the
word. By the first century BC, it was thought that the library contained
700,000 papyrus rolls, 120,000 of them poetry and prose, all stored and
labeled and cataloged in their own tailored linen or leather jackets.

This industrial-scale exercise in cultural imperialism left its impress
on Homer, and the key to the Alexandrian changes is in the large number
of marginal notes in Venetus A. The Byzantine scholar in about 950 copied
out the text the Alexandrians had bequeathed to him. In his wide margins,
he wrote down many of the remarks they had made, not only about Homer
but about previous commentators on him. It is Homer as a mille-feuille:
one leaf of scholarship laid on top of another for centuries. Other medieval manuscripts have their own additional notes, or *scholia*, and some of
the papyrus fragments, including the Hawara *Iliad*, also have marginal
notes from these editors.

It is difficult to escape the idea that the Alexandrian editors, who seem to have limited themselves to commentary rather than cuts, wanted to make Homer proper, to pasteurize him and transform him into something acceptable for a well-governed city, to make of him precisely the dignified monument that the family of the young woman in Hawara had placed beneath her head in death. There was a long tradition of treating Homer like this.

In Plato's *Republic*, written in about 370 BC, Socrates maintained that Homer would be catastrophic for most young men in the ideal city. Poetry itself was suspect, and dangerous if it disturbed the equilibrium of the citizen, but in some passages Homer stepped way beyond the mark. He quotes the beginning of book 9 of the *Odyssey*, when Odysseus is about to sit down to dinner in the beautiful palace of the king of the Phaeacians.

Nothing, Odysseus says, is more marvelous in life than sitting down to a delicious dinner with your friends, the table noisy and the waiter filling the glasses. "To my mind," Odysseus says cheerfully, looking round him at his new friends who have saved him from the unharvestable sea, "this is the best that life can offer." Not for Socrates or his pupil Plato: "Homer is the greatest of poets and first of tragedy writers; but we must remain firm in our conviction that hymns to the gods and praises of famous men are the only poetry which ought to be admitted into our State."

That frame of mind undoubtedly governed the editing process in Alexandria, and its presumptions appear at every turn. Toward the end of book 8 of the *Iliad*, Hector is making a speech to the Trojans. It has been a long and terrible day on both sides. Among the many dead, Priam's son Gorgythion had been hit hard in the chest with an arrow.

> Just as a poppy in a garden, heavy
> with its ripening seeds, bends to one side
> with the weight of spring rain;
> so his head goes slack to one side,
> weighed down by the weight of his helmet.

Night is now falling, and Hector is encouraging the Trojans to prepare themselves for the following day. He has been like a hound in the battle, pursuing the Greeks as if they were wild boar, slashing and scything at their legs in front of him, his eyes glittering in the slaughter like the god of battle. The corpses have piled up on the field like the swaths of a hay meadow newly mown and yet to be gathered. There is scarcely room for a body of men to stand together. Hector, though, has summoned the Trojans "to a place that is clear of the dead" and now speaks to them of the state they are in. They should feed their horses, light fires, roast the meat of sheep and oxen, drink "honey-hearted wine" and eat their bread. In Troy itself, the old men and the young boys should stand on the walls and the women light great fires in their houses, all to keep a watch so that the Greeks should not "ambush" them. The word he uses is *lochos*, the same as will be used in the *Odyssey* to describe the Greeks hiding in the Trojan Horse, and which has as its root *lechomai*, meaning "to lie down." The implications are clear: the Trojans stand to fight; the Greeks do so cheatingly, creepingly. The ambush, the covert attack, is the kind of violence the Greeks would do. This is Hector speaking as the man of the city, defending it against the treachery of its assailants, a man who in almost every line is the voice of his community.

The Alexandrian editors accepted these noble statements without demur. In these passages Hector fitted the idea of restrained nobility which the Hellenistic Greeks required of Homer. But Hector then moves up a gear and goes on to speak of the next day and of himself. The Greeks are no better than "dogs, carried by the fates on their black ships." Hector will go for Diomedes in the morning, and Diomedes will lie there, "torn open by a spear, with all his comrades dead around him." And Hector himself will be triumphant: "I myself wish I might be immortal and ageless all my days, And that I might be honored just as Athene and Apollo."

A peppering of special marks in the margin, hooks and dots, all carefully transcribed by the Byzantine scholars, signals the Alexandrian editors' anxiety at the vulgarity of these lines.

This apparent self-promotion and self-assertion—can that really be what Homer intended for him? In the third century BC, Zenodotus, the first librarian at Alexandria appointed by the Ptolemies, rejected the line about the fates and their black ships. Aristarchus, his great second-century successor, agreed with him. And when Hector went on to claim immortality, Aristarchus thought his words "excessively boastful," not the done thing, and highly suspect. In Aristarchus's mind, although not entirely clearly, these lines were probably not Homeric.

It is as if these editors were trying to make Homer into a proto-Virgil, to turn Hector into Aeneas, to transform the Greek epics into tales of irre-

A page from the Byzantine Venetus A manuscript of the
Iliad with editorial anxiety marks in the margin.

proachable moral instruction, and in doing so to reduce their emotional and
psychological range. But Homer was greater than his editors, rougher, less
consistent and less polite, a poet who knew that a war leader in his speech on
the eve of battle will be both a man of civilization and its raging opposite.

Compare Hector's words with the speech made by the British officer,
lieutenant colonel Tim Collins in the Kuwaiti desert about twenty miles
south of the Iraqi border on 19 March 2003, the eve of the allied invasion
of Iraq. Collins had found a place where he could address the men of the
First Battalion, the Royal Irish Regiment. In his Ray-Bans, with his cigar
in his hand and a certain swagger, speaking off the cuff to about eight

hundred men standing around him in the middle of a dusty courtyard, he spoke as Homer had Hector speak.

"We go to liberate, not to conquer," Collins began, half remembering echoes of the King James Bible, Shakespeare and Yeats, all mingling with the modern everyday in his ear.

> We are entering Iraq to free a people and the only flag which will be flown in that ancient land is their own. Iraq is steeped in history. It is the site of the Garden of Eden, of the Great Flood and the birthplace of Abraham. Tread lightly there. If there are casualties of war then remember that when they woke up and got dressed in the morning they did not plan to die this day. Allow them dignity in death. Bury them properly and mark their graves.

Alongside that restraint and magnanimity toward the enemy, and the sense that he is speaking as the representative of a great civilization himself, is something else. "I expect you," he said, addressing his young soldiers, most of them from poor Catholic northern Irish backgrounds,

> to rock their world. Wipe them out if that is what they choose . . . The enemy should be in no doubt that we are his nemesis and that we are bringing about his rightful destruction . . . As they die they will know their deeds have brought them to this place. Show them no pity . . . If someone surrenders to you then remember they have that right in international law and ensure that one day they go home to their family. The ones who wish to fight, well, we aim to please.

Hector wants his men to rock the Greeks' world. There is an element of pretension and self-aggrandizement in both of them, but the modern British officer and the Bronze Age poet both know more than the scholar-editors in their Alexandrian halls. Homer's subject is not elegance but truth, however terrible.

The Alexandrians were keen on more than a moralized Homer. Their huge and careful gathering of texts from across the ancient world and from any passing ship was a complex inheritance, a braided stream they tried to purify and make singular, to make one Homer where previously there had been many.

They did their job with scholarly decorum, sometimes deleting lines from the text they bequeathed to the future, usually in their commentaries doing no more than casting doubt on what Homer was meant to have said, marking the text with a skewer, an *obelos*, in the margin, as if to pin the error to the spot. If Homer got things wrong—killing off a warrior who then reappeared in the battle a few lines later; if he repeated a line or group of lines with no variation; if it seemed as if something had been pushed into the poem at a later date; or if Homer's ancient words simply didn't make sense to Hellenistic editors—these were all grounds for severe judgment in Alexandria. Homer had to be kept up to his own standards.

Before that Alexandrian edit, Homer was a not a single monumental presence in the ancient world but a voluble, chattering crowd of multiple voices. Ancient authors quote lines from Homer that do not appear in the post-Alexandrian text. Occasionally a piece of papyrus will have an odd or variant equivalent for a well-known line. Different Greek cities had their own different Homers. Crete had its own, as did Cyprus, Delos, Chios and Athens. Alexandrian scholars knew versions from Argos in the Peloponnese, from Sinopē on the Black Sea coast of what is now Turkey and from the great Greek colony of Massalia far to the west, beneath what is now Marseilles. There were more epics than merely the *Iliad* and the *Odyssey*, filling in the gaps of the story which the poems we know only hint at. Homer was said to have written them all. Aristotle had a different version of Homer from Plato's and prepared another for his pupil Alexander the Great, to take with him on his world adventures into Asia. Homer ripples around the ancient Mediterranean and even farther afield, taking on local color, not a man or a poem but flickering, octopus-like, varying, adopting the colors of the country he found himself in. None of these local versions survives as more than a reference or two in ancient scholarly notes, but they hint at a reality that would have made William Cowper's or Alexander Pope's hair stand rigid. Homer, before Alexandria, was multiplicity itself.

It's as if in that Alexandrian moment Homer's radiant, ragged beard and hair were trimmed and neatened for a proto-Roman world of propriety and correctness.

Roughness characterizes the world before the great pruning. In this way Homer is unlike any historical writer. The usual idea—that copying makes a text increasingly corrupt through time—must be abandoned and the opposite assumption made. As Homer traveled on through time, passing in particular through the rigorous barbers' salon of the Alexandrian scholars, the more regular he became. In the words of Casey Dué, professor of Classics at Houston and editor of the Harvard Homer multitext project: "The further back in time we go, the more multiform—the more 'wild'—our text of Homer becomes." Homer is not orderly. Hope to trace him back to his essence, to the tap root, and you find yourself lost among the tangle of his branches. Homer's identity was in his multiplicity, his essence was in his lack of it, and he soon sinks back into the world from which he came.

Homer is never there. He is the great absentee, always slipping between the fingers, a blob of mercury on a bed of wax. Nothing reliable can be said about him: his birthplace, his parents, his life story, his dates, even his existence. Was he one poet or two? Or many? Were the Homers women? Samuel Butler, a great Victorian translator of the *Odyssey*, thought that its poet must have been a girl from Trapani in Sicily, "young, headstrong and unmarried," partly because she was "so exquisitely right" in her descriptions of "every single one of [her] women," partly because she made such girlish mistakes. Would a man ever have thought, for example, that a ship should have a rudder at both ends? Homer does, twice, in the *Odyssey*, book 9, lines 483 and 540.

This Homeric unpindownability has inspired eccentrics. Craziness abounds. Medieval Italians, who could not read Greek, used to keep copies of the *Iliad* and kiss them for good luck. Lawrence of Arabia thought he was qualified as a translator of the *Odyssey* because, among other attributes, he, unlike most Greek professors, had "killed many men." No point in trying to read Homer unless you had blood on your hands. One scholarly work in Italian has revealed that Homer was Swedish and that his Mediterranean was in fact the Baltic. Another recently showed that the *Iliad* is an ancient guidebook to the stars. According to a careful and immensely detailed study written by a Dutchman, Homer was from Cambridgeshire, the Trojan War happened on the Gog Magog Hills near Cherry Hinton, "Sparta" was in Spain and "Lesbos" was the Isle of Wight. Henriette Mertz, a Chicago patent attorney, thought that Calypso lived in the Azores, that Scylla and Charybdis were Homer's descriptions of tidal movements in the Bay of Fundy, Newfoundland, and that Nausicaa and her father lived in the Caribbean.

None of this is new. Plutarch (AD ca. 46–120) thought Calypso's island was five days' sail from Britain out in the North Atlantic, perhaps in the Faroes. Earlier still, many lives of Homer were written in the ancient world, some now preserved in precious early medieval manuscripts that are stored in some of the great repositories of Europe. They are rich in creative detail, but, like so much else to do with Homer, all of them were made up. In the library of the Medicis in Florence you will find a fourteenth-century manuscript that describes the way in which Homer lived and worked and sang his poems on Chios, the desiccated rusk of an island off the Aegean coast of Turkey. According to a ninth-century manuscript now in the Biblioteca Nazionale in Rome, he was born in Smyrna, on what is now the Turkish mainland. Others say in Ithaca, as the grandson of Odysseus, or so the Pythia in Delphi told the emperor Hadrian when he inquired; or in the Argolid, where Agamemnon had ruled in Mycenae; or in Thessaly, in the harsh and half-civilized north of Greece, the northern zone on the edge of civility from where Achilles came; or, as a manuscript now in Rome claims, in Egypt, because his heroes had the habit of kissing each other and that was an Egyptian practice. Even, in time, the Romans themselves claimed him as one of theirs. An eleventh-century manuscript now in the royal library in the Escorial outside Madrid adds Athens to the list. Many claim he was born, or died, or at least lived for a while, on the island of Ios in the Cyclades. In other words, he came from everywhere and nowhere.

The life of Homer lurks in this way in the subconscious of the European imagination. He is present in the archives but mysteriously absent. And hanging over all the suggestions in these ancient lives, which are thought to draw on ideas of Homer that emerged in about the sixth century BC, is a deep air of doubt. Did Homer really come from any of these places? Homer, even in the tradition of the ancient lives, seems to exist as a kind of miasma, a suggestion of himself, more an idea than a man, a huge and potent nonbeing.

But from these muddled, uncertain texts one or two beautiful suggestions do emerge. In the ninth-century life of Homer now in the Biblioteca Nazionale in Rome, the author—himself anonymous—compiled the verdicts he could glean from the past, and quoted Aristotle from a book called *On Poets* which is otherwise now lost. "The people of Ios, Aristotle said, record that Homer was born from a spirit, a daimon, who danced along with the Muses." His mother, a girl from Ios, had got pregnant with the daimon. So it was as simple as that: like Jesus and Achilles, Homer was half human. And his flesh was infused not with mere godliness but with the spirit of poetry. Just as Aesop never existed but was a name around which traditional fables gathered, Homer was the name given to the poems his world composed.

The word Aristotle used for this moment of fusion carries some wonderful implications. The Greek for "dance with" is *synchoreuo*, meaning "to join in the chorus with." The *choreia* of which the Muses and Homer's daimon father formed a part was a singing dance—words, music and movement together. The same word meant both the tune they danced to and, by extension, any orderly circle or circling motion. Even the islands of the Cyclades, of which Ios is one, arranged as they are in a wide circle on the horizon around the sacred island of Delos, were thought to be a *choreia*. It was, in essence, any beautiful turning in motion together, especially of the stars. Buried in this half-mystical genealogy is the understanding that Homer's poems are the music of the universe.

Another life, said to have been written by Plutarch, the Greek historian of the first century AD, and perhaps genuinely drawing on Plutarch's lost books, says straightforwardly that Homer's fatherland was nowhere on earth; his ancestors came from "great heaven" itself: "For you were born of no mortal mother, but of Calliope." Calliope was the muse of epic poetry. Her name means "beautiful voice," and she was the daughter of Zeus, the all-powerful king of the gods, and of Mnemosyne, the goddess of memory. This is not the language we now use. It is even a little off-putting, too high, too reminiscent of murky paintings on ignorable ceilings, but it says what seems to be the truth. There was no human being called Homer; his words are the descendants of memory and power, the offspring of the muse who had a beautiful voice. The myth itself identifies something that biography and geography can only grasp at. Homer is his poetry. No man called Homer was ever known, and it doesn't help to think of Homer as a man. Easier and better is to see him abstractly, as the collective and inherited vision of great acts done long ago. The poems acknowledge that. In the first lines of both the *Iliad* and the *Odyssey*, they call on the muse as their own divine mother, the source of authority and power, to tell the tales the teller is about to begin.

The name Homer—which is pronounced in Greek with a short *o* and a long *e*, *Homeeros*, making it stranger than you had imagined, from a more distant world—may mean "blind," at least in the dialect of Greek spoken on Lesbos. From the name came the tradition that Homer was blind, although that too was fiercely disputed by the ancient authors.

Or it may mean something stranger still: a "connector" or even "bond." Homer, perhaps, was the man who joined, in the way of the poet, things that might otherwise have lived apart: different elements of the inherited stories or those stories and the audiences who listened to his telling of them.

There is another tradition, related to that one, which runs through all his ancient biographies. Homer was not his original name, perhaps only given him when he went blind or became a hostage (another possible etymology). His original name in this version was Melesigenes, perhaps because he was born by the river Meles, which runs through Smyrna, now Izmir, or more intriguingly because the name can mean "caring for his clan." This Homer is to be seen as the man who cared for his people, his inheritance, his race descent, the way he came into being, his origins. Homer is what looked after the source, what found, remembered and transmitted truth from the distant past. In that meaning of his name, his essence is not his smart newness, his ability to connect, but the antiquity of the tales he tells. He is the embodiment of retrospect.

All poetry is memorial. Much of it is elegy. The earliest to have been found was dug up by Victorian archaeologists in Sumer, in what is now Iraq, on a tablet marked with wedge-shaped cuneiform symbols pressed into the wet clay before it dried. The fragmentary poems in the clay were written in about 2600 BC, perhaps two thousand years before the Homeric epics were first written on papyrus. But that first written Sumerian poetry is not about the springtime of the world. Poetry begins by looking back to the beautiful past with a song about Ashnan, the goddess of grain, and her seven sons, opening with these chantable, formulaic repetitive lines.

U re u re na-nam
Gi re gi re na-nam
Mu re mu re na-nam

In those days, now it was in those days,
In those nights, now it was in those nights,
In those years, now it was in those years

As far back as you can reach, poets have been looking back, their poetry living in the gap that opens between now and then. Another song, from Ur in Iraq, written down at about the same time, instructs the singer to

attend to what is old, and not allow it to be neglected.
Let nothing be neglected in practice,
Let him apply himself to the art of singing
Let the scribe stand by and catch the songs in his handwriting
Let the singer stand by and speak to the scribe from the songs
So that they will be made to last in the scribal college
So that none of my praise-song should perish
So that none of my words should be dropped from the tradition.

This song is what Melesigenes, Homer's hidden name, actually means. You might think of Homer as the skilled reteller of his people's stories. But he is more than that; the poems are the passed baton itself, ancient meaning enshrined in the remembered word.

One more story, often repeated in the fictional biographies of him that were written throughout antiquity, hints at Homer's unfittedness for the ordinary world. It exists in many versions, but the most articulate has survived in a manuscript transcribed in the eleventh century AD and now in the great royal library in the Escorial outside Madrid.

Homer is at the end of his life, sitting on the beach on the Cycladean island of Ios, after a life of traveling and singing his poems in many places in the Greek world. This is not his home. As he sits there, alone and blind, he hears some fishermen coming up the beach toward him. They have been at sea, and Homer calls out to them: "Fishermen from Arcadia [it is unexplained why it should be Arcadia in the Peloponnese when he is in the Cyclades], have we caught anything?" There is something charming, or perhaps self-ingratiating, in that "we." But they reply unkindly. "All that we caught we have left behind and all that we missed we carry." By which they mean that their fishing had been useless, but as they sat out at sea with nothing to do, they searched each other's bodies for lice. Those lice they had caught, they killed and threw into the sea; those they missed were still on them in their clothes.

It was a joke, a riddle, a tease for a blind old man, but he didn't understand it, and, crushed by the loneliness and depression that came in the wake of that failure to comprehend, he died on Ios, where he was buried under an epitaph he had written himself.

> Here the earth conceals that sacred head,
> The setter-in-beautiful-order [*kosmitora*] of heroic men,
> the godly Homer.

According to that much-repeated story, it was the triviality of the joke, a ridiculing of incapacity, even a lack of nobility in others, that finally killed him. This is Homer as the Great Outsider, blind, from beyond our ken, the figure who does not belong in the world where everyone knows everyone else, the man who has yet to enter the restaurant or the drawing room. He is outside our normality, scarcely even aware of the merry din within, with an austerity about him, a grandeur and an urgent, other reality.

Homer—allied to his neighbor and contemporary Isaiah, another great speaker of wisdom, whose dates and identity also stretch across many generations from at least 1500 to 600 BC—is the archetype from which every great seer is descended: he is Lear on the heath, Rousseau in a reverie on his island in the Lac de Bienne, the Ancient Mariner who waylays the wedding guest at the bridegroom's door, but who will never enter that feast. Homer exists in his other world, almost unknowably separate from us in time and space, a realm whose distance allows ideas of transcendence to develop around him. His distance from us is itself an imaginative space which his own greatness expands to fill.

This is no modern effect; it was the effect Homer had on the ancient Greeks, as a voice from the distant past, even a voice from the silence, the voice of greatness untrammeled by any connection with our present mundanities. Homer doesn't describe the world of heroes; he *is* the world of heroes. As his epitaph said, he made their *kosmos*, a word which in Greek can mean "order," "world," "beauty" and "honor." It is used in the

Iliad when the commanders set their men in order for battle. It is used to describe the order in which a poet sets the elements of his tale. Those qualities are all different dimensions of one thing. Everything one might associate with the heroic—nobility, directness, vitality, scale, unflinching regard for truth, courage, adventurousness, coherence—is an aspect of the cosmic and all of it is what "Homer" means.

5 · FINDING HOMER

It seems clear, from the kind of Greek in which the Homeric poems are written, that the main text preserved by the Alexandrians came from Athens, where Homer could be heard almost daily, in recitals by rhapsodes, professional artists who strung together choice passages from the epics, learning by heart parts of the inherited text and, in a way not entirely approved of by the traditionalists, selling their services for dinner parties or entertainments. Homer was also used as a manual in school, the poems treated as tales of great men and women, of nobility in crisis, and of the choices people must make when faced with the deepest challenges of their lives. Homer for classical Athens was an encyclopedia of moral choice.

The Homeric poems were also performed with enormous elaboration at the quadrennial festival of the Panathenaia, where, at least according to Eustathius, a twelfth-century Byzantine bishop of Thessalonica, the reciters of the *Odyssey* wore sea-purple and of the *Iliad* earth-red costumes, "the purple on account of Odysseus's wanderings at sea, the red on account of the slaughter and bloodshed at Troy." If the *Odyssey* men were soaked in the royal purple dye of the Phoenicians and those of the *Iliad* in the blood of the heroes, nothing could be clearer about the role Homer played in classical Athens's idea of itself. At their most holy and self-conscious moment, the Athenians gathered for total immersion in the Homeric stories, drinking up the tales from which most of the great tragedies drew their plots and characters, thinking of Homer as the source of what they were.

A clan of reciters from Chios on the eastern side of the Aegean, calling themselves the Homeridae, claimed to be Homer's descendants and to have his precious poems in manuscript handed down to them by the great man, their ancestor. Whether there is any truth in that claim is unknown, but, under the Athenian surface, the main constituent of the Greek in which the epics are written is Ionic, which was spoken in Chios and other parts of western Anatolia. And there is an early piece of evidence for Chios in the so-called *Homeric Hymn to Delian Apollo*, written in Homeric hexameters, when the singer himself says:

> Remember me in after time whenever any one of the men on earth, a stranger who has seen and suffered much, comes here and asks of you: "Who do you think, girls, is the sweetest singer that comes here, and in whom do you most delight?" Then answer, each and all of you, with one voice: "He is a blind man, and lives in rocky Chios: his songs are forever supreme." As for me, I will carry your fame as far as I roam over the earth to the well-placed cities of man, and they will believe also; for indeed this thing is true.

The *Iliad* also knows that country, not only the shape of the land around Troy but the habits of the wind, the form of islands and the nature of the sea there. If Homer needs to turn for a comparison to a specific place, the choice he usually makes is there too.

Chios lies only seven miles off the Turkish coast. Its dry limestone gorges push deep into its mountains, and, on the bench of flat arable land beside the sea, acre after acre is covered in olive groves, vineyards and the dark, irregular mastic bushes, the source of a clear chewable gum, much valued in antiquity.

The huge harbor at Chios town is almost empty of shipping now—a few yachts, a ferry, one or two container ships—but is still surrounded by the cafés on the port side, the banging of dominoes on tables, the bales of stuff awaiting collection. Behind them are the crumbling neoclassical villas of the Chiote merchant class, who in the nineteenth century made their fortunes trading around the Mediterranean. Chios is what it always has been: a commercial island, outward-looking—there are still some powerful shipowning families here—and with its foundations resting on the products of the earth, the red wine, loved by Virgil, famous across the whole Mediterranean for its blackness, and the pungent, peppery green island oil.

Far to the south of Chios town, a rare and extraordinary ghost of the Homeric world can be recovered. A narrow road curls its way down the length of the island. Drought is all around you, a blazing sky and burningly bright rocks. In among the rocks are the cisterns, the beautiful dark and buried places of cool and conservation, an eye of water at their heart, roofed in stone, protected from the sun. In a landscape of such exposure and harshness, the cistern seems like the guarantee of continuity.

All this defines a dry world. It doesn't rain in Chios from the beginning of June until the end of October. What rain has fallen in the winter sinks into the ground and emerges from the rock reservoirs as springs. There the soil gathers, and the fertility builds in a landscape that is otherwise bones. The result is a kind of sharpness, superdefinition, a world polarized between the inhabited and the bare, the habitable and the desolate.

In places like this, the growing of human sustenance can only be governed by the presence of water. Where the springs (*vryses* in modern Greek) emerge is where the vegetable gardens are. "I am going to the springs" means "I am going to the gardens." The roots of that word stretch far back into ancient Greek, from *bruein*, which when it describes water means "to gush out," "to bubble up," "to spring." But more than that, *bruein* means "to be full to bursting," "to swell," "to abound," "to be luxuriant," "to teem with produce." It is the verb of emergent life.

Beyond the gardens full of grapes and figs, pomegranates, plums and blackberries, those miraculous concentrations of sugar and juice in the damp corners of the island, often away from houses, the dry country stretches, the world of drought in which everything that grows infiltrates its roots between the rocks and is defended against the grazing and browsing teeth of the animals that would devour it. The leaves that survive are either bitter or armored in thorns. Even the thorns are branched, thorns with thorns on them. Settlement here cannot choose to dispose itself carelessly as it can in a temperate or wooded country. Life must be concentrated: the city, the village, the gathered place is a necessary response to a landscape in which life is thin on the ground.

Almost at the southern tip of the island, Emporio is little more than a scatter of one or two buildings and a taverna, a stub of a quay at which the fishing boats are tied up, a looped horseshoe of a harbor, a gray beach on which the Aegean laps. Its name means "the trading center," the emporium, which may also have been the name of this small settlement in antiquity. Here, in June 1952, came two of the great men of Homeric studies in the second half of the twentieth century: a young English archaeologist, John Boardman, then deputy director of the British School at Athens, with the young architect Michael Ventris, the man who would soon decipher Linear B, the written language of Mycenaean Greece. They walked up from the harbor—"a well-girt man carrying nothing in his hands can today reach the acropolis from the harbour side in twenty minutes without serious loss of breath"—and high above the valley, on top of a dry, conical hill overlooking the little harbor, they found an ancient settlement, a rocky citadel, heavily walled against raiding pirates, the workmanship of the masonry, Boardman reported, "wretched throughout."

It was no great city but a rather poor and abandoned village, probably built in about 800 BC. Outside the acropolis walls there remain some small, stepped and paved, walkable streets between one- or two-roomed houses. There are stables and granaries beside them. The scale is domestic, and because nothing was built here later, everything is clear on the ground, looking much as it did when abandoned in 600 BC. The tall white spires of the asphodels glow on the stony, lizardy hillsides. Inside the acropolis walls there is a small temple to Athene (Boardman and Ventris found little votive shields in there, given by fighting men to the warlike goddess) and a *megaron*, a large columned room about sixty feet long and twenty wide, a gathering hall, with the stone bases of three wooden columns down its center. Perhaps eighty people could have met here. It is not unlike a Saxon or Viking mead hall, in which *Beowulf* or the sagas would have been heard or sung. It is the great house of the settlement, the only one inside the acropolis walls, and with a commanding view from its columned porch down across the hill to the harbor below. Boardman found little inside, a few pieces of pottery with a "heavy cream slip," the handle of a wine jug, but stand in here now and you can start to feel your way toward the Homeric world of the eighth century.

Beyond the lee of the island, the Aegean sparkles under the north wind. On the far shore, gray mountains step back into the Asian mainland—a promise of scale and richness outside the constraints of island life. The eighth-century sea is full of threat, and even in the sunshine, as cigarette smoke disappears in the brilliance of the light, Emporio feels carefully held back, marginal, defensive. It is cleverly designed so that the harbor can be seen from the acropolis, but the acropolis is almost invisible from the harbor. You can watch the people down there in the taverna, where the fish are smoking on the griddles, and they will not know.

Boardman thought that about five hundred people might have lived here, in about fifty houses spread over ten acres. Their lord and master would have occupied the *megaron*, and there the heroic songs would have been sung. There is no grandeur. It is a rough, overt power structure. The plain below the acropolis may be covered in olives and mastic bushes, and its harbor is there so that these people can reach out to lands beyond those horizons, but this miniature city is up here for protection. Emporio is both closed and open, a place to withdraw into and from which to venture out. It is a place belonging to robber-traders, at least half piratical, needing to rely on imported grain for its sustenance, perhaps from Egypt, perhaps from the Black Sea, and to export its wine and oil and gum for its currency, but inseparable from violence. Here it is possible to feel that Homer is the product of an essentially marginal world, away from the great civilizations, the lords of Emporio fascinated by the great but not able to count themselves among them.

If Homer was an ancient inheritance in the eighth century BC, as I believe it was, already a thousand years old, this is the sort of place in which that memory would have been treasured and nurtured, where the Keatsian sense of enlargement and the surge of greatness would have been experienced by the young men hearing the stories, no doubt inspiring their own visions of love and violence. Just as much as Athens or Alexandria, places like this would have been links in the chain.

Only the phlomis and the thorns grow on the eastern shore of Chios; the only colors are the sand-washed blue of the sea and the rust stains in the limestone of the cliffs. Here and there the cushion tufts of a low thistle show purple in its nest of thorns. On a stony path just above the sea, with a swell breaking on the shore, I found a young kid, perhaps born that spring and now laid out on a rock, dead and as dry as parchment. It had been preserved by the drought. Its leather collar with bell was still around its neck, its yellow plastic ear tags pinned into its ears, its hooves tucked up under its chest, where its ribs, like flat, blanched pencils, just protruded from the coat. The teeth were made prominent by the shrinking of the lips, but otherwise it was almost perfect, as if in the drought one day it had simply lain down and died. Touchingly, its head was turned as if it were trying to lick its own flank. The eyes were gone, and you could look through their sockets into the skull. It was the Homeric world: brutal, perfect, without euphemism, but somehow enshrining a longing for something better, softer, more forgiving.

The Homeric poems, or at least versions of them, were written down somewhere very like this, perhaps in about 725 BC, or maybe as much as a century later. Precision is almost certainly irrelevant; there can be no ruler-drawn horizon at which the written Homer begins.

If Homer is from this moment, the poems are the product of a culture emerging from a dark age, looking to a future but also looking back to a past, filled with nostalgia for the years of integrity, simplicity, nobility and straightforwardness. The *Iliad* is soaked in retrospect. The *Odyssey*, the twin and pair of it, is filled with heroic adventurism and the sense of possibility, as if it were an American poem and the *Iliad* its European counterpart.

There is no doubt that the poet of the *Odyssey* knew the *Iliad*. The *Odyssey*, with extraordinary care, is shaped around the preexistence of the *Iliad*. It fills in details that are absent from the earlier poem—the Trojan Horse, the death of Achilles—but never mentions anything that is described there. That discretion and mutuality is present on a deeper level too. So, where the *Iliad* is a poem about fate and the demands that fate puts on individual lives, the inescapability of death and of the past, of each of us being locked inside a set of destinies, the *Odyssey*, for all its need to return home, consistently toys with the offer of a new place and a new life, a chance to revise what you have been given, for the individual—or at least the great individual—to stand out against fate.

The two poems talk across that divide. The *Iliad* is rooted in the pain of Troy, the singular place and the sense of entrapment that it brings to everyone involved. The *Odyssey* is constantly free and constantly inventive. That difference is reflected in the two heroes. Achilles is fixed into rage, into the need to fulfill his fate, fixed into having to revenge the death of his friend Patroclus. Odysseus is always slipping out, the man who has been everywhere, seen everything, done everything, but also thought of everything, invented everything and changed everything.

These are the two possibilities for human life. You can either do what

your integrity tells you to do, or niftily find your way around the obsta-
cles life throws in your path. That is the great question the poems pose.
Which will you be? Achilles or Odysseus, the monument of obstinacy
and pride or the slippery trickster in whom nothing is certain and from
whom nothing can be trusted? The singular hero or the ingenious man?

The *Iliad* embraces an earlier, rawer, more heroic and more tragic
past. The *Odyssey* looks forward, takes modern dealing and adventuring
and casts a magic spell over it so that it becomes a strange and idealized
version of the trading and colonizing life. The *Iliad* is a picture of what we
think we once were and maybe long to be; the *Odyssey* a version of what
we are and what we might yet be. There is no need to put a date on those
perspectives; their prospect and retrospect are everlasting dimensions of
the human condition. In any age, the present is no more than the saddle
of level ground at the pass, an instant of revelation in front of you and
abandonment behind. Like all great art, Homer is essentially transitional,
emergent, hung between what is lost and what does not yet exist.

In a way that remains permanently and inevitably uncertain, the Phoenician alphabet arrived in the Greek world, probably in the ninth century
BC, from the trading ports of the Near East. Powerful currents were running between the Near East and the Aegean. Craftsmen, foods, spices,
herbs, precious metals, ways of working that metal, myths, metaphysical
ideas, poetry, stories—all were flooding in from the east, and the alphabet came with them. Unlike the earlier complex scripts, the simple Phoenician alphabet wasn't confined to high-class scribes, and the Greeks soon
bent it to their own use, adapting Phoenician letters for vowels and for *ph-*,
ch- and *ps-*, which do not occur in Phoenician. Like the songs of Homer
themselves, the Greek scripts they developed varied from place to place,
but of all the scraps and fragments of early Greek text that have survived
from the eighth century, none is more suddenly illuminating than a small
reconstructed object from the island of Ischia, at the far western end of
the Greek-speaking world, guarding the northern entrance to the Bay
of Naples.

Ischia now is a dream of well-being, a sharply dressed salad of an
island, rising to a high volcanic peak in Mount Epomeo, rimmed in lidos
and those in search of rheumatic cures, but with a lush greenness which

must have seemed to any Aegean sailor like an oasis of welcome. It is a version of Calypso's island, balmy, seductive, inviting, somehow suspended from mundane realities. The sun comes up over the shoulder of Vesuvius on the mainland and lights the lemon trees and the figs. Mounds of bougainvillea and ipomoea clump and tumble down the hillsides. A milky haze hangs all morning over an almost motionless sea. Bees hum in the rosemary flowers, and crickets tick in the grass.

Ischia offered the early Iron Age Greeks more than exquisite comfort. When the first settlers came here in about 770 BC from the Aegean island of Euboea, they set up the earliest, most northern and most distant of all Greek colonies in Italy. They chose it because the northern tip of the island provides the perfect recipe for a defensible trading post: a high, sheer-walled acropolis, Monte Vico, with sheltered bays on each side, one protected from all except northerlies, the other open only to the east. Between the two a shallow saddle is rich in deep volcanic soils where a few vine and fruit trees still grow among the pine-umbrellaed villas and the swimming pools. Here, beginning in the early 1950s, the archaeologist Giorgio Buchner excavated about five hundred eighth- and seventh-century BC graves that reveal the lives of people for whom the Homeric poems were an everyday reality.

This little Greek stone town was called Pithekoussai, Ape-island, perhaps from the monkeys they found here on arrival, or more interestingly as a name suitable for people who were seen from the mainland as vulgar and adventurous traders, laden with cash, irreverent and with uncertain morals, enriching themselves on the edge of the known world (*pithekizein* meant "to monkey about"). It was an astonishing and wonderful melting pot, four thousand people living here by 700 BC, nothing halfhearted about it, nor apparently militaristic. People from mainland Italy, speaking a kind of Italic, were living here, with Phoenicians from Tyre and Sidon, Byblos and Carthage, Aramaeans from modern Syria and Greeks. The archaeologists found no ethnic zoning in the cemetery. All were living together and dying together, buried side by side. There was little apparent in the way of an ethnic gap between these people. It was a deeply mixed world. Iron with the chemical signatures of Elba and mainland Tuscany was worked here in the blacksmiths' quarter and sold to clients in the Near East. Trade linked the island with Apulia, Calabria, Sardinia, Etruria and Latium as well as the opposite Campania shore. No other

Greek site in Italy has objects from such a vast stretch of the Iron Age Mediterranean.

Buchner found no hint in any of the graves of a warrior aristocracy. The only blades were a few iron knives, awls and chisels. The leading members of the Pithekoussai world were from a commercial middle class, some with small workshops for iron and bronze, many with slaves of their own. The style of burial marks the difference between those classes: the slaves hunched fetally in small and shallow hollows, no possessions beside them; their masters, mistresses and their children laid out supine, in plain and dignified style, accompanied by simple but beautiful grave goods.

Much of their pottery came from Corinth and Rhodes, and what they didn't import, they copied. Small Egyptian scarabs were often worn as amulets by the children and went to their graves with them, along with stone seals from northern Syria and one or two Egyptian faience beads. There are some fine red pots made in the Phoenician city of Carthage on the North African coast, and silver pins and rings from Egypt. A tomb of a young woman buried in about 700 BC was found with her body surrounded by little dishes from Corinth and small ointment jars, seventeen of them, around her, a dressing-table-full. Men also had little fat-bellied oil jars with them, some no more than an inch high and an inch across, pocket offerings, maybe used in the funeral rites. A fisherman was buried with his line and net; only the bronze fish hook and the folded-over lead weights of the net have survived. These men were all buried in the way of Homeric heroes, their bodies cremated on wooden pyres and then interred with the charred wood and their possessions beneath small tumuli.

Nothing is coarse or gross. Big-eyed sea snakes and fluent, freely drawn fish decorate the gray-and-ocher pottery. There are flat-footed wine jugs, suitable for a shipboard table. One big dish is decorated with a chariot wheel, perhaps another faint heroic memory. Some pots are decorated with griffins from patterns that had their distant origins in Mesopotamia, others with swastikas that probably originated just as long ago in the Proto-Indo-European cultures of the Caspian steppe.

Fusion and mixture, a kind of mental mobility, is the identifying mark of this little city. It was not a luxury civilization, but as you spend a morning walking around the empty, cool marble halls of the Pithekoussai Museum in the Villa Arbusto, peering in at the pots, you can feel the

The design on the shipwreck *cratēr* from Pithekoussai in Ischia.

stirring of life in this distant and adventurous place 2,700 years ago. It doesn't take much to see the wine being mixed in these bowls, poured from these jugs or drunk from these cups, nor the glittering fish hauled up in these nets or the goods loaded on distant quays and beaches and sold from here to curious buyers on the mainland of Italy.

And the museum holds its surprises. One late-eighth-century *cratēr* originally made in Attica, a bowl for mixing wine and water, depicts this world in trouble. On its gray and rapidly painted body, a ship floats all wrong in the sea, turned over in a gale, its curved hull now awash, its prow and stern pointing down to the seabed. Everything has fallen out. Wide-shouldered and huge-haunched men are adrift in the ocean beneath, their hair ragged, their arms flailing for shore and safety. Striped and cross-hatched fish, some as big as the men, others looking on, swim effortlessly in the chaos. A scattering of little swastikas does little to sanctify this fear-filled waterworld. One man's head is disappearing into the mouth of the biggest fish of all. It is a disaster, fueled by the fear the Greeks had of the creatures of the sea, alien animals which, as Achilles taunts one of his victims, "will lick the blood from your wounds and nibble at your gleaming fat." The scene is no new invention; it is painted with all the rapidity and ease of having been painted many times before.

There is no need to attach the name of Odysseus to this; nor of Jonah, the Hebrew prophet swallowed by a fish, his story exactly contemporary with this pot. It is merely the story of life on the Iron Age seas, the reality of shipwreck, the terror of the sea as a closing-over element filled with voracious monsters. In a later, Western picture, the large-scale catastrophe of the ship itself would have been the focus. Here it is pushed to the outer margin and made almost irrelevant; the central characters are the men, their hair and limbs out of order, the experience of human suffering uppermost. In that way, this is a picture from the Homeric mind.

Then, in a room hidden deep in the museum, you find the other transforming dimension of Pithekoussai: these people wrote. Shards from the eighth century BC are marked or painted with tiny fragments of Greek. One has the name Teison, perhaps the cup's owner. A second, on a little fragment of a cup, says "eupoteros"—meaning "better to drink from." A third, also in Greek, written like the others with the letters reading from right to left as they are in Phoenician, and with no gaps between the words, says, fragmentarily, " . . . *inos m' epoies[e]*." The verb *poieo* has the same root as "poetry," and the inscription means "someone whose name ended in -*inos* made me"—Kallinos, Krokinos, Minos, Phalinos, Pratinos? This is no scratched graffito, but painted as part of the geometric design. It is another first: the oldest artist's signature in Europe.

By 750 BC at the latest, writing had seeped into all parts of this expanding, connecting, commercial, polyglot world. Pithekoussai is not unique. Eighth-century inscriptions, many of them chatty, everyday remarks, with no claim to special or revered significance, have survived from all over the Aegean and Ionian Seas. These aren't officious palace directives, but witty remarks, sallies to be thrown into conversation.

And, as a wonderful object on Ischia reveals, Homer played his part. It was found in the tomb of a young boy, perhaps fourteen years old, who died in about 725 BC. He was Greek, and unlike most of the children was cremated, an honor paid to his adulthood and maturity. In his grave his father placed many precious things: a pair of Euboean wine-mixing bowls from the famous potters of their home island, jugs, other bowls, and lots of little oil pots for ornaments.

The greatest treasure looks insignificant at first: a broken and mended wine cup from Rhodes, about seven inches across, gray-brown with black decoration and sturdy handles. Scratched into its lower surface on one side, and not at first visible but dug away a little roughly with a burin, are three lines of Greek, the second and third of which are perfect Homeric hexameters. Not only is this the oldest surviving example of written Greek poetry, contemporary with the moment Homer is first thought to have been written down; it is also the first joke about a Homeric hero.

In the *Iliad*, during a passage of brutal bloodletting and crisis for the Greeks, the beautiful Hecamēdē, a deeply desirable Trojan slave-woman, captured by Achilles and now belonging to Nestor, mixes a medicinal drink for the wounded warriors as they come in from battle: strong red wine, barley meal and, perhaps a little surprisingly, grated goat's cheese, with an onion and honey on the side. Hecamēdē did the mixing in a giant golden, dove-decorated cup belonging to Nestor, which a little pretentiously he had brought from home: "Another man could barely move that cup from the table when it was full, but old Nestor would lift it easily."

Near Eastern stories tell of giant unliftable cups belonging to heroes from the far distant past. And in the tombs of warriors on Euboea from the ninth century BC there are, along with arms and armor, some big bronze cheese graters, now thought to be part of the warrior's usual field kit, perhaps for making medicines, perhaps for snacks.

So this little situation—the Nestor story, the unliftable cup, the Euboean inheritance, and the presence at a drinking party of wonderfully desirable women—has deep roots. Remarkably, they come together in the joke and invitation scratched on the Ischian cup. "I am the cup of Nestor," it says,

> good for drinking
> Whoever drinks from this cup, desire for beautifully
> crowned Aphrodite will seize him instantly.

The Pithekoussaian trader was turning the Homeric scriptures upside down. This little cup was obviously *not* like Nestor's cup, the very opposite in fact: all too liftable. Its wine was *not* to cure wounds received in battle. It was to get drunk at a party. And drinking it would *not* lead to an old man's interminable reminiscing over his heroic past. No, the cup and the delicious wine it contained would lead to the far more congenial activity of which Aphrodite was queen: sex. This elegant little wine cup, treasured far from home amid all the burgeoning riches, gold and silver brooches, success and delight of Pithekoussai, a place supplied with beautiful slave-girls taken from the Italian mainland, was for the drinking of alcoholic aphrodisiacs. The inscription was an eighth-century invitation to happiness.

The distant past might often seem like the realm of seriousness, but the Ischian cup reorientates that. The first written reference to Homer is so familiar with him, and so at ease with writing, that in mock Homeric hexameters it can deny all the seriousness Homer has to offer. Homer and his stories were so deeply soaked into the fabric of mid- to late-eighth-century BC Greek culture that dad-style jokes could be made about him. And that makes one thing clear: here, in 725 BC, is nowhere near the beginning of this story. The original Homer is way beyond reach, signaling casually from far out to sea.

There is only one aspect of grief associated with the sophisticated optimism and gaiety of this story, and it is inadvertent. The father offered this cup to his fourteen-year-old son in the flames of the funeral pyre, where it broke into the pieces which the archaeologists have now painstakingly gathered and restored. Death denied the boy the adult pleasures to which these toy-verses were inviting him. And that is another capsule of the Homeric condition: the Odysseyan promise of delight enclosed within the Iliadic certainty of death.

6 · HOMER THE STRANGE

The Pithekoussai wine cup marks the limits of the written Homer. It is the edge of a time-cliff; step beyond it, farther back in time, and the ground falls away. In that disturbingly airy and insubstantial world out beyond the cliff face, before the eighth century BC, Homer is unwritten, existing only in the minds of those who knew him.

It is a disorienting condition for our modern culture: how can something of such importance and richness have had no material form? How can the Greeks have trusted so completely to their minds? At home in Scotland, I sometimes go up to the edge of the sea cliff above the house, looking down to the fulmars circling in the four hundred feet of air below me. Again and again, the birds cut their effortless disks in that space, turning in perfect, repetitive circles, in and out of the sunlight, scarcely adjusting a feather to the eddies, but calm and self-possessed in all the mutability around them; and I have thought that in that fulmar-flight there may be a model of the Homeric frame of mind. You don't need to fix something to know it. You know it by doing it again and again, never quite the same, never quite differently. You may even find, in that tiller-tweaking mobility—a slight adjustment here, another there—that you know things that the rigid and the fixed could never hope to know. The flight is alive in the flying, not in any record of it. And perhaps we, not Homer, are the aberration. Of about three thousand languages spoken today, seventy-eight have a written literature. The rest exist in the mind and the mouth. Language—man—is essentially oral.

Until the twentieth century, no one had any idea that Homer might have existed in this strange and immaterial form. It was the assumption that Homer, like other poets, *wrote* his poetry. Virgil, Dante and Milton were merely following in his footsteps. The only debate was over why these written poems were in places written so badly. Why had he not written them better? Both the *Iliad* and the *Odyssey* are riddled with internal contradictions. No self-respecting poet would allow such clumsiness.

The great eighteenth-century Cambridge scholar Richard Bentley—the dullest man alive, according to Alexander Pope, "that microscope of Wit,/Sees hairs and pores, examines bit by bit"—thought that Homer wrote "a sequel of songs and Rhapsodies, to be sung by himself for small earnings and good cheer, at festivals and other days of Merriment; the Ilias he made for the men and the Odysseis for the other Sex. These loose songs were not connected together in the form of an epic poem till . . . about 500 years after." Homer was no longer a genius; he was the work of an editor-collector, perhaps not entirely unlike Professor Bentley himself.

Later microscopes of wit thought there was not even one author, but a string of minor folk-poets whose efforts had been brought together by the great Athenian or even Alexandrian editor-scholars. The Prince of Poets had been dethroned. The scholars had won. And so the nineteenth century was animated by the debates between Analysts and Unitarians, those who thought Homer had been many and those who continued to maintain that he was one great genius.

The argument lasted for over a century, largely because of the sense of vertigo a multiple Homer induced. If Homer was dissolved into a sequence of folk-poets, one of the greatest monuments of Western civilization no longer existed. Nevertheless, these were the preconditions for the great discoveries about Homer made in the early twentieth century by the most brilliant man ever to have loved him.

Milman Parry is a god of Homer studies. No one else has made Homeric realities quite so disturbingly clear. Photographs show what his contemporaries described, a taut, focused head, a man "quiet in manner, incisive in speech, intense in everything he did." There was nothing precious or elitist about him, and his life and mind ranged widely. For a year he was a poultry farmer. Along with the technicians at the Sound Specialties Company of Waterbury, Connecticut, he was the first to develop a

Milman Parry, 1902–1935.

recording apparatus that didn't have to be interrupted every four minutes to change the disk. He took his wife and children with him on his great recording adventures in the Balkans and at night sang songs to them that mimicked and drew on the epic poems he had heard in the day. At Harvard, where he became an assistant professor, he took to washing his huge white dogs in the main drinking-water reservoir for the city, stalking about the campus in a large black hat with "an aura of the Latin quarter" about him, regaling his students with the poetry of Laforgue, Apollinaire, Eliot and e.e. cummings. Supremely multilingual, at home in Serbo-Croat, writing his first articles and papers on Homer in French, this was the man who pulled Homer back from its academic desert into life.

Parry was born in June 1902 and brought up a Quaker in the sunny sterilities of Oakland, California. From that clean, germ-free youth he plunged off into ancient Greek at Berkeley, and while still there, writing the thesis for his master's degree, jumped to the idea that Homer was neither a great poet making these poems from nothing nor a collection of minor folktales somehow strung together, but the combination and fusion of those two ideas: a poet working within a great tradition which had deep roots and multiple sources. The poems were composed by a man standing at the top of a human pyramid. He could not have stood there without the pyramid beneath him, and the pyramid consisted not only of the earlier poets in the tradition but of their audiences too, the whole set of assumptions and expectations in which the poems swam. Homer—try thinking of it as a plural noun—were the frozen and preserved words of an entire culture. At different moments in their evolution, the songs would have sounded different, but there is no need to assume that they would have been cruder or worse. At any one moment the singer is standing on the human pyramid beneath him. Hear them as they should be heard, and you will have the sound and meanings of the distant past in your mind and ear.

Parry was a romantic, who loved the ancientness of the past for itself and for its stark difference from twentieth-century America. The motivations apparent in Keats are in Parry too. For the classical scholars of eighteenth- and nineteenth-century Europe, brought up in an elite and aristocratic culture, Homer may have seemed like a contemporary, his words on honor and self-sacrifice to be taken as relevant instructions for the noble life. The only task was to clean Homer up, to make Homer more like them, to classicize him, to rid him of his repetitiveness and his awkward lack of savoir faire, to translate him, as Pope had done, with many delightful felicities overlying the raw Greek.

For the brilliant young American from Oakland, that could never have been the starting point. Homer for Parry is almost unapproachably strange and distant. Only by recognizing that distance could he be understood. Parry's guiding light was Ernest Renan, the star of the dinners at the Repas Magny. Renan had insisted on understanding the past on its own terms. "How can we grasp the physiognomy and the originality of an early literature," he had written,

> if we do not enter the personal and moral life of the people who made it, unless we place ourselves at the very point in humanity which was theirs, so that we see and feel as they saw and felt; unless we watch them live, or better, unless for a moment we live with them?

This liberal, anthropological understanding of what Homer might be— quoted and requoted by Parry in his papers—was far ahead of anything other Anglo-Saxons were thinking, and the key to that penetration of the past was in the nature of the verses themselves. Parry's central question was this: what does the nature of the poetry say about the world in which it was composed? He focused on two qualities: the way in which heroes and objects are accompanied by almost unvarying and sometimes inappropriate adjectives and epithets, the building blocks of unvarying "formulas"; and the role of words in Homer which "Homer"—the eighth-century BC scribe who wrote the poems down—almost certainly did not understand.

In 1922 the classics faculty at Berkeley told Parry that there was no chance he would get a doctorate by following up on his master's thesis on the formulas in Homer. It was not what an American classicist did. For a year Parry worked with his chickens, but he recognized that his future studies would find most encouragement with the anthropologists in Paris, and when he was twenty-two he went there to do his doctorate at the Sorbonne. What he set out to analyze may seem arcane, but it is in fact a route into the mind of the Bronze Age, an archaeology of the word. First, abandon any idea of the classic poet. The poems are not objects conceived by a single, gifted person, but inherited, shaped and reshaped by a preceding culture, stretching far back in time, something as much formed by tradition as the making of pots or the decoration of their surfaces. Homer is the world of tradition-shaped poetry, not of realism, as unlike reality as opera and profoundly guided by its own conventions. And the governing fact in that epic world is the music of the poetry.

The Homeric epics are essentially the music of hexameters—the Greek word *hexameter* means "six measures"—because in each line there are six "feet" for which the words must be chosen to fit the preexisting pattern. This verse is measured language. Within each of the six feet, the language can fall in different ways. Feet made up of a long and two shorts (a phrase like "This is the") are called dactyls, after the Greek word for a finger, *daktylos*, a word which both mimics the shape of the human finger—a long bone followed by two short ones—and is a dactyl itself. A foot of two longs ("hemlocks") is a spondee—*spondee* is the Greek word for a libation—an offering poured out with certainty and directness for a god, and which is a spondee itself. Most feet can be either dactyls or spondees, but the rules of epic insist that the fifth foot is usually a dactyl ("pines and the") and the final foot always a spondee.

Here, with those rules in mind, is an English hexameter by Henry Wadsworth Longfellow.

—   u u |—u u |—u   ^   u |— u u |—   u u |—   —

This is the | forest pri | meval. ^ The | murmuring | pines and the | hemlocks

Variation is always to hand: the dactylic "murmuring" could be the spondaic "moss-girt." The pines have to be surrounded by hemlocks because dactylic "rivulets" would not be allowed at the end of the line, but Longfellow could have chosen the spondaic "wood prim-eval," to make an even weightier line,

—   u u | —   — |—u ^ u |— — |—   u u |—   —

This is the | wood prim | eval. ^ The| moss-girt | pines and the | hemlocks

But he may have felt that the breeze was not blowing through that American landscape quite as he wanted. Flexibility within the pattern is at the core of the system. This is not an iron prison but a means of making memorable music, of allowing music to carry a tale.

Each of the lines has a natural break (marked here by ^ after "primeval") called a caesura, and the line naturally falls into two halves on either side of it. In reality, there are many variations in Homeric verse, but this is the underlying structure, a combination of variety and rhythmic certainty, governing the way each line develops. It is the sound of epic, entirely unlike the way anyone would ever have spoken, but embodying for the Greeks the heroic world.

Parry established that an astonishingly high proportion of the poems composed in this rhythmically repetitive form was made up of prefabricated elements that had been evolved to fit the metrical pattern of the hexameter. Anyone telling the story of the *Odyssey* or the *Iliad* in verse would have had, ready to hand, words and expressions that could easily be put into this form. Just under a third of all the lines in Homer are like this, either repeated entirely or containing phrases repeated elsewhere. Saying the same thing, or a version of the same thing, over and over again lay at the foundations of the Homeric world.

If Alexander Pope in eighteenth-century England thought the excellence of poetry lay in "What oft was thought/But ne'er so well express'd,"

Homer's ideal is precisely the opposite: saying the true things in ways that are deeply familiar: what oft was thought and almost always expressed in exactly the same way. Homer, in its genes, was set against newness, turning to the fixed music of the hexameters and the phrases inherited from the past for the validation of its truths. This poetry can be thought of in the same light as weaving patterned cloth or building wooden ships. The past, through endless tests, successes and failures, came up with ways of using and joining materials that work, that are robust, reliable and true, that can cope with seas or storms at night, that have a grace and commodity about them, whose threads can glitter in the candlelight and which are, of their essence, inherited.

Nowhere is the formulaic method of the verse clearer than in the way Homer uses the name of a hero or god, attached to a descriptive adjective or phrase, to fill in the second half of a hexameter, the space between the midline break, the caesura, and the end of the line. You can represent the gap Homer needed to fill again and again by the phrase "the murmuring pines and the hemlocks." Each of the thirty-seven most important heroes and gods of the *Iliad* and the *Odyssey* has a formula attached to his or her name which exactly fills that gap. One after another they queue up to occupy it: *polytlas dios Odysseus*—much-suffering godlike Odysseus is there thirty-eight times; followed closely by *podarkēs dios Achilleus*, swift-footed godlike Achilles; *boöpis potnia Hera*, cow-eyed goddess Hera; *thea glaukopis Athene*, goddess owl-eyed Athene; *anax andrōn Agamemnon*, lord of men Agamemnon—and so on through the whole cast. Equally formulaic phrases often fill the other part of the line—"and so in reply he spoke," "and so she said when smiling"—so that entire lines, and entire sequences of lines, are filled up not with words chosen for their individual strength, poignancy or relevance, but as a means of keeping the music constant, keeping the characters present and alive in the surface of the poem.

Once you grasp this core repetitive mechanism—often obscured in translations of Homer—these poems become profoundly strange, sinking back away from us in time and mentality, to a point where story and character are visible only though the mask of the formulaic, as unreal as a Noh play, as mysterious as an unheard liturgy. The stories of the warriors at Troy and the wanderings of Odysseus become as alien as a tale told in hieroglyphs or cuneiform. This is the Renan effect, seeing the past for its strangeness, not imposing our own clarity or suppositions on something from the other end of human consciousness.

"The poetry," Parry wrote, "was not one in which a poet must use his own words and try [as] best he might to utilize the possibilities of the metre. It was a poetry which for centuries had accumulated all such possibilities— all the turns of language, all the words, phrases, and effects of position, which had pleased the race."

So powerful was the need to keep the music whole, that these metrically convenient phrases are often used even when they make no sense. The heavens are "starry" in the middle of the day; linen is "gleaming" when it is about to be washed; Odysseus is called "much-suffering godlike Odysseus" by the shade of a man he recently killed, now in Hades; Aegisthus, the adulterous lover of Clytemnestra and murderer of Agamemnon, is "blameless"; ships are "swift" when they have been turned to stone. But the hexameters roll on, sustained by these formulaic expressions, a music whose sense of its own overarching greatness matters more than any local meaning. By the time of "Homer"—often put in quotes by Parry— the heroic epithets had become virtually meaningless. Achilles was not really "swift-footed" when lurking in his tent for book after book of the *Iliad*, refusing to fight for the Greeks; Odysseus was not really "suffering much" when performing as only one among many of the Greek commanders at Troy. These words, in Parry's analysis, had become useful line-fillers because that is what the music of the hexameters, the tradition itself, required. They had nothing to do with what the poem meant.

This was a radical dismantling of the inherited Homer. Ever since the Alexandrians, Europe had tried to rescue Homer from his own errors. Parry, alive with all the early twentieth century's fascination with the strange truths to be found in non-Enlightenment cultures, now plunged him back into a deeply preclassic world, taking him apart in the process. Parry was accused of being the "Darwin of Homeric scholarship," the man who had turned a god into an ape. But he is more like Homer's Gauguin or Stravinsky, creating a poet for a Jungian world, allowing for the validity of his prerational methods, finding there beauty which the classic tradition was blind to and wished to excise. Parry thought Homer beautiful in the way an African totem or a Polynesian mask might be beautiful. Europeans since the Renaissance might have looked on Homer as one of the furnishings of the gentlemanly life. Parry saw himself as no part of that tradition, and for him distance and inaccessibility stood at the root of Homer's meaning.

Parry had summoned a strange and troubling Homer from the depths, a poet entranced by his inheritance, almost blind in front of it, spooling out what the past had given him, "a machine of memory with limited aesthetic scope," as the Californian critic James I. Porter has described him, "his materials emerging from the deepest lava flows of epic time." This is Homer as Hawaiian volcano, oozing the past like the juice from the earth's mantle. Parry even suggested that the poems were full of words, often in old forms of Greek, that may have fitted the music of the hexameters but which "Homer," the Ionic poet from Chios in the eighth century BC, did not himself understand. There are 201 words in the *Iliad* and the *Odyssey* that occur only once in Homer and never again in the whole of Greek literature. That number goes up to 494 if you include proper names, their roots deep in ancient forms of Greek, many of them spoken in Thessaly in northern Greece, but which in Chios and through the Ionic fringe of Anatolia were no longer used. Many have never been translated— unintelligible to the Greeks of fifth-century Athens or third-century Alexandria, their meaning still only to be guessed at.

But for Parry, this was all evidence of the tradition at work, of Homer being more interested in epic music than its meaning. The past must be given its due, and one aspect of that past was the unintelligibility of its language. Only then would you understand the relationship of the singer and his tradition: "The tradition is of course only the sum of such singers. One might symbolize it by the idea of a singer who is at once all singers." He quoted Aristotle's *Rhetoric* on the ideal for an epic poet: "One's style should be unlike that of ordinary language, for if it has the quality of remoteness, it will cause wonder and wonder is pleasant." Mystery is power, and the not-entirely-understood seems greater than what is clear. Parry's vision of Homer is very nearly like the unintelligible ritual of the Latin mass sung to uncomprehending peasants across medieval Europe: words that were meaningful because they could not be understood. Eliot's passing thought in his 1929 essay on Dante that "genuine poetry can communicate before it is understood" is less radical than this. Parry sees Homer as a culture riding into the future on poetry whose deepest parts are entirely inaccessible.

His professors at the Sorbonne told him something he hadn't quite grasped: everything he had been pursuing was a sign that Homer was not originally a written but an oral text. This formulaic composition was the mark of a sung poem, so dependent on preshaped elements that a singer could compose it as he performed it. Such songs were neither monstrous feats of memory nor improvisations, invented from one moment to the next, but tales told with the help of ancient formulas, devised long before, which the singer could rely on as steady metrical elements in his lines. He did not have to learn any poems, but he had to learn what the tradition could teach him, the ability to make poems on the hoof.

This may seem a presumptuous comparison, but it is clear to me that anyone who has ever stood up in front of an audience, of any kind, and made a speech, knows what is meant by composition-in-performance, particularly if you have made the speech before, or over the course of a few months had the chance of making it a few times to different audiences, in different atmospheres and for different purposes. You know, in essence, the stories you have to tell, the morals you would like to draw. You know the moments where pathos is available and those where people will laugh. You know what has worked before and what has died as it left your lips. You know, above all, but just how you know is difficult to know, how to establish a kind of gut-dialogue between you and the audience, to feel them feeling what you are saying, to understand point by point what might be the right development of the tale.

It is not improvization, because you know at least where you might be going. You have your formulas, conscious, semi-conscious, unconscious, the tics that make you who you are, that are your inheritance. You have passages that run in familiar ways, that allow the intuition to consider the shape of what you are making, the way you might go next, the goal it must aim for. And you have your ingredients, your set terms, the passages where you need not invent, where you can say what was said before, and those passages where invention seems to come easily to the mind, not in the sense of making up a new substance for the story, but in finding words that will work for it. All this is easier when there is some darkness in the room.

This is not to say that I speak in hexameters or devise complex reflective schemes and ironies, that I keep in train a thousand characters over 14,000 lines. But at a very basic level I understand that between memory, the present moment and the spoken word, is a kind of three-part dance.

When my children were small, we used to play this Homeric game. Last thing at night, I would tell them long rhythmic poems about our lives and our holidays, the little adventures we had in boats or trains, all designed to send them to sleep. Nothing was repeated more often than the story of taking the night train to Scotland, feeding off the atmosphere of excitement and anticipation we got from it every summer and Christmas. The poem was never quite the same from one telling to the next, but it used all the easy techniques of repetitive phrasing and a thumping rhythm which, as Milman Parry said of his own storytelling to his children when they came with him to Bosnia, are the overused recourse of the bad epic poet and almost untouched by the good.

But this is epic verse as it is made today in England, in the evening, upstairs in the bedroom, traditional, formulaic, with lumps of the culture embedded in it, full of memories, lullingly soporific. I never wrote anything down at the time, and I have typed this now straight onto the keyboard as it came to mind, nothing predetermined, except the formulas and the memory of having done something like it often before.

> That was the night and it was very very dark
> That the children found their way to the station
> and there at the station waiting in the dark
> was the long long train that they knew from before.
> Dark was the train and wonderfully shiny
> the lights from the station shining on its flanks
> and the lights in the cabins glowing inside
> and there as the children stood in the station
> watching the train that was dark in the night
> they said to each other Can we climb aboard?
> Can we find our way to our beds in the train?
> And their father said No to them, No not yet.
> Wait till the guard opens the doors.
> So they stood in the cold and longed for the warmth
> Of the long night train as it made its way north.
> Together they stood and huddled in the dark
> Waiting for the moment when the doors might open
> and then at last they heard far away

The banging of doors and the shouting of men
as each of the guards got out his big key
and opened the doors for the night to begin.

I usually fell asleep before they did, lulled by my own pump-engine rhythm, but this is Homeric in its parataxis, its telling of the story with no subordinate clauses, accumulating one detail after another, its rapidity, its formulaic phrases taking up reliable positions in the pattern of the lines, its cherishing of memories and heroizing of the ordinary, its love of the shared experience between speaker and listener, its cavalier way with facts.

What can you say? Only that this sort of rhythmic, inherited storytelling is part of the human organism, and that the world in which the *Iliad* and the *Odyssey* began was an outgrowth and fulfillment of this basic capacity, one in which the telling of your own great tales was not something done by a father at bedtime but in the gathering of people for whom these stories were the foundation of their lives, the thing that might last when everything else might not.

Between 1933 and 1935, prompted by his Parisian professors, Parry made his journeys through the remote mountain villages of Yugoslavia. It was quite a caravan: his assistant, a Harvard student, Albert Lord, several typists and interpreters, and Nikola Vujnović, a singer himself from Herzegovina, who would ease the way with the people they met. They met and listened to over seven hundred singers, each with their *gusle*, the single-stringed violin that accompanied the words. Almost 13,000 separate songs were written into eight hundred notebooks, and hundreds more recorded on 3,500 twelve-inch aluminum disks. When he returned to Harvard, Parry delivered to the library almost exactly a ton of archive material.

The excitement was real. Here was the past made flesh and blood, stubble and cigarettes, sawing out its epics in front of them. On market day they would drop in at a coffeehouse and make inquiries. Were there any *guslari* nearby? Were they good? Could they come? One morning at Bijelo Polje, a small town in the hills of northern Montenegro, they found,

Bégan Lyútsa Nikshitch, a Turkish bard
from Montenegro, "a tall, lean and impressive person."

lying on a bench in a coffeehouse, a Turk smoking a cigarette with an
antique silver cigarette holder. He was Bégan Lyútsa Nikshitch, "a tall,
lean and impressive person" who spoke to them like a warrior from the
depths of the past.

Bégan knew a certain Avdo Medédović, a peasant farmer who lived
an hour away, and he was insistent that the Americans had to hear him.

Finally Avdo came, and he sang for us . . . We listened with increasing
interest to this short homely farmer, whose throat was disfigured by a
large goiter. He sat cross-legged on the bench, sawing the gusle, swaying in
rhythm with the music. He sang very fast, sometimes deserting the melody, and while the bow went lightly back and forth over the string, he
recited the verses at top speed. A crowd gathered. A card game, played by
some of the modern young men of the town, noisily kept on, but was
finally broken up.

The next few days were a revelation. Avdo's songs were longer and finer than any we had heard before. He could prolong one for days, and some of them reached fifteen or sixteen thousand lines. Other singers came, but none could equal Avdo, our Yugoslav Homer.

The *guslari* always sang their long epic songs of battle and disaster with a kind of hard energy, loud, at a high pitch, the singer's whole frame gripped with the effort. This was no smooth crooning but a passionate engagement of mind and body.

It takes the full strength of the man to sing in this way. The movement of the body in playing the instrument, the laboring of the lungs needed for the breath needed for the volume of song, the strain on the muscles of the throat and mouth that go to forming the words, make the singing a toil, and a good singer after a half hour of his song is drenched in sweat.

Nothing about the sound of the *gusle* is charming, and the way in which the poems are sung has little apparent melody. The string of the instrument screeches from one line to the next, the *guslar* chants his lines without any attempt at a flourish or grace notes. This is not an exhibitionist performance. It is more serious than that, the voice of concentration, as he composes with his formulaic phrases and passages, the meter heavily emphasized in every phrase he uses. It is the words that matter, their recounting of tragedy and suffering. But the unbroken presence of the instrument is there not for its tune but for its strangeness, the signal it makes that this is another world.

Each singer sang usually for between twenty and forty minutes, sawing away at the *gusle* on his lap, singing up to twenty lines of his song every minute, more slowly at first, speeding up as he reached the crisis of the tale and then stopping for a cup of coffee, a cigarette, a glass of burningly fierce plum raki or simply for a break. They didn't always get to the end of their song before the session tailed off into the night. Some singers did not even know the endings of their songs, and when they did come to the last part, they were always more various than the beginnings.

In June 1935 Halil Bajgorić, a thirty-nine-year-old stockman from a remote mountain village in Bosnia, sang them a long song about a young and resourceful hero, called "The Wedding of Mustajbey's Son Bećirbey."

Even as he began, after a thirty-second introduction on the *gusle* alone, setting the rhythm, establishing the meter in his mind, it was clear that Bajgorić's tale was driven along by the formulaic pattern, not only at the level of individual phrases but in the shape of scene after scene.

Bajgorić's epic is simple, but it shares many things with Homer. First, as in Homer, the adventure begins with the break of day and the waking of the hero.

> Oj! Djerdelez Alija arises early,
> Ej! Alija, the tsar's hero,
> Near Visoko above Sarajevo,
> Before dawn and the white day
> Even two full hours before dawn,
> When day breaks and the sun rises
> And the morning star shows its face.

In epic, it is not enough to say "One morning..." It needs expansion, space opening out around the story, the luxury of time expanding around the singer. And it can joke about that need for a little more time.

> When the young man gets himself up,
> He kindles a fire in the hearth
> And on the fire he puts his coffee pot;
> After Alija brews the coffee,
> One, then two cups he pours himself—
> One, then two, he feels no spark,
> Three, then four, the spark then seizes him,
> Seven, then eight, until he has enough.

Finally, its hero sufficiently stoked with caffeine, the formulaic sequence can begin: the preparation of "a long-maned bay horse" for the journey, the horse made beautiful with all her trappings, "Like a careless young shepherdess up on a mountain/Clothed in her hood and motley jacket," the fitting of the hero with his beautiful equipment, his swords and daggers, his elegant pistols, one from Venice, one from England, to the point where he can set out on his journey, swim a great river while still mounted on his precious mare—she knows what he wants without him saying so—until at last he arrives at the city where "He quenche[s] his thirst with dark red wine/And he smoke[s] two pipefuls of tobacco."

Translate the Homeric situation to the valleys of early-twentieth-century mountain Europe, and the poem translates itself. That is Parry's point: this poetry was the product not of a unique glowing genius but of a world in which the spoken epic is the vehicle that carries the meanings of the past into the present and in which the need to tell the poem again and again is itself the most powerful force in its shaping. Formulaic verse is a response to social need.

Parry was entranced by the world he had stumbled on. "The moment he cherished most," his student Albert Lord wrote later,

> occurred toward the end of one of his earliest days in the Serbian hills, during the summer of 1933. They had settled at an inland village and at length come across a *gouslar*, the first epic poet Parry had ever known, an old man who claimed to have been a warrior in youth and to have cut off six heads. All afternoon he sang to them about his battles. At sunset he put down his *gousle* and they made him repeat a number of his verses. Parry, very tired, sat munching an apple and watching the singer's grizzled head and dirty neck bob up and down over the shoulder of Nikola, the Herzegovinan scribe, in a last ray of sunlight. "I suppose," he would say, in recalling the incident, with crisp voice and half-closed eyes, "that was the closest I ever got to Homer."

It is as powerful a moment in the history of Homeric understanding as the evening when Keats and Cowden Clarke peered into Chapman's Homer, or when Carl Blegen in the summer of 1939 found the smashed fresco of the singer, destroyed in the fire three thousand years before. Parry, listening to these men and their grating instruments, their sawing voices, heard in them the transmission of epic across the generations, the thousands of years. It was the moment in which the vacuum of life before the written word had suddenly acquired a substance.

Through Nikola Vujnović, the Herzegovinian singer, Parry asked Halil Bajgorić where he had learned his songs. All came from his father, he said. But how had he actually learned to sing and play when he was a boy? Halil described how he would sneak the *gusle* away from his father, and in another room, when his father was sleeping, he would sing a little.

> NIKOLA: But why did you feel the need to sneak the *gusle* away from him?
>
> HALIL: Because I wanted to know how [to play], I saw there was a place for him among the people because he knew how to sing. He'd come there, when there were gatherings among us, when there were weddings, some celebrations, and I'd go with him. And he'd come there, and there would be a lot of people, and the people all made room and said, "Singer, come on up to the front and sit by the man brewing coffee."
>
> NIKOLA: Aha.
>
> HALIL: Then, by God, I too wanted to learn to play the *gusle*.

This is how it must always have been: the father at the center of the listening circle, the boy on the edge of it seeing his father in a different light from the usual man at home with his breakfast, the current of the heroic recognized by the boy, the stirring of ambition to have that scale of existence in his own life, the tentative beginnings in secret, his imagining of the audience, his first attempts in public, the increasing confidence with which the formulas might become his own, that miraculous sensation when he felt he could divert the stream through his own life and mind.

"The verses and the themes of the traditional song form a web in which the thought of the singer is completely enmeshed," Parry wrote later, establishing the primacy of the tradition over the individual poet. "The poetry stands beyond the single singer. He possesses it only at the instant of his song which is his to make or mar." "His to make or mar" is the idea in the mind of the young Halil, practicing with his father's *gusle* in the hidden room.

They asked one singer called Ibrahim Bašić, known as Ibro, a seventy-year-old woodcutter from central Herzegovina, where he got the words for the songs. If he told a tale a second time, did he repeat it word for word? Yes, Ibro said, word for word.

NIKOLA: What is, let's say, a word in a song? Give me a word from a song.

IBRO: Here's one, let's say, this is a word:

Mujo of Kladusha arose early, / At the top of the slender, well-made tower.

NIKOLA: But these are lines.

IBRO: Well yes, but that's how it is with us; it's otherwise with you, but with us that's how it's said . . . But here's one, let's say this is a word: "Mujo of Kladusha arose early"—that is a word for "arose early"; "Before dawn and the sun is arising"—that's also a word for "arose early."

Words are not individual, separated lexical objects but poetic lines, half lines, formulas, metrical units and story units that can slot into the song. This is building a wall not brick by brick but panel by panel. Getting up with the dawn, preparing the chariot, arming the warrior, equipping the ship, rowing for the wind, swift-footed Achilles, much-suffering Odysseus— these are the words in which Homer speaks. To repeat a song "word for word" is to choose any one of these formulas as they come to mind. The tradition is not a fixed object like the written text of *Paradise Lost* or the *Aeneid*; it is a braided stream of possibilities pouring into the present out of the past, essentially multiple, recomposed from its given elements every time it is sung, and in that retelling conceived of as remaining the same. It is a curiously Platonic conception of a story, as if the epic's essence were in a pure, immaterial, preexistent form, of which the actual words that are sung are an almost incidental bodying forth into our mundane reality.

"Plato thought nature but a spume that plays/ Upon a ghostly paradigm of things," Yeats said, and you could say the same of Parry's Homer: Homer thought his poem but a spume that played upon the ghostly truths that came from long ago.

Parry was convinced that he had pushed the modern understanding of Homer back beyond the eighth-century BC horizon at which writing arrived in the Greek world. He thought he knew that in the formulaic composition-in-performance of the Yugoslav *guslars* he had heard the way in which the *Iliad* and the *Odyssey* had been composed. Homer was clearly the most extraordinary practitioner—the songs from the Balkan mountains were thin and empty compared to the *Iliad* and the *Odyssey*—but this was the practice of which Homer was the master.

"The more I understand the South Slavic poetry and the nature of the unity of the oral poem," Parry wrote late in his life,

> the clearer it seems to me that the *Iliad* and the *Odyssey* are very exactly, as we have them, each one of them the rounded and finished work of a single singer . . . I even figure to myself, just now, the moment when the author of the *Odyssey* sat and dictated his song, while another, with writing materials, wrote it down verse by verse, even in the way that our singers sit in the immobility of their thought, watching the motion of Nikola's hand across the empty page, when it will tell them it is the instant for them to speak the next verse.

Parry had crossed the boundary into the mental world occupied by Homer. He was thirty-three when he returned in triumph to Harvard with his ton of notebooks and aluminum disks. A life's work stretched ahead of him, but in December 1935, on a visit to his mother-in-law in Los Angeles, he died in a stupid accident when a revolver mixed in with his clothes in a suitcase went off and killed him. Something resembling the book he was planning to write about Homer and the *guslari* was written much later by his assistant and student Albert Lord, after a long and fruitful career spent fulfilling the promise of the visionary man who had once led him to the Balkans.

A rainy early-autumn day in the Hebrides, the cloud down low over the islands, a sheen of wet on the grass. We have been gathering sheep for the September markets. The sea around us is bruised by the wind. Hardly a word has been spoken all morning, as the four of us have been strung out in a line across the hillside half a mile long, two or three hundred yards between each of us, our arms flailing at the gloomy and reluctant sheep. The sky is torn into shreds and patches. The only words have been the violent insults thrown at the dogs.

Now the lambs are down at last in the pen on the beach, ready to be taken off by dory and fishing boat tomorrow morning. The sheepdogs nip at them through the bars. The shepherds, Kennie, Nona and Toby, are all leaning on the hurdles of the pen and discussing the animals in front of us, their fleeces shriveled and lank in the rain. They are not as good as anyone had hoped.

NONA: It was the wet spring that did it.

TOBY: That was what kept them back.

NONA: Aye, and the dry summer.

TOBY: Aye, that would have kept them back too.

NONA: And it's been cold these last few weeks.

TOBY: That wouldn't have helped.

NONA: No, they are not as good as they might have been.

TOBY: But there are some big ones in here.

NONA: Monsters some of them.

TOBY: There's some good lambs in there.

NONA: Look at that horned ewe with her twins.

TOBY: There's some very heavy lambs here.

KENNIE: It'll be heavy work getting them into the dory.

TOBY [TO HIS DOG]: Come into heel, will you.

NONA: You are not going to get that quality every time.

TOBY: No, not every time, that's right.

KENNIE: No, not every time. You can't hope for it every time.

This was a chat, a break from work, with a roll-up and a cup of tea and caps on the backs of heads, but it is the talk that has been had since the Neolithic. Its buried musicality, the repetition of its phrases, the antiphonal give and take of each repeating gesture—all of that presses up under the surface of the words. Perhaps this is the natural way we have of speaking, just hesitating on the lip of the musical, but it is a quality of language that is usually shut down and denied in a written culture.

Parry's new understanding of the Homeric poems undoubtedly pushed them into the preliterate centuries before 800 BC. Homer comes from an oral and aural world, a world of public speech and shared listening. But how far back? And how much of that ancient world could survive in the telling and retelling? Can one really reach back through the words of Homer to that moment in about 1800 BC when the Greek-speaking people, whatever they were called, came south to the Mediterranean world of sailing ships and stone-walled cities?

There is a real difficulty: the reliability of these storytellers. They inherited the past, they were conscious of that inheritance, but how much did they transform what they had been given? Milman Parry and his team asked the Serbian singers if their stories had any truth in them, a question, it soon became clear, that did not entirely make sense to them.

Ibrahim Bašić, the *guslar* known as Ibro, answered casually enough: everything in his songs was true, except for details he added to make them more fitting. His stories might have required heroic furniture— swords, horses—to sound right, but that didn't make them any less "true." It might even have made a story "truer," more like the heroic past Ibro had in mind. These songs were epics, extensions of memory over deep reaches of time. They weren't history. They celebrated a heroic ethos, and their purpose was not to preserve events. They existed in the "now," standing as a bridge between the present moment and the distant past.

There is one extraordinary discovery from Crete, made by the American-Greek scholar James Notopoulos, a follower of Parry and Lord, that relegated the question of historical truth in ancient epics to a category that was at least moot. Notopoulos was a professor in Hartford, Connecticut. His father had been a poor Greek immigrant from the Peloponnese who became rich by building and operating theaters in small-town Pennsylvania. At Oxford, James had become entranced by Homer and Parry's discoveries. An intense romantic, he was remembered by his students gazing dreamily at the ceiling through clouds of pipe smoke during Greek classes in Hartford. But he was also a precisionist, capable of "making the wince into an art-form" when a pupil failed to pronounce the Greek properly or get the meter right.

In 1953, with a Guggenheim scholarship, Notopoulos traveled to the far west of Crete, one of the most heroic landscapes in Europe. In the wild and stony mountain province of Sfakia, gorges are sawed thousands of feet down into the barren, dry White Mountains. I have seen fences around sheepfolds there held up with the rusted barrels of old machine guns, and have sat eating my lunch in a café while at the table next to me a man first cleaned his automatic pistol and then fired it out of the door to see that it worked.

Notopoulos arrived only eight years after the end of a war in which the Cretans had maintained bitter and heroic resistance against the German occupiers. He found Sfakia in a "ferment" of song. Everywhere the American ethnographer went, men were singing about the 1941 airborne invasion, the cruelty of the Germans, their burning of villages, their shooting of the innocent, the heroism of the Sfakiots themselves, the sons no less heroic than their fathers and grandfathers, and the bitter reprisals carried out by them against their own traitors and fifth columnists. The long island tradition of daring manliness, the kidnapping of brides, the maintenance of unforgivingly violent blood feuds and of loathing for the outsider—Roman, Arab, Venetian and Turk—was pouring out in this new generation of song. It is a suggestive connection: are the years after a war the great moment for epic? With the dreadful realities of the crisis over, can the miasma of epic descend?

The mountain bards in their black tasseled kerchiefs, knee-high boots and baggy trousers sang as Parry had led Notopoulos to expect, formulaically and repetitively, composing in performance, versions of songs sung in the morning different from how they were sung at night. Notopoulos recorded them all. One of his bards was a young man, Andreas Kafkalas, only thirty-nine, particularly gifted in what Notopoulos called "spontaneous improvisation," the ability to sing a story for the first time without rehearsal.

After one of his epics about the German invasion and occupation, Notopoulos said he was surprised Kafkalas had not mentioned anything to do with General Kreipe, the commander of the German garrison on Crete. No, Kafkalas said, but in response to the American's prompting, he thought he could sing a poem about him now. Notopoulos turned on the recording equipment, and Kafkalas began. His tale was about as long as one of the shorter books of the *Odyssey*. His formulas filled whole passages of the song, all in the traditional fifteen-syllable Cretan line. How did he know, Notopoulos asked him later, to put fifteen syllables in a line? "I didn't know the line had fifteen syllables," he said. "I don't count the syllables, I feel them—it's the melody that shapes the lines." The tradition was singing through him.

The kidnapping of General Kreipe was the most famous act of bravura

special operations in the whole story of occupied Crete. Two British officers, Patrick Leigh Fermor and Billy Moss, had captured him, their whole
enterprise conceived in Cairo but dependent on the networks of *andartes*,
the Cretan resistance fighters. One evening in late April 1944, on the road
between the general's HQ at Archanes and his quarters outside Knossos
in central Crete, the two Englishmen and a band of *andartes* stopped the
German car, a new Opel, hit the driver, dragged him onto the road (he
was later killed) and bundled the general into the back of the Opel with a
knife at his throat. The two British officers sat in the front, Moss imper-
sonating the German driver, Leigh Fermor Kreipe himself, with the general's hat on his head.

After a terrifyingly anxious drive through Herakleion, passing slowly
through twenty-two German checkpoints, inching along streets filled
with the men of the garrison who had just come out of the cinema, they
drove out into the wild lands at the foot of Mount Ida, abandoned the car
and headed off on foot into that harsh, dry and fissured mountain. For
the next twenty days, as the Germans attempted to encircle them, looking for them with spotter planes but never detecting them, the general
was led west halfway across mountain Crete, the party hiding in sheepfolds and caves in the daytime, stumbling on difficult mountain paths,
often in the rain, at night, until they finally came down to a small bay
west of Rodakino on the south coast. There they boarded a British motor
launch that had been summoned by radio and, high on excitement and
triumph, with their general safely aboard, made off for Alexandria.

I walked the whole of their route, from where they dumped the car to
the little bay where they embarked near Rodakino. It took me two weeks.
I slept in chapels and vineyards, I burned in the sun in the daytime, froze
at night at six thousand feet on top of a snowy Ida and was often lost in
the dry, echoing gorges coming down to the valleys. Griffon vultures
swung across the sky. I ate cherries in the villages and for days at a time
brushed through the dry, scented smoke of the Cretan garrigue. My boots
after two weeks' walking were shredded by the limestone shards of the
mountains, my body crawling with lice from the places I slept, but my
mind was filled with the mountain distances of that epic and beautiful
island. A shepherd taught me a phrase—*Yiassou pantermi Kriti!*: (Bless
you, desolate Crete!)—as the only words to be said when facing the long,
dry emptiness of the mountains, stretching as a desert into the haze. It is

a brutal world, and later in 1944 the Germans executed brutal, slaughtering attacks on the people of mountain Crete. In every one of the villages through which the Kreipe group passed, in between the cherry trees and the figs, the little tavernas and the shady plane trees, there is a tall marble memorial on which the names of their dead are listed.

The Leigh Fermor party never got as far west as Sfakia, but Kafkalas told his tale with only a little hesitation. He had heard it from another Cretan when in the hospital in Athens. And now, he told Notopoulos, he was singing the song to him "to fulfil the obligations of Cretan hospitality." But the song Kafkalas sang was an intriguing oddity. Almost nothing survived in it from the original story; truth had disappeared under a slew of the heroic. A single (untrue) English general (untrue) arrives in Crete and summons a hero from Sfakia, Lefteris Tambakis, to see him. (Untrue: Tambakis was a real figure, but he had never been anywhere near this operation.) The English general draws himself up to his full height, weeps over the cruelties being done by the Germans to the people of "desolate Crete" and reads out the order to the Sfakiot hero that Kreipe is to be captured dead or alive. (All untrue—no such order existed.)

For the honor of Cretan arms, Tambakis knows what to do. In disguise he goes to Herakleion and finds a beautiful girl there. (He didn't.) She is the secretary to the German general. (He didn't have one.) He tells her that if she helps him, her name will be immortal in Cretan memory. She will join the catalog of heroes. She agrees and "sacrifices her woman's honor" with the German general. Kreipe—called Kaiseri in this song—whispering across the pillow, tells her his plans. (Of course he didn't.) She passes them on to Tambakis, and Tambakis goes to meet the English general at Knossos. (There was no meeting there.) The ambush is laid. The *andartes* get "a long car" with which to block the road (they didn't), but Tambakis himself waits there on a beautiful horse. (No horses were involved, but they always are in old Cretan songs.) The English general is by now pretty marginal to the story. The Cretans stop Kaiseri's car, strip him naked (they didn't), he begs for mercy for the sake of his children (he didn't, but this is a motif that usually appears at these moments in Cretan poetry), and they start on the long trek over Mount Ida. Dogs (not used) and airplanes, called "birds of war," hunt for the kidnappers, but to no avail. They arrive in Sfakia (they didn't), where the people try to kill Kaiseri (they didn't) before a submarine (it was a launch) sweeps him off to

Egypt. Hitler is in despair. (He probably was in June 1944, if for other reasons.) "Never before in the history of the world has such a deed been done."

Nine years had passed between these events and this telling of them. Nothing in the *Kreipiad* is true beyond the kidnapping of a general and his leaving for Egypt. Whole characters and a different Sfakiot geography, plus the luscious fantasies of a Mata Hari seductress-spy, are laid over the top of any historical truth. If this is what could happen to a modern story in nine years, how could anyone hope that anything true might survive in the *Iliad* or the *Odyssey*?

At almost exactly the moment James Notopoulos was hearing the *Kreipiad* sung to him in Crete, and the idea was collapsing of an inheritance transmitted through song from the deepest past, precisely the opposite conclusion was being reached at the other end of Europe. In September 1953 a group of forty Celtologists gathered at a conference in Stornoway on the Outer Hebridean island of Lewis, flown in from all over Europe by the British Council. The key session in Stornoway was boringly advertised as "Paper on Folktales with Live Illustration." No one guessed that they were about to hear something that would turn the Parryite orthodoxy on its head.

Also asked to the meeting, as its star turn, was a seventy-year-old stonemason from a village on South Uist, two ferries and a long drive away down the Hebridean chain. Duncan Macdonald was a small man with an air of untroubled self-possession. He was not Duncan Macdonald but *Donnchadh mac Dhòmhnaill 'ic Dhonnchaidh 'ic Iain 'ic Dhòmhnaill 'ic Tharmaid* (Duncan the son of Donald the son of Duncan the son of Iain the son of Donald the son of Norman). They were descendants of the MacRury family of hereditary bards who had sung for the chiefs of the Macdonalds at the now ruined and abandoned castle at Duntulm, on the shores of the Minch, within touching distance of the northern tip of Skye. His father and brother were storytellers, his mother a famous singer, her brother a much-loved piper and poet. He was one of the most gifted storytellers in twentieth-century Europe, heir to the great traditions of Celtic storytelling which stretched far back into the Gaelic past.

Anything about the singers Milman Parry had found in the Balkans could be matched by this inheritance, and Duncan did not disappoint. It was not the first time he had been the focus of attention for the folklorists, and on this afternoon in Stornoway he told a tale—it was "The Man of the Habit," lasting about an hour—which he had told to transcribers four times before, in 1936, 1944, 1947 and 1950. This afternoon the delegates were given a booklet containing a transcription and an English translation of the way he had told it in 1950.

He began, as one of his hearers said, in Gaelic that was "polished, shapely and elegant . . . Everything he recited was given both weight and due consideration." But, as slowly emerged, this mild-mannered stonemason's confidence in the tradition was matched by the extraordinary precision with which he told his tale. Scarcely a word was different from the printed version they held in their hands—a few tiny mistakes, substituting *subhachas* ("gladness") for *dubhachas* ("sadness"), one or two interjections that were different and some synonyms changed, but on the whole the seven-thousand-odd words of the story were exactly as he had told them three years earlier. On analysis, all five of his versions were as good as identical. He had learned it like this from his father and had told it like this ever since first learning it. The family had held it in mind as a kind of remembered heirloom, a hero tale, composed at least two hundred years earlier—there is an account of it from 1817—which remained alive not just as a plot but in precisely the same words, transmitted unaltered from generation to generation.

In a world overtaken with the Parry hypothesis of composition-in-performance, this was revelatory. Duncan Macdonald had provided another way of seeing Homer, not as the poet who had written the *Iliad* and the *Odyssey* as his own works of art; nor as the poet who adapted and transmuted what he had learned to the situation he found himself in; but a poet who worked with a curatorial exactness, resisting the changes imposed by the passing of time, preserving antiquity in detail. For this kind of poet, stories were reliquaries in which precious wisdom and cherished understandings could be kept despite all the mutability of world and time. A poem enshrined memory. Its music denied death.

In Homeric Greek this understanding of the role of poetry focuses on a particular phrase: *kleos aphthiton*, in which *a-phthitos* means "without fading," "undying," "eternal," "everlasting"; and *kleos*, in the most revealing of all Homeric significance-clusters, means "story," "fame," "honor" and "glory." In the Homeric mind, those four things are one. The tale told is itself a form of honor; honor exists in the telling of a tale; fame is to be found in the heroes of tales; their glory in life is the substance of honor; the tale of honor is the denial of death. Only if the tale resists the erosions of time can it make any claim to be the vehicle for glory. Undying fame is both the substance and the purpose of the Homeric poems.

In the years since then, ethnographers have discovered all over the world traditions of oral poetry that do not rely on the Parry method of composition-in-performance, that are not entirely formulaic, but that trust in the power of human memory to preserve with real precision the names, stories and words of the past. Duncan Macdonald's son wrote down 150,000 words of stories he had heard from his father before he died. The great eighteenth-century illiterate poet Duncan Ban MacIntyre knew at least six thousand lines of his own poetry. According to the Scottish Homer scholar Douglas Young, there was an octogenarian crofter from the Hebridean island of Benbecula, a man called Angus McMillan, who

> had in his head more than seventy tales lasting at least one hour each, and some novels lasting seven to nine hours, one of them running to 58,000 words, which is nearly as long as Homer's *Odyssey* . . . [He] could talk for eight hours at a stretch, almost without a pause. On the nearby island of Barra, Roderick MacNed is reported to have told tales every winter night for fifteen years without ever repeating himself. On the Scottish mainland, in Lochaber, John Macdonald recorded over six hundred tales, each of them a comparatively short story complete in itself. An Irish taleteller recorded over half a million words of tales he knew.

The idea of human memory in monumental form allows one to push Homer beyond the ninth or tenth centuries BC. The epic poem, seen as the deepest of all recording mediums, releases Homer from time constraints, allowing his tales to plunge far back into the centuries before writing. It is a kind of time-release not unlike standing on a peak in Darien, seeing the Pacific widths of the past expanding before you. Parry was only partly right; it now seems clear that his model is one way, but not the only way, that Homer works. Homer unites and combines the formulaically made with the acutely remembered and the sparklingly invented. In the substance of its poetry, Homer is the inherited tradition in its multiple forms: both alive as the poem composed in performance and fixed, as monumental as the stone over a grave mound, the memorial of great things done long ago. Multiple in origin, multiple in manner and multiple in meaning, Homer in this light both knows the deep past and moves beyond it. He is both South Uist and Sfakia. And so the question emerges: what is it that Homer remembers?

7 · HOMER THE REAL

Homer is haunted by the threat of transience, by the way memory fails and meanings drift in the face of time. That slide into insignificance summons his tenderest and most lyrical moments. So in book 6 of the *Iliad*, when the battle is well under way and all is in a roar, "the terrible noise" of it stoked by the commanders on both sides, a brazen, brutal shouting, something else emerges. The Greek warrior Diomedes, second only to Achilles as a man with an appetite for killing, is pumped with rage and the need for death. He is conducting his drive, his *aristeia*, through the Trojan ranks. Death awaits anyone he meets.

Quivering with battle-lust, he comes across a young warrior from Lycia, an ally of the Trojans. This is Glaucus, whose name means "the gleaming one," a word used by Homer to describe both the sea and the eyes of the wisdom goddess Athene. Here, surely, is Diomedes's next victim. But instead of surrender or any display of weakness, Glaucus appears to him, like other heroes, "shining" and "glorious." Diomedes guesses he might be a god, and as such intensely dangerous. He isn't, he is mortal, and so Diomedes asks him about his ancestry, who his father and grandfather might have been.

It is a traditional conversation, important for a hero, as his own self-esteem is bound up with the knowledge that his victims are themselves of good lineage, but also a kind of time mark: two warriors meeting in battle are not merely themselves; they are the vehicles for their own pasts. A man is his ancestry, and just as this poem is the poem the tradi-

tion is now singing, these men are the future their fathers and grandfathers dreamed of.

Nevertheless, Glaucus resists the expectations. "Why ask about my
birth?" he asks Diomedes in return, and a pause, a slowness, pools out
into the flow of violence and grief. The noise of war rolls on in the background, but immediately, here, in the present, with you the listener looking on, a scene unfolds that exists in its own bubble of quiet, delivering a
kind of precious and individualized oasis amid all the horror. In some of
the most famous lines in the *Iliad*, Glaucus reflects on the meaning of life
and death.

> As the generation of leaves, so too is the generation of men.
> And as for leaves, the winds scatter some on the earth,
> But the new wood puts forth others, and spring comes again.
> So it is with men: as one generation is born, another dies.

For Glaucus, all life goes back into the earth and returns again. Earth's
abundance and earth's indifference are the same thing. But this resolved
simplicity in the face of death, a philosophical calm and a knowledge that
the armies of men gathered on the Trojan plain are "as many as the leaves
and flowers that appear in the spring"—that is not the usual Homeric
attitude. Glaucus may think of himself as one leaf in the centuries of leaves,
a transient phenomenon, an irrelevant individuality, but that acceptance of
transience is not what most of the poem thinks or most of the heroes in it.
For them, and for Homer, impermanence is life's central sorrow and the
source of its most lasting pain.

It is also what the poem itself is intended to cure. In scene after scene,
Homer quietly shows its listeners that it knows more and remembers
more than men usually know or are able to bring to mind. The whole of
the *Iliad* is a hymn to the scale of remembering of which epic is capable.
The world forgets, but the poem remembers, and that knowledge is the
source of Homer's repeated sad-eyed, bloodhound irony on the nature of
life. Only the gods can know as much as the poem knows.

Almost at the beginning of the *Iliad*, the first time the Trojans move
out of the city and onto the plain to confront their enemies, to face either
death or the possibility of renown and glory, Homer describes the landscape beyond the gates. On the open plain there is a tomb, a high burial

mound or tumulus, of the kind found across the whole of Bronze Age Eurasia, from Bahrain to Sweden and from Sussex to the deserts of Kazakhstan. It is the tomb of Myrine, a mythological Amazon warrior queen, who conquered Anatolia and died in battle. The poet knows the story, but the Trojans have entirely forgotten it. Myrine has disappeared from their minds; instead they know the site as "Thicket Hill." The great mound has today sunk from memory. Only Homer and the gods know that a great woman is buried there.

> Near the city but far out in the plain, there is a steep hill with clear
>   space around it so you can pass on either side; this men call Batieia,
>   but the immortals call it the grave mound of Myrine.

Homer knows something else, a delicate and transient fact about Myrine. She was *polyskarthmos*, a dancer, "much-skipping" as the word means literally, and "very frisky," a phrase used for calves or lambs playing on the springtime grass. Epic poetry serves us well by redeeming from the distant past such a fragile and transient thing as the gaiety and dance steps of a long-dead warrior queen.

Though human memory lasts only three generations at best, the poem becomes an act of memorialization, fixing the past into an everlasting song. Agamemnon may lust after the possessions that victory offers him, objects "such as will remain in the minds of men who are yet to be." But he is wrong about that, because we have no idea what those looted goods were, knowing only what the poem has preserved.

Epic is different from life. The present moment might be seen as a blade, cutting the past from the present, severing *now* from *then*, but poetry binds the wounds that time inflicts. As Odysseus says, the Muse provides "her own way" for poets and storytellers, a path of song, on which events from the past will continue to live in a present reality. It is inconceivable that the epics, for all the pressures of composition-in-performance, did not attend to inherited realities, beyond the moment in about 700 BC or soon after when Homer was first written down. The poems are littered with hints and suggestions of the ancient. Iron, which by the time of Emporio and Pithekoussai was the material out of which farm instruments were made, is often treated in Homer as the most precious and rare of metals, to be carried home as booty in the same class as gold and bronze, the stuff of strange dark jewelry and, as Hector says of Achilles's iron heart, capable when heated of a mysteriously powerful reddened glow. That is exactly the position of iron in the Bronze Age before 1200 BC. Homeric warriors carry "silver-riveted swords," which are found in the graves at Mycenae from the sixteenth century BC but scarcely later. Shields in the form of either large figures-of-eight or huge towering constructions behind which a man can hide as if behind a city wall—these are both Homeric pieces of equipment that are never found by archaeologists from contexts later than the fourteenth century BC. Helmets made of boars' tusks sewn to a leather backing, each helmet requiring the tusks from at least forty boars, are found in Mycenaean graves and in Homer but never in contexts nearer the Iron Age. This is the equipment of a profoundly ancient world.

In the *Odyssey*, Homeric bards sing to gatherings of elegant aristocrats and their followers, attentive around the formal hearth, in complex, many-roomed and multifloored palaces, in which kings and their queens happily ordain a well-ordered life, the like of which are not found in archaeology after the cataclysms of 1200 BC, but which are the baseline of the Mycenaean civilization before it. Much of that poem addresses the agony of rootlessness, the lack of civility in an ill-governed house, the failure of Greeks to be civilized; but the rest of it portrays what looks like a Mycenaean world, a world in which the war is over and the Greeks have come to rest. These poems must at least have passed through a palatial phase for them to be so familiar with the workings and architecture of that life. And in the *Iliad* one element in particular of that palace environment seems to guarantee that at least in part Homer belonged to the palatial phase of Greek Bronze Age civilization.

In the late nineteenth century and again in the mid-twentieth century, the greatest of all Aegean archaeologists—Heinrich Schliemann, Arthur Evans and Carl Blegen—working at Mycenae, at Knossos in Crete and at Pylos in the Peloponnese (with others following at Chania, Thebes and Tiryns), found a series of clay tablets in which some kind of writing had been scratched before they dried. Small, gray, slightly roughly made things, these tablets were clearly not public objects. They are clay notes and records for private reference, not public display.

At Pylos, they came from within a few yards of where Carl Blegen found the fragments of the wonderful fresco showing the poet with his lyre and the bird of poetry taking wing in front of him. For decades no one could interpret the scratched signs, but in the early 1950s, through a combination of American and English analysis (feeding off the cryptography techniques developed in World War II), it became clear that the language they were written in was a form of Greek that was in use between about 1400 and 1200 BC. These Linear B tablets (Linear A was a similar, earlier, Cretan script, yet to be deciphered), once they had been understood, turned out to be the checklists and storeroom accounts of clerks working in the administrative offices of these early Greek palaces. They were everyday files, dealing with employees, religious functionaries, chariots and other military equipment, food stores, domestic animals, regional officials and palace servants.

Judging from impressions on the clay, they had been kept either tied together in bundles or in baskets on shelves, which had collapsed in heaps on the floor during the final conflagrations of these palaces, the heat by chance baking and preserving the clay. Nothing on any of them even faintly resembled nonbureaucratic life, let alone the energized emotional realities to be found in Homer. It was a filing system, which like the workings of most bureaucracies remained hidden from the mass of the population: an essential part of the way the world works, entirely obscure to the mass of people inhabiting that world.

In what became known as the Archive Room at Pylos, Carl Blegen, on the very first morning of his dig in 1939, began to uncover the cache of Linear B tablets. By the end of that first season, his team had found six hundred. In the southern corner of the same room, traces of burned wood and seven small and very badly corroded hinges were found. Other similar hinges had been found at Knossos by Evans in 1900. Both sets of hinges and the little nails attached to them were too small to have belonged to a box of any size. They could not have been the remains of hinged containers for the tablets, because few such tablets could have fitted inside them. No one could guess what lids or doors they were for.

Only when another discovery was made in 1982 did the significance of these tiny clues become clear. Off the coast of Lycia, at Ulu Burun, about six miles southeast of Kaş in southwestern Turkey, a local sponge diver stumbled on the wreck of a Bronze Age ship. A piece of firewood on board, freshly cut, was dated to 1306 BC.

The objects the wreck contained provided the most time-shrinking set of insights into the world of the eastern Mediterranean in the fourteenth century BC. The ship had been sailing west toward the Aegean from the Near East, heavily laden with ten tons of large copper ingots from Cyprus and a ton of tin ingots, perhaps brought to the Mediterranean coast from the great tin mines in Afghanistan. The standard copper-to-tin ratio for making bronze is 10:1. The metals in the Ulu Burun cargo could make enough bronze weapons to equip an army.

Together with those bulk goods was an extraordinary collection of riches: glass ingots, logs of Egyptian blackwood—a kind of ebony—ostrich eggshells, perhaps to make cups, inlaid seashell rings, elephant tusks, more than a dozen hippopotamus teeth and the shells of tortoises which the excavators think were the soundboxes for musical instruments. Little pots contained coriander and nigella seeds, rose-scented oils, olive and almond oil. There was gold jewelry from Canaan and Egypt, and precious mugs and cups made from tin. The ship carried equipment for building, fishing and war, presumably for sale, or perhaps to be distributed as gifts to those in power, and also the personal possessions of the people on board. Most of them seem to have been either Cypriot or Canaanite, traders coming west with the luxury goods of the East, but there were three men on board who had different origins. One wore a sword of which the nearest equivalents have been found in Sicily and Albania, as well as a bronze pin, and had some spears and a stone mace, of which the nearest parallels have been found in Romania and Bulgaria, on the western shores of the Black Sea. This was a man from the shadowy north, traveling in the Mediterranean, also now making his way back west, perhaps to Greece, perhaps to his homeland.

Alongside him were two men from Mycenaean Greece, their possessions appearing in pairs, carrying with them the kind of bowls and plates they were used to at home, as well as their razors, their bronze knives and the engraved stones, their seals, with which they signed off documents and packages by pressing the engraved surface into clay balls attached to the binding strings. From mainland Greece, many seals and sealings survive. Perhaps these two men were accompanying some of these precious goods back from the Near East to the court of their king in Greece. In Egyptian and Hittite royal documents, such ambassadorial figures, overseeing the exchange of valuable goods between brother-kings, are a constant element in Bronze Age diplomacy.

The late-fourteenth-century BC realities of the Ulu Burun wreck—all now to be seen in the beautiful, cool, darkened rooms of the museum in

Bodrum—were accompanied by one other extraordinary and revelatory object: a writing tablet made out of two boxwood leaves, with ivory hinges at one side, and hollowed-out panels on the inside of each leaf into which wax could be poured to make the writing surface. The bed of each panel is roughly cross-hatched to make a good, binding key for the wax. The closed tablet could be held shut with fixings on its outer edge, and that is probably how it was when the merchant ship went down; the outer surface of the tablet is far more worn than the inside. The wax itself entirely disappeared in the thirty-three centuries the tablet spent in the sea. Nor was any stylus found with the Ulu Burun tablet, perhaps because it was made of wood or horn, but metal ones have been discovered in Anatolia, with a writing point at one end (the Greek word *graphein*, later meaning "to write," originally meant "to draw with a point" or "to scratch"), and at the other a flat spatula for revision, smearing out marks in the wax.

The mysterious hinges at Pylos and Knossos were, it now seems, the only parts of portable writing tablets that survived the fires that brought the life of those palaces to an end. But the situation those objects describe—writing as the reserve of a specialist minority in royal households; folding tablets in which written messages, unintelligible to the majority of people, could be carried abroad to foreign courts; the tablets stored for keeping in the writing offices of the palace administration—finds a vivid echo in a moment from the *Iliad*.

It is the story the Lycian warrior Glaucus tells Diomedes when they meet in battle and Diomedes asks him who his ancestors were. Glaucus's grandfather, he says, was a beautiful young hero called Bellerophon. He was living in Corinth, at the court, when the queen of Corinth fell in love with him. She was originally from Lycia, in western Anatolia, where her father was king. At the sight of Bellerophon she became crazed with lust, but he held her at bay. Her frustration mounted, and she came to the point where if she could not sleep with him she wanted him killed. She went to her husband and told him that Bellerophon had tried to seduce her, to sleep with her against her will. If the king had any dignity at all, he would have him murdered.

The king balked at the idea of performing the killing himself, but instead "he quickly sent him off to Lycia, gave him some fatal tokens, scratching many deadly soul-tormenting signs in a folding wooden tablet, and ordered him to show them to the queen's father, who was king of Lycia, so that he might die."

Bellerophon, without being able to read it himself, was carrying his own death warrant with him into exile. When he reached Lycia he showed the mysterious signs to the king, who was able to read them, and then subjected him to a series of murderous tests. But Bellerophon behaved so heroically, overcoming every challenge, that he emerged triumphant and came to father three children, one of whom was Glaucus's own father.

The world of this tiny, famous incident is almost Arthurian: its elevation of honor, its secret lusts in palace corridors, its conscious stepping beyond the ethics of the battlefield. It is, in fact, a deeply traditional folktale, elements of it found all across the preserved literatures of the Near East. But what of the writing, those mysterious and dangerous signs? What does this description of writing say about the Homeric moment?

The Greek king could have had something written, presumably by a scribe, but Bellerophon could not read what it was. Writing was something that belonged to royal administration, not to members of the court. The text was also inaccessible to the poet telling the tale, and seems mysterious, half magical to him. The king in Lycia could read it or have it read to him, but still it has the quality of a spell, those many dangerous signs crammed into the folding wooden tablet Bellerophon brought him.

This story is, in other words, an illiterate description of something written, seen more as an object than a message, its means of communication arcane and beyond ordinary understanding. It is a tiny glimpse into the Mycenaean world, profoundly different from both the Greek world after 750 BC, when ordinary wine drinkers could scratch hexameters into wine cups, and from the Greek world between 1200 and 750, when no one could write at all and there were no palaces or archive rooms within them. The Bellerophon tale, in other words, is the mark of the *Iliad* being at least as old as the palatial culture of Mycenaean Greece.

But that is far from the end of it. A Mycenaean palace might have been the world in which the *Iliad*—or an *Iliad*—was sung. It is not the world the *Iliad* describes or in which it began. That world, in which a Greek warband confronts a non-Greek city; in which Greek adventurers find themselves at sea in a world of settlement and order, profoundly unlike their own mobile, predatory, unsettled lives; in which they know about gold and weaponry and fine things but look on palaces and cities as belonging to others—that world can only have been earlier.

Clues to these ancient ghostly layers are everywhere in Homer. As the great American archaeologist of the Bronze Age world, Emily Vermeule, professor of archaeology at Harvard, said of the Homer she loved, deep tradition "floats all through the songs as dust through air." About 20 percent of the whole of Homer looks as if it was originally composed in a Greek that was earlier than the Greek of the Linear B tablets, that is, before 1400 BC. That antiquity can be seen above all in the way what are called preverbs relate to the verbs they modify. In Linear B, as in later classical Greek, a phrase the equivalent of "the situation described earlier" might be written as "the aforementioned case." In Homer (and in other early languages of the Indo-European family) it often takes the form of "the afore case mentioned." The preverb floats free of the verb. A "predetermined outcome" can in Homer, but not in later Greek, be a "pre outcome determined." This small clue makes it clear that Homeric Greek is in many parts earlier than the Greek of the Linear B tablets.

It has long been a puzzle to Homeric scholars that some lines in Homer don't scan properly. But they can be made to scan if you assume that certain words had another letter in them: the *digamma* or *wau*, which was pronounced like the English *w*, and which had mostly disappeared by the time of the Linear B tablets, and is absent from the text of Homer as it has been preserved. Agamemnon is *anax andrōn* (the lord of men) in the text that has survived; the phrase only scans if you assume that it was originally *wanax andrōn*. The Greek for wine is *oinos*, but its original form is more familiar: *woinos*. These words that only work in their early form include the descriptions of the giant man-encircling shield carried into battle by Ajax. That kind of shield had been replaced by a little round shield as early as the fourteenth century BC, but the Iliadic words that had originally accompanied it survived in epic. Battle equipment, word-form and verse-form all point in the same direction: Homer's foundations are in prepalatial antiquity, a poem stretching at least as far back as the seventeenth century BC.

That is the evidence in the language, but archaeology feeds into this too, nowhere more spectacularly than in the objects discovered in the Shaft

Graves at Mycenae. Go to the beautiful halls of the National Archaeological Museum in Athens—make it midweek in midwinter, and you will
have them entirely to yourself—and what you will find there is an electri-
fying encounter with the past. The Shaft Grave treasures are from the
seventeenth and sixteenth centuries BC. The dead and their possessions
were laid on the floor of a deep shaft, which was then roofed over and a
mound built above it. They are from the time before any great fortresses
or palaces were built in mainland Greece. The famous gates and ramparts
at Mycenae and at Tiryns are all later. The blazingly rich objects in the
graves come from a Greek warrior world, where all value was to be found
in the glory of the individual body and its accoutrements. This is an
essentially mobile world, in love with horses, chariots, ships, weaponry,
hunting, adornment, beauty, gold and song. The people in the graves were
undoubtedly entranced by the contemporary richness and glamor of
the Minoan civilization in Crete and the almost unimaginable wealth of
Egypt. Evidence of borrowings—or thefts—from those cultures is everywhere in the grave goods. But the Shaft Grave world was not yet palatial.
From all the evidence found by more than a century's intensive archaeology, it was the bodies of the great, not the city of Mycenae in the sixteenth
century BC, that were rich in gold. These kings and queens must have
rustled with gold, jangled with it as it hung from their ears and wrists,
amazed onlookers with it, standing before them in high, pointed diadems
and perfect, imperishable gold foil.

This body-enriched but monumentless life is strikingly like the world
of the Greek warriors in the *Iliad*. When the German businessman and
romantic Heinrich Schliemann first dug into the Mycenae graves in the
wet autumn of 1876, he wrote to his friend Max Müller, describing how
he was reduced to *weighing* what he was finding.

There are in all five tombs, in the smallest of which I found yesterday the
bones of a man and woman covered by at least five kilograms of jewels
of pure gold, with the most wonderful, impressed ornaments; even the
smallest leaf is covered with them. To make only a superficial description of the treasure would require more than a week. Today I emptied
the tomb and still gathered there more than 6/10 kilograms of beautifully ornamented gold leafs . . . I telegraphed today to *The Times*.

It is held up as one of Schliemann's great errors that he identified the warriors he found in those graves with the Homeric heroes. It is still thought to have been the crassest of his anachronisms, since the orthodoxy continues to think, as the classical Greeks did, that the Trojan War was fought in around 1200 BC, and that the Shaft Graves at Mycenae are at least 350 years too early to have had anything to do with that war. But that dating has nothing to secure it beyond the guesses made by the classical Greeks. Evidence of destruction at Troy itself has been found at a series of archaeological horizons from 2200 BC to 1180 BC. Any one of them might have been the war of the *Iliad*, except for this one reason: Homer in the *Iliad* describes the Greeks as a prepalatial warrior culture, very like the world of the gold-encrusted kings buried in the Shaft Graves at Mycenae. The Greeks as seen in the *Odyssey*, which in these lights can only be the later poem, colored by the great period of Mycenaean palaces, have clearly begun to adopt the habits and structures of the Near Eastern palace culture. Nothing of that, though, appears in the *Iliad*. There is certainly no better reason to associate Homer with the Troy of about 1200 BC than with a city many centuries earlier.

And so this book, like Schliemann, has a different suggestion to make: the Shaft Graves at Mycenae are contemporary with, or probably slightly later than, the deepest levels of the Homeric poems. The objects in the graves are their own best evidence of a pre-urban, marginal, heroic world whose inhabitants look very like the people Homer portrayed.

The faces on which Schliemann stumbled are the faces of men as they are found in the *Iliad*. The usual image of the most famous mask, with the ears laid out to the side, gives the wrong impression, reducing the severity it intends. As you can see from the creases in the gold, those ears, much of the beard and the upper rim of the mask should be folded away from the face, leaving the features naked and prominent.

It is a battle face, not a portrait of an individual but the face of the warrior king: brutal, excluding and potent, as intense as any Renaissance inquisitor, nothing more resolute than that wide, closed mouth and the jaw gripped behind it. It is the face-helmet of fixed glory. Stare into its rebarbative blankness, appeal to it, and it will not respond. Its gold shines; it does not care. It can hurt, but you cannot hurt it. Here is Agamemnon in his *aristeia*, his power-drive toward supremacy, his best moment, his excellence, his moment of prowess. And in that focus of power his strange, coffee-bean eyes can be seen as either closed in self-absorption and self-regard or slitted in concentration. There is vanity here—his mustache tips are just tweaked upward; a little sprig of hair grows just below the lower lip—but at root this face is the pitilessness of dominance.

Hold that face in mind and read Agamemnon's demeanor in book 11 of the *Iliad* as he wades through "the slayers and the slain." Under his violence, men fall like trees under a woodman's ax. He drives his spear through a Trojan's forehead, "and the spear is not stopped by the helmet, heavy with bronze, but passes through it and through the bone, and all the brain is splashed inside." The next man is speared in the chest "by the nipple," and the third killed with a sword-cut close to the ear. The next two, brothers, beg Agamemnon not to kill them. They speak to him "weeping, with gentle words," offering him bronze and gold and iron from their father's house, but "ungentle is the voice they hear," *ameiliktos*, meaning "unsoothed," the opposite of "darling." He stabs one of the boys in the chest and slices off the arms and then the head of the other with his sword, the head rolling through the surrounding crowds of warriors like a round stone. Agamemnon is a fire in the forest and a lion in the mountains. His hands are spattered with the filth of blood. The chariots of those he has killed run driverless through the battlefield, the horses "longing for their incomparable charioteers," but those men are now lying on the earth, "more loved by the vultures than by their wives."

Every Trojan warrior stands away from Agamemnon, trembling like a hind that sees a lion devouring her young and can do nothing to protect them. Agamemnon is that lion, eating the inward parts of those he kills. He kills a man, Iphidamas, just married, whose wife would now have "no joy of him," and then, in a frenzy of repetition, Iphidamas's brother, whose head Agamemnon cuts from his body with his sword. It has been a fiesta of severance, a destruction of human beings, but more than that, a destruction of human bonds. Agamemnon is edge-honed violence, his victims essentially their ligatures and sinews. It is the meeting of blade and connective tissue.

Only when wounded in the arm does Agamemnon withdraw from his unforgiving crusade. As his wound begins to dry, pain starts to afflict him: "And just as when the sharp pain strikes a woman in labour, the piercing dart sent by the bitter goddesses of childbirth, so sharp pains break in on the strength of Agamemnon." Those words are a measure of the grace and wisdom of this beautiful and terrifying poem. The pain suffered by the unforgiving agent of death and termination is like the pain of a woman as she gives birth to new life. What Agamemnon has done is to cut the connections between men and their fathers, men and their brothers, men and their wives, even men and their horses. But as his comparator for that slicing away of meaning, Homer summons the agony of childbirth, the root connectedness of humanity.

The Shaft Grave Greeks, in this vision, are the people of the blade and the mask, the Trojans of the loom and the embrace. One slices and rejects, the other weaves and holds; but Homer stands beyond and embraces them both. He makes a poem of death that is itself a thing of woven beauty. That is the essential picture of the *Iliad*, a great history cloth, a tapestry of sorrow, in which the noncity is set against the city, where the marginal and contingent confronts the settled and the secure. The poem is hinged to that difference: the loved against the abused, the creative against the destructive forces of life. And the fact of the poem itself is a kind of super-weaving, a weaving of severance and weaving into one shining cloth of understanding.

You can find that love of complexity in the Mycenaean halls of the Athens museum. Take, for example, the interlaced spirals on one of the beautiful golden cups, almost certainly a hospitality cup for drinking on shared, ritual occasions. Its decoration dramatizes those moments. The spirals are formed into upper and lower bands. Trace individual lines in the patterns, and you will find that the spirals in one set of lines roll from right to left, those in the other from left to right. Each tightens into a knot, meets its opposite there and then spirals out and onto the next encounter. At the same time lines from each band reach out and intertwine with lines from the bands above and below.

This is a culture entranced with the meeting, engaging, twisting, intertwisting and emerging of different cross-currents. Spirals are everywhere, in the gravestones showing spearmen in chariots hurtling into battle, on pots and on architectural masonry, on the beautifully chiseled platforms for the thrones of Mycenaean kings, on a golden breastplate bubbling with the swirl of life. The spirals might be taken as abstractions of the waves of the sea, but they are more than that: a recognition that this pattern of bind-and-release, alternating connectedness and separateness, is intimate with the nature of existence, of the thinking mind, the experiencing heart, the world that weaves and severs.

In book 14 of the *Iliad*, as deep trouble is afflicting the Greeks, Nestor, the old king of Pylos, stands outside his own shelter in the Greek camp and looks dazed at the confusion around him.

> As when the open sea is deeply stirred by the ground-swell
> But stays in one place and awaits the rapid onset of tearing
> Gusts, not rolling its surf onward in either direction
> Until Zeus drives the wind down to decide it:
> So the old man ponders, his mind caught between two courses.

That is as near as poetry could get to what archaeologists call the "antithetical spirals" that colonize such large areas of Mycenaean decoration and thought: dynamic, self-interlacing, not fixed but entranced by the very concepts of mobility, complexity and dynamism.

But there is a delicate and fluttering sensibility here too. In Grave III, where Schliemann found the remains of three women and two children, crowned with the most astonishing sun-embossed diadems of gold foil, their dresses scattered like spring meadows with gold roundels and flowers, he also found a set of impossibly flimsy golden scales, the bar from which the two pans hung made of foil so thin that anything more than the weight of a butterfly would have bent it. And on those scales, the Mycenaean craftsmen had impressed into the metal precisely that: fat-bodied butterflies, their wings fitting the scales on which they rested.

All this makes one thing clear: there is no need to assume that this early, prepalatial *Iliad* was some kind of brutalist crudity of bloodlust and violence, indifferent to the subtleties of moral atmosphere that are part of the deep weave of the poems. The early *Iliad* was as alert to irony, tragedy, poignancy and humanity as the *Iliad* we know. As Emily Vermeule once told a gathering of American classicists:

> Philologists often dislike, and reject, the idea that the early *Iliad* was
> good, and so beloved that great poetic effort and training were devoted
> to conserving it with all its archaisms and outmoded armor. They often
> prefer a late genius Homer who unified the design and gave new subtlety

to the characters. This is because we still like to believe in progress, and that each generation somehow improves over the one before it; so, Homer should be as close to the civilized and lovable Us as we can make him, not some primitive singer of the remotest past . . . [But] poetically and archaeologically, early is not always the same as primitive.

Look, for example, at the two most pitiful and most fully realized deaths in the *Iliad*, those of Achilles's dear friend Patroclus and of Hector, the champion of Troy. The same lines are given to their moment of dying, and only to them.

> He speaks, and as he speaks the end of death closes in upon him,
> And the soul, fluttering free of his limbs, goes down into Death's house
> Mourning its destiny, leaving behind its youth and manhood.

The Greek of those lines is as ancient as any in Homer, and yet they are also among the most poignant. The little soul leaves with nothing but regret. Death is not a release into beautiful immateriality but an expulsion from vivid life. Death is exile from light. The lovely limbs and eyes of Hector and Patroclus are now inert and glazed; the soul is nearly nothing without them.

Later images on Greek pots sometimes show a tiny, mothlike figure, more wing than body, hovering on the head or shoulders of the heroes who just died. Emily Vermeule, in a connection typical of her bright genius, reported an experiment performed by a doctor in Düsseldorf who had placed the beds of his dying patients on extremely sensitive scales, so that he could measure their weight immediately before and after death. The difference, he found, was twenty-one grams, three-quarters of an ounce, the weight of the soul.

How can these objects and images not be evidence of a Homeric sensibility in sixteenth-century BC Mycenae? The love-denying mask of Agamemnon; the vision of the mayfly-soul, sadly departing the man in whose body it had found such radiant life; the antithetical interlace of a mind caught between two courses; the presence of tenderness allied in your everyday life to desperate violence.

Again and again in his similes, Homer knows that life is fragile, love suffers hurt and death comes; and that the moments on a hillside in the springtime, when the flowers are emerging in the turf, the sheep are giv-ing milk and what looks like a mist of new leaves is just breathed into the dark of a winter wood, are more precious than any gathering of metal from slaughtered enemies or the rape of their wives.

There is no need to patronize the past or to assume that we somehow have a fineness of moral vision to which the warrior culture of Homer and the Shaft Graves had no access. But can one push on beyond this moment of the early Greeks in Greece? Does Homer have his roots in anything earlier than what can be found at Mycenae? He does. But here the path bifurcates: from Greece and the Aegean, the undoubted setting of the Homeric poems, one road leads north and west into Europe and the borders of Europe and Asia; the other goes south and east toward the great palace civilizations of Crete, Egypt, Mesopotamia and the eastern shores of the Mediterranean. Homer exists at the confluence of those two giant streams; in many ways his subject is what happens when those two streams meet and mingle. Homer, often seen as the template from which many later encounters of west and east are drawn, is better understood as the great meeting of north and south, what happens to northern adventurers in a southern world. That meeting lies at the roots of Greek civilization, and stemming from it is much of the later history of Europe.

8 · THE METAL HERO

In the Stone Age, before man went in search of metal, you could have picked up nodules and nuggets of copper lying on the surface of the earth or glimmering in the sandbanks of any stream. In some places, like the great copper body at Parys Mountain in Anglesey, copper was so thick in the groundwater that perfect branches, plant stems, leaves and nuts of the metal could be found in the dirt, where the mineral had somehow replaced the organic matter buried there.

All over Eurasia, that native copper was beaten into disks and rosettes, badges and brooches, and occasionally little needle-sharp awls and burins for working leather. In about 8000 BC in Anatolia, in Syria and northern Mesopotamia, people began to smelt it, the first smiths, magicians of heat and strangeness, drawing the metal out of the ores in which it is usually found. The heat of a pottery kiln is enough to release the metal from its oxides and sulfides, but even so the glowing emergence of a material that stayed flame-bright when cool can only have summoned a kind of awe. It may even be that the Arthurian story of the sword in the stone is a folk-memory of this emergent miracle: gleaming strength drawn from a rock.

From about 5000 BC, people all over Europe and Asia started hardening the copper, perhaps first by chance, by mixing arsenic with the metal when it was molten. But copper and these copper-arsenic alloys were rather soft, not the revolutionary material that after 3000 BC would transform Eurasia. Only then did someone, probably in Anatolia, discover that if you added tin to copper, you could produce a metal that not only would take a high shine—a brazen, visual hardness—but was physically hard and could be sharpened to a fierce and lasting edge. This tin-copper alloy was bronze, and it would change the world. There is some tin in Anatolia, but in most places it is rare or absent, and across the bulk of the bronze-making world it had to be imported from elsewhere. Still nobody is certain where that tin for the Bronze revolution came from: perhaps from Bohemia in the Czech Republic, maybe from Cornwall, but more likely from Afghanistan. Whatever the origins of the tin, travel and connection become central to the culture of Europe. For the first time in the European Bronze Age (2500 to 800 BC), the exotic became desirable and the distant prestigious. It became a world of interconnectedness, a culture founded on mobility, with ideas, beliefs and ways of life all traveling along the seaways and river routes of Europe and western Asia.

"The broad picture," as the Bristol archaeologist Richard Harrison has written, "is of a continent with an imaginative map of itself that knew, through objects from faraway places, that other worlds existed and that they shared values as well as objects." A necklace of Baltic amber, found in a grave in Wiltshire in England, was made of beads shaped in Mycenae. The Nebra sky disk, found in central Germany, was made of Austrian copper, Cornish tin and Cornish gold. A Bronze Age wreck off the south coast of Devon carried a Sicilian sword. A piece of amber has been found at Bernstorf in Bavaria, inscribed with a word written in Linear B, the Greek spoken in Mycenae, along with gold diadems that resemble those from Mycenae itself. Afghan lapis lazuli appears in Greek graves. Folding chairs in Danish graves were made on patterns that recur in Greece and in Egypt.

Were these movements of things accompanied by people? Or was it only that objects were passed from hand to hand across Europe? Shipwrights in Bronze Age Scandinavia made craft that bear a striking resemblance to Greek prototypes. Carvings of otterlike animals on some Swedish tombs look very like the creatures engraved on Mycenaean signet rings. How did those ideas get there? Did Bronze Age Greeks actually make their way to Denmark?

The teeth of an early Bronze Age man who was buried not far from Stonehenge in southern England bear trace elements that show he grew up somewhere in the Swiss Alps. Near him another man was buried, his relative, perhaps his son, with the same slightly faulty bone structure in his feet, whose teeth revealed that he had grown up in southern England. Cross-continental journeys were certainly possible in the Bronze Age, but was the whole of this proto-Europe alive with adventurers and travelers? Or people whose journeys were not of their own volition? Chemical analysis of the teeth enamel from twenty-four people roughly buried in a series of late Bronze Age pits at Cliffsend in Thanet in northeast Kent, from around 1000 BC, shows an extraordinary set of international origins. Just over a third were from Kent (strontium and oxygen isotopes in drinking water carry unique chemical signatures), another third from southern Norway or Sweden, a fifth from the western Mediterranean and the rest undetermined. Many of these people left their birthplaces when they were children between three and twelve years old. One old woman buried in Thanet was born in Scandinavia, moved to Scotland as a child and at the end of a long life finished up in Kent. Almost certainly these people were slaves.

Certain clusters of human genes (the haplogroup E3bIa2), which have their heartland in the copper-mining districts of Albania and are found in the people living there now, rarely appear elsewhere in Europe, except in two specific concentrations: one in the modern inhabitants of Galicia in northwest Spain, the other in the people of northwest Wales, both important centers of copper mining in the early Bronze Age. It seems inescapable that these genes are the living memories of Bronze Age people traveling the width of a continent to exploit the magical metal.

Bronze began to transform the Near East and to have its effect in China, the Indus Valley and the Aegean. Troy, on the far northern edge of that urban belt, became a trading city, controlling routes to the north. City-states emerged, along with writing, bureaucracies, specialist traders and central authoritarian government. Woven textiles were traded up into the Caucasus in return for copper from increasingly well-developed mines. In a belt that stretched east across the Asian continent, and of which Troy and the beautiful cities visited by Odysseus are the emblem and embodiment, urban civilizations emerged.

At the same moment, but farther north, the new metal had an equally powerful effect on human history. A different, nonurban Bronze-based culture emerged. A cluster of economic, social, military and psychological changes came about in a wide swath of country which stretched from the steppelands around the Caspian Sea through the Balkans and on into northern Europe. These changes created the civilization of which Achilles is the symbol: not a city world but a warrior elite, ferociously male in its focus, with male gods and a cultivation of violence, with no great attention paid to dwellings or public buildings, but a fascination with weaponry, speed and violence. The heroes of this warrior world were not the bureaucrats of the cities farther south, or the wall builders, or the defenders of the gates, but men for whom their individuality was commemorated in large single burials, often under prominent mounds, on highly visible places among the grazing grounds cleared for their herds. Meat mattered in this warrior world, largely as a symbol of portable wealth when on the hoof and as the material for feasting when dead and cooked.

This semipastoral economic and political system was the breeding ground for a dynamic and mobile warrior culture which would eventually spread throughout Eurasia. There were many local variations and idiosyncrasies, and a complex chronology, full of time lags, which mean that the same cultural phase occurs at different times in different places; but for all that, a single world of Bronze Age chieftainship stretched across the whole of northern Eurasia from the Atlantic to the Asian steppe. It is a world hinged to the idea of the hero, quite different from the developed, literate cultures of the eastern Mediterranean, and it is the world from which the Shaft Grave Greeks emerged in about 1700 BC.

In his Greek heroes, Homer gives voice to that northern warrior world. Homer is the only place you can hear the Bronze Age warriors of the northern grasslands speak and dream and weep. The rest of Bronze Age Europe is silent. Echoes of what was said and sung in Ireland or in German forests can be recovered from tales and poems collected by modern ethnographers, but only in Homer is the connection direct. The relationship travels both ways. Homer can illuminate Bronze Age Europe, and Bronze Age Europe can throw its light on the Homeric world.

In places where you might least expect to find them, echoes of the world of Achilles come drifting up at you. And the weapons are at the heart of it. I have seen them now in museums in Wiltshire, in Naples and Syracuse, Bodrum, Athens and Nafplio, and in St. Petersburg, Paris, Edinburgh, London and Boston, where collectors and excavators have gathered them. Anywhere you seek out Bronze Age weaponry, the same power gestures greet you from across the room: the seductive, limousine length

Bronze spearheads, eighth century BC, found in 1908 in a large clay pot near Syracuse, Sicily.

of the blades, the oxidized green of the bronze, often now the color of a mottled sea, the willow-leaf javelin points, the sheer length of the long swords with their golden hilts, the deep-socketed spear heads, the socket running as far back along the shaft as the spear head protrudes beyond it, the metal occasionally still wrapped in oiled cloth to preserve it.

If you look at one of these blades with Homer in mind, you see it for what it is: the tapering fineness of its double edges, coming to a point more gradually than anything in nature, those everlasting cutting edges going on and on like the leaf of a fine, imagined iris; or a slow-motion diagram of death being delivered; the strengthening midrib, narrowing along the blade but running to the very tip, so that it arrives there as delicate as a syringe; and the reinforcement at the root of the blade, a possible weak point where the shaft first narrows, vulnerable to the body of the victim twisting and kicking with the pain.

These blades are pure ergonomy, designed for a purpose, elegantly coalescing the necessary functions, the cut and the shove, two slicing edges and a penetrative rod for the best possible pushing of metal into flesh, and then the widening of the wound past the point, so that the man will bleed and die.

These are the wonder-weapons of the *Iliad*: "They clothe their bodies in gleaming bronze and Poseidon the Shaker of the Earth leads them, carrying in his strong hand his terrible long-edge sword, like lightning, which no one can stand up to in dreadful war. Terror holds men aloof from it."

These weapons are horrifying and beautiful, repulsive and attractive in the way the *Iliad* can be, for their lack of sentiment, the unadorned facts they represent, but also for the perfection with which they are made, their seamless match of purpose and material. The swords that have been found in Mycenacan graves are always exceptionally well-balanced things, the weight in the pommel counteracting the weight in the blade so that they feel functional in the hand, body-extensions, enlarging the human possibilities of dominance and destruction. The lances would have been useful in the hunt, to be thrown or to jab at cornered prey, but these swords mark a particular horizon in human history: they are the first objects to be designed with the sole purpose of killing another person. Their reach is too short for them to be any good with a wild animal thrashing in its death terror. A sword is only useful if someone else agrees to the violence it threatens; it will get to another man who is prepared to stand and fight. Some of the most beautiful decorated swords are found scarcely used, ceremonial objects to be carried in glory. But most of the rest show the marks of battle; the edges hacked and notched where another sword clashed onto them, worn where those edges were resharpened for the next time.

An air of threat and beauty hangs about them, even in their glass cases, labeled and sanitized, consigned to a curated past. They seem sometimes like caged predators, their violence lurking a quarter of an inch beneath the surface. Anyone who has ever walked out with a gun they liked, or even a rod well set up, will know something of this, its beautiful fittedness to your needs, "as snug as a gun," as Seamus Heaney described the pen he chose instead of it, the sense a weapon has of extending your power over the material world, its promise, or at least taunting suggestion, of what it will be like when the fish takes the hook and the rod bends, and you feel in your hand that other creature's struggle against your dominance; or when the bird you have been tracking crumples and folds with the shot, its head and wings useless, howling toward earth, where the body lands football-like, a muffled heavy thump.

Our modern sensibility might wrinkle its nose against the pleasure the warrior world took in violence, but Homer cannot be understood unless that pleasure is also understood. Homer has a specific word for that death thump: *doupein*, meaning "to sound like the heavy thud of a corpse as it falls." It is always set against its opposite, *arabein*, "to rattle and clash," the sound that armor makes when a man is felled. That pairing is a formula that fills a whole line, recording again and again the death of enemies: "*doupēsen de pesōn, arabēse de teuche' ep' autōi*" (With a thud he falls, rattling his armor around him). The thud and the rattle mark the falling apart of a man's life, its coherence removed by death, the effect delivered by the gleaming bronze, the triumph of the new metal dominance, its penetrative masculinity and its cultivation of power. The sharpened blade transformed human relations.

Only once in my life have I had a knife held to my throat. It was thirty years ago. I was twenty-five years old and in Palmyra in the Syrian desert. In the early evening I was walking alone in the palm groves on the southern edge of the oasis, down the rutted tracks that curved through the trees beyond the ruins of the temple of Baal. The sun was coming through in rods, lighting up the bunches of fruit high in those trees, and between the shafts of light the air was soft and gray, almost milky. The warmth of the evening was feeling its way between my shirt and skin. A little boy passed me and said "Hallo" in English, brightly and sweetly.

I was thinking how beautiful this place was after all the openness of the desert, coming as we had on a hard, rough track from Damascus, and was paying no attention to where I was wandering, kicking up the dust on the track with the toes of my boots. But the light was going, and after a while I thought I should return to where I was staying, the Hotel Zenobia, a mile or so away on the far side of the famous ruins, in the grid of streets of the modern town.

And so I turned back up the track, the way I had come. I could see the footprints my boots had made as I came down there. But I reached a crossing, where another track cut over, and could not immediately remember which to take. A young man, a little older than me, but shorter, with rather thick hair combed to one side, was leading his bicycle toward me.

"Hotel Zenobia?" I asked him. He looked up at me. "Hotel Zenobia?" I asked again.

A look of understanding came into his face, and he smiled, turned his bicycle around and led me along the track he had just come down. We had the usual, fruitless nonconversation between people who cannot speak each other's language. After a few minutes we came to another crossing, and he seemed a little uncertain. I looked in his face to see if I could guess where he thought we should go, but as I did so he dropped his bicycle, grabbed me by my wrists and started to push me to the ground in front of him. It was always going to be hopeless, he being the shorter, and I held him and his arms away from me. He tried to trip me, as schoolboys do, by putting his foot behind mine, but to no end. It was faintly ludicrous, the two of us there in a kind of tussling nonembrace, on some track in the middle of an oasis in the Syrian desert. But there was anxiety in his eyes, now that I looked into them.

I broke free of his hold, running back the way we had come, turned right at the first crossroads and ran on, hoping but not knowing that I was on the track to get out of the palm grove and into the openness around the ruins. I ran on, the path curving here and there between the different blocks of the plantation, until I came to a fork in the road. Which way? I had no idea, and stopped, trying to recognize the route home. But as I stopped he caught up with me. I looked down at him and saw that he had a large stone in his hand; he had been thinking of throwing it at me. But the instant I saw the stone he dropped it and took out a knife, the blade no more than four or five inches long, but coming to a point, the edges honed, scratched where he had sharpened them on a file.

He raised the knife to my throat and held the point just where you would put your fingers for a pulse, where the neck begins to curve around under the jaw. I could feel the metal point on my skin, but it did not cut me. Keeping it there, he led me back down the track we had both just run along. I didn't feel any conscious fear. My breathing was slowing, my mind going cold, disconnected. He wanted to be somewhere we would not be disturbed. We turned off the track into a little patch of scrubby ground between the palm trees. There were some plastic canisters here, perhaps for oil. Neither of us spoke. He made me undress, holding the knife into the side of my neck as I did so. Surely I should have hit him then? Looking back on it now, I wonder why I didn't. Why not just hit his face with my fist, knock him down and kick him once he was on the ground? Isn't that what the warriors in Homer would have done? Break his skull, murder the man who threatened me with his knife? Wasn't that the only dignified thing to have done?

But I didn't. I behaved in the way that the "foolish children" of the *Iliad* behave, submitting to the knife, too frightened at what that blade might do to my face and body to risk fighting him. Women and children in Homer are always called foolish because they do not risk death by confronting the enemy; they submit and suffer like sheep under a worrying dog. I knelt in the dust as he raped me, a pitiable little doglike action from behind, the point of the knife jiggling in the side of my neck with his frantic movements, my mind observing this from afar and realizing that the moment of greatest danger was not yet over, that after he had done with me, all the possibilities of loathing, resentment and shame, not to speak of the chance that I would report and identify him, might mean he would kill me.

I prepared for that moment as I felt him coming over my thighs and buttocks. It all seemed entirely prosaic, neither consciously frightening nor dramatic, not anything that would raise my pulse. This was my experience of the ordinariness of death, that everything that had made me what I was up to that moment—my father and my father's father, my love of home, of the orchards and wheatfields that the Iliadic warriors always remember, and my wife in England—all of that was now perhaps to come to an end, without strangeness or mystery, but as one of the essential facts of being and nonbeing, of my life being bound up with the continued existence of the pulse in my body. I felt entirely animal, as if I and my body were coterminous, everything about me dependent on the blade of that knife not cutting into me and draining my life into the Syrian dust.

In those few minutes, I moved through the full spectrum of Homeric reactions, from the childlike stupidity of acceptance of violence to the manlike recognition that I should risk killing him in order to be myself. This was when the fight for life would happen; this was my introduction to the world with which the Homeric heroes are so familiar; their life dependent on the death of those who are out to destroy them.

We stood up, I dressed, he did up his trousers, holding the knife in his hand, and I walked back alongside him, smiling, talking about Palmyra, just out of arm's reach. We came to his bike, and he picked it up, the knife still in the hand that held the handlebars. I made sure I walked with the bike between me and him. I kept talking to him, looking at him with my eyes, smiling, acting ease and acceptance, waiting for the moment when he would stop again, and come for me, preparing for that, not in anything resembling rage or fear, but a stilled, intent cold-mindedness. As we walked along, I looked for the stones on the track which, when the time came, I would pick up and use to crush the skull bones between his eyes.

It was getting dark. We passed the point where he had first caught up with me. The farther we got, the safer I knew I was. We reached the edge of the palms and the blue of the open desert. He pointed me to the road I should have taken, and then he turned away to the right, walking with his bike into the shadows of the trees. I went on across the desert toward the town and the hotel, where I stood for longer than I knew in the shower, recognizing that I had understood something that evening: the banality of one's own death, so much less terrible than the death of someone you love; its mysterious combination of everything and nothing; its lack of beauty or poignancy; the extreme calm that threat can summon; the clarity with which, when threatened with death, you must threaten death in return.

I knew nothing of Homer then, but I know now that these are all aspects of Homeric understanding. They emerge from a world in which use and imposition are part of the everyday fabric of life. The poems are not the overheated fantasies of palace-based thrill seekers. There's no *ooh-ah* here. Homer's groundedness in the plain facts of killing is one of the guarantees of its truth.

A few years later I went in deeper pursuit of this northern, nonurban, metal warrior world, led first by the hint of a footnote in a book by Adolf Schulten, the German archaeologist who devoted his life to the recovery of antiquity in southern Spain. In 1922, in the first volume of *Fontes Hispaniae Antiquae*, he suggested that he knew the location of Hades, the underworld, which in the middle of the *Odyssey* Odysseus and his men visit in order to learn the way home from the old, blind seer Tiresias. It was, I recognize, a quixotic thing to do, to fly there, rent a car, drive through the concrete scurf of the modern Spanish coastline, to find the place where

Odysseus, a fictional character in a phantasmagorical story from the Bronze Age, was said to have encountered some of the deepest truths Homer had to offer. It is the sort of behavior you might find in a Tom Stoppard play or a High Victorian memoir, but as things turned out, in my few days of walking around the river valleys and dry cork oak pastures on the high borders of Andalusia and Extremadura—that most marginal imaginable of Odyssean landscapes—I felt as if I were cutting deep trenches into the Homeric world.

When I first read the *Odyssey*, no moment was more powerful for me than Odysseus's visit to the underworld. Inner and outer landscapes were more intimately fused there than in anything I had ever read. The great man's crew of time- and sea-worn sailors have been on Circe's island but are now cold and frightened, at the limits of the world. The coast of Hades is desolate, fringed with tall poplars and with willows whose seed falls from the trees before it is ripe. This place is everything the world of heroes is not: dark, colorless, silent and mournful.

Crowds of the dead surface to confront the crew. The ghosts, the *psyches*, shuffle toward them; their limbs are "strengthless." All the varieties of death emerge: the old who have suffered much, the girls with tender hearts, the brides and unwed youths, and "great armies of battle dead, stabbed by bronze spears, men of war still wrapped in bloody armour." They cannot speak. They do not have the life juices which would allow them to speak.

For the dead, there is no other choice than Hades. This is not punishment but simply the place where in the end all people, however good and however holy, must go. Hell is the absence of life, the removal from the world of love and warmth which is the defining glory of life on earth. Hell is the house of loss. Only when Odysseus sprinkles in front of him all the good and fruitful things of the world—milk, honey, wine, water, white barley flour—and adds to them the hot blood of newly slaughtered lambs, and only when he allows the ghosts to sip at that lifeblood, does the power of speech, the sense of human communicativeness, return to the spirits.

One by one they approach him, drink and speak: his friend Elpēnōr; Tiresias; and his mother. Odysseus longs to embrace them all, but as he moves to hold them, they "flutter through his fingers, sifting away like shadows, dissolving like a dream." They are nothing in his arms. *Psyches* are merely people from whom the life-defining qualities of people, their physical presence in the world, have been stripped away. Here are people in the gray, fleshless state to which death has reduced them. It is a vision of the beautiful, the regal and the desirable sunk to nothing but rustling, flittering spirit.

As Odysseus stands there, with the tears running down his cheeks, he sees, coming toward him, the ghost of Achilles, the greatest of all the warriors, the fastest and fiercest among them, worshipped almost as a god by the other Greeks at Troy, and now the greatest among the dead. His face is mournful, and Odysseus tries to console him. Achilles answers coldly and passionately: "Never try to sweeten death for me, glorious Odysseus." The word Achilles uses for glorious, *phaidimos*, is used throughout Homer to describe the heroes. But here in hell, it has a particular resonance. Its roots are in the word for shining or brilliance. As the dead Achilles speaks, it is the world of lightlessness addressing the world of light and glimmer, the shining world from which Odysseus comes and from which Achilles is forever excluded.

This is one of the pivotal moments of the Homeric epics, the dead hero of the *Iliad* addressing the living hero of the *Odyssey*, the man of singular and unequaled heroism, who has already suffered his fate, speaking across the borders of hell with the living, slippery, "many-wayed" man, *polytropos Odysseus*, whose life and destiny still have some glittering way to run. Death is addressing life and envying it.

Achilles makes the great central statement of the poems. "If I had a chance of living on earth again," the ghost says through his tears, "I would rather do that as a slave of another, some landless man with scarcely enough to live on, than lord it here over all the dead that have ever died." This is the Achilles whose pride had defined him in life, whose honor and sense of his own greatness had driven hundreds of men to their death, who had chosen death and a short life as the foundation of his glory. In the *Iliad*, Achilles had glowed with destructive beauty; he was a flaming star, a fire burning through a wood. His hands were "like consuming fire, his might like glittering iron." His eyes burned like a furnace-core. His protective goddess, the gray-eyed Athene, had lit an unwearying fire that burned over his head. At every turn in his life he was quick and unforgiving. He was elemental in his strength, like a river unsusceptible to argument or compromise. But now, for this ghost, this burned-out, ashy wraith, any taste of life, of any kind, however humble, is preferable to the half-lit half-existence of senseless wastedness to which he is condemned. The purity of death holds no attraction for the Homeric Greeks. Their world is one in which the felt, sensed and shared reality, the reality of the human heart, is the only one worth having.

As a measure of Homer's skill as a dramatist and topographer of the emotions, he has Achilles address Odysseus again, the two of them still in tears, with the question that burns in the heart of any ghost in hell: "But tell me the story," Achilles says—the Greek word is *mythos*, meaning the "word," the "rumor," what men say, but also the plot, the pattern of the story—"of the lordly boy." He is referring to his son Neoptolemos, whose name means New War. Had he followed the Greeks to the wars? Had he fought as a son of Achilles might be expected to fight? Was he a boy a man might be proud of? Odysseus, drenched in love and pity for the dead hero, tells him all he knows of the beauty and courage of Neoptolemos: his calm when waiting with Odysseus in the belly of the Trojan Horse, his unwavering courage and, perhaps more important, how the boy had ended the war unharmed and even unscarred, never stabbed by either spear or sword, but sailing home in his ship with his share of the spoils and "a noble prize." He does not mention that in other stories of the Trojan War, Neoptolemos was the most savage of all killers at the fall of Troy, murdering Priam at the altar of Zeus and killing Astyanax, Hector's child, by throwing him from the walls. In one version, Neoptolemos kills Priam by battering him with the dead body of his grandson.

Achilles does not hear this but nevertheless can say nothing in response to what Odysseus does say. It is too much for any father, even the greatest of heroes. He can only walk away across this beautiful, monochrome hell, which is covered, like all stony wasteland in the Mediterranean, with stands of tall, pale asphodels. It is a moment to describe the desolation of death and the unbridgeable gap between the world of light and the world of dark. Achilles both possesses his son in his memory and knows he can never possess him again. Neoptolemos is not here, and Achilles can be nowhere else. Here, defined by death, is the central grief of experience. Odysseus tells his listeners what Achilles did next.

> So I spoke, and off he went, the ghost of the great runner,
> Loping with long strides across the field of asphodel,
> Speechless in triumph at all that I had told him of his boy.

Adolf Schulten suggested that this scene occurred at the far western end of the Bronze Age world, in southwest Spain, because that is where the goddess Circe had told Odysseus to go: "Set up your mast, spread the white sail, and sit yourself down; and the breath of the North Wind will bear your ship onwards." Bronze Age ships, on a broad reach, with the mainsail braced hard to port, could drive west with a north wind, the fastest of all points of sailing. "But when in your ship you have crossed the stream of Oceanus," Circe continued, "where is a level shore and the groves of Persephone—tall poplars and willows that shed their fruit— there beach your ship by the deep swirling Ocean, but go yourself to the dank house of Hades."

These are plain instructions. Odysseus's ship must sail beyond the gates of the Mediterranean, out through the Straits of Gibraltar, into the Atlantic Ocean, where the tides swirl and circle in a way unknown to Mediterranean sailors, and there find a beach with strange, cold, oceanic trees whose fertility deserts them under the salt winds. These are the trees of Persephone, the queen of death who is also queen of life, a vegetation goddess taken by Hades, king of the underworld, to be his consort, and in whose kingdom she presides over the sufferings of human souls. Odysseus will know he has arrived when he finds her trees whose seeds would never be ripe.

But Circe is more explicit still: "There into the ocean flow Pyriphlegethon and Kokytus, which is a branch of the river of Styx; and there is a rock, and the meeting place of the two roaring rivers." Homer's geographic imagination understands scale and substance, and these are the giant rivers of hell: *Pyriphlegethon* means "blazing" or "raging like a fire," used of cities when men torch them; *Kokytus* means "howling" or "shrieking"; it is the sound made by Priam and the women of Troy when they hear of the death of Hector; *Styx* means "hateful" and "loathsome," the word used again and again for war, death and destiny. In rivers that make their way down to the great surrounding ocean, sorrow and fearsomeness slide out of the huge, dark, hidden continent called Hades.

Schulten thought he knew where this was. West of the Guadalquivir, and west of the straits of Gibraltar, two rivers flow out into the Atlantic at Huelva: the Rio Tinto—the name means the "red river"—and the Rio Odiel. Where they meet in the estuary at Huelva, a great hoard of Bronze Age weaponry, now in Madrid, was dredged up in 1923. The confluence of those rivers is below a conspicuous rock where the monastery of Santa Maria de la Rábida has stood since the Middle Ages, and where in 1492 Christopher Columbus made his final prayers before sailing west for Cathay.

It may not be much, but there were undoubtedly Mycenaean connections in southern Spain; Mycenaean ceramics have been found at Montoro on the Guadalquivir, east of Córdoba. If there were connections to the Cornish tin supply, the sea routes came past here. It is possible that the estuary at Huelva is Homer's gates of hell.

I was there alone one autumn, the south wind blowing warm and delicious out of Africa. There are beaches where, as it says in the *Odyssey*, "they stowed their gear and laid the mast in the hollow hulls," waiting to see what would come to them at the ends of the earth. There is a flat shore, as Circe promised; a rock, or at least a large mound; two rivers, but neither is roaring nor made of fire. The estuary waters are brown and polluted. Slimed stumps of old quays stand up to their shins in the water. Waders teeter on the water's edge. The trees are no longer the seed-spreading willows but clumps of eucalyptus and palms in rows. Phoenician, Egyptian, Greek and Cornish objects have all been dredged from these shallow waters, but if this is the gate of Hades, the shores of a light-less eternity, you would hardly guess it.

But go inland, and the landscape starts to change. Both the Rio Tinto and the Rio Odiel push on to the north of Huelva. These river valleys were one of the most important sources of metals in the Bronze Age because the hills on either side are filled with veins and big ore-bodies of copper, tin, gold and silver. Both rivers in their upper reaches are deeply changed by the metal country they run through. The *Odyssey*, with its man-eating monsters and vicious whirlpools, is a gothic poem, full of the nightmarish and the terrifying, the imagined sufferings of its heroes, but these garishly colored mineral valleys share that atmosphere: the toxic, the metallic, the otherworldly, the lifeless and the threatening all fused into some kind of recipe for hell.

Stop the car, walk down to one of these riverbeds and you will find the world drenched in strangeness. It is a gaudy and bloody trench, earth transmuting into another planet. The rocks and water are both iron red. Sandbanks in the river look as if they are the hulks of abandoned iron beaches. These are not the neat pleasure-landscapes of an island kingdom

but are big, harsh, continental, inherently violent. Flakes of white quartzite shine through the water between ribs of rock that veer from red to
tangerine to ocher and rust to flame-colored, flesh-colored, sick and livid.
In between those red rocks are green snakeskin copper-rich boulders,
glinting gray-eyed green minerals from within the orange depths.

The rivers themselves are deeply and naturally poisoned. This is the
earth polluting itself. Where it has dried it has left white chemical resi-
dues, scurfy scabmarks of receding poison tides. Only one kind of strange,
green, long-haired weed can live in it. Apart from that, the water is cloud-
less, mineral red but entirely clear. This is a place in which almost nothing can live, in which fruit would drop before it was ripe. Those swirling
fronds of green hair, seven, eight, nine feet long, are swept downstream
around the flakes of rock. Underwater, the whole bed of the stream is
coated in a thick dust of iron poison, iron solids precipitated from the water,
a fungal metal scum. Where, in a back eddy, the current slows, a crusted
porridge of the bloody slurry gathers in the pools, and no fish rise.

An occasional dragonfly hangs its diamond-blue wings over this hell-
water, but never with a mate. No songbirds. High above, some distant
hawks. Perfectly white flies lie dead, caught in the mineral slicks. If Homer,
in Chios, heard of this, of course he would have put Hades and Persephone here. I have never seen a place more suited to them.

At the mining town of Rio Tinto itself, there is a museum where the
mysteries of this metal world are on display. If you want to rediscover the
Bronze Age entrancement with minerals in the raw, this is the place. In
neat, old-fashioned glass cabinets you will find some of the strangest
things the natural world can offer: fractured blue-silver flakes of galena;
silver-gold cubes of iron pyrites; bulbs of calcite, erupting and diseased like
glaucous eyeballs. Cinnabar is a stone blood-pudding, its red shot through
with purples and blacks, the background for lilac amethysts. Green malachite is here, with azurite its close cousin, a Prussian blue only to be found
in Alpine gentians. Sometimes the pyrites coat the skin of a rock in what
is called *calco pitita*, as if a breath of gold had been blown over the stone.
But nothing is more like the jewels of a hell palace, or poetry from the
depths, than the rainbow stripes of Goethite, the crust of an indigo, lilac
and green-gold planet.

The extraction of mineral ores here can only have been hell. The metals
were mined from the overlying rock in difficult, cramped, dangerous and

unforgiving conditions. Much of the ore was loosened by setting fires in the underground chambers, the heat splitting the rock, which could then be pulled away by hand or levered off with antler picks. Otherwise, it was simply beaten with hard stone hammers that were waisted to take a rope binding, which have been found in the ancient mines, their ends battered with the work they had done before they were cast aside. Human limb bones are occasionally found beside them deep in the ancient workings.

Twenty miles from Rio Tinto, in the dry hills near the village of El Pozuelo, at a place called Chinflón, a Bronze Age copper mine remains much as it was left when the seams were abandoned about three thousand years ago. It is not easy to find, about an hour's walk from the nearest road through poor, scratchy cork oak and eucalyptus hills. This is high and silent country, nearly sterile with its metals, scarcely visited now, a universe away from the industrialized agriculture of the coast. There are deer slots in the dust of the track, and the views are enormous, twenty miles in all directions over the burned forested ridges, taking in at their limit the vast bloody gash of the modern quarries at Rio Tinto. There are pale-winged buzzards in the sky, dust seems to be everywhere and salt sweat runs into your eyes and onto your lips.

The top of the hill at Chinflón is still smothered in the gray-greenish toxic spoil from that ancient mine. Red and orange rock flakes prod up through it. Coppery gray-green lichen spreads over the stones. Because of the way the rock strata are aligned, the flakes run along the crest of the hill in a series of narrow parallel ridges, so the summit is spiked skyward, like the vertical plates on the back of a Stegosaurus. Between those flakes is where the metal-bearing veins of malachite and azurite came to the surface, and where the Bronze Age men dug away for it, mining into a series of slits, pursuing the vein as it sank away from the air and the light, scrabbling with their heavy hammers, diving after the metal like dogs down burrows.

There is a modern chain-link fence surrounding the workings, to prevent you from getting at them, but you can fumble and scrape your way under it easily enough. Within the rough enclosure are the deep but narrow rock trenches cut into the earth, twenty or thirty feet long, six feet wide at their widest; others just wide enough for a ladder to lead down into their dark. They push seventy or eighty feet below the surface. Coppery, blue-leaved plants grow on the mine lip, as if the metal had entered their veins. Clots of quartzite sit there like fat in pâté. Steps are cut into the walls of these red, dark mineral hollows, the rim of each step slightly higher than its cupped floor so that the hold feels safe enough as you go down. But you descend gingerly. In one of them, nineteenth-century iron chain-ladders are set into the little cut cliff-faces, where later miners hoped to find what their predecessors had abandoned. The air feels cool as you drop into the shadow, lowering yourself into the rock-bath, the sweat cooling on your back, the mine wrapping its walls around you. At the bottom, in the half-dark the slits are wet and mossy, comforting, mysteriously juicy, liquid, the walls of Hades seeping with grief. Any noise you make is echoey. But the sides of the walls are vulnerable. There is not much a pick would be needed to dig out. Touch them, and rock pebbles clatter down below you into the dark, ricocheting off the lower walls. I collected flakes of greenish, snakeskin rock, the minerals in them glimmering as they turned through the light from above.

All mines are full of spirits. In the lead mines in County Durham, the men always spoke of the rock as an animal, ready to push at you as you made your way along an adit or down a shaft. In Cornwall the tin miners called the mine spirits the Knockers, as they knocked back at any man cutting away at the metal-bearing veins. They were the mine itself speaking. In sixteenth-century Germany, according to the great Renaissance theorist Georgius Agricola, these spirits were "called the little miners, because of their dwarfish stature, which is about two feet. They are venerable looking and clothed like miners with a leather apron about their loins."

Most of the time the Knockers were gentle and friendly, hanging about in the shafts and tunnels, only turning vicious if the miners ridiculed or cursed them. You needed to treat them with respect. Whistling could offend them, as could intentionally spying on what they were doing. They liked to be left in the shadows or the depths of the mines, or even behind the rock, knocking from inside it. Many miners placed small offerings of food or candle grease in the mine to feed and satisfy them. If you were good to them, they would show you where to find the metal.

As Ronald Finucane, the historian of the medieval subconscious, has said, ghosts "represent man's inner universe just as his art and poetry do." Ghosts are what you fear or hope for. The mine, if the gods favored you, could provide a sort of magically immediate richness not to be found in the surface world. But all was hidden until you found it. And that reward-from-nothing was reflected in the miners' attitudes toward metals. In Cornwall, they thought that iron pyrites when applied to a wound would cure it. Even water that had run over iron pyrites was said to be medicinal. Cuts washed in it would heal without any other intervention. But also in Cornwall, and in the parts of the United States where Cornish tinners immigrated and took their ancient beliefs with them, Knockers were thought to be ugly and vindictive. Miners who were lamed were known to be victims of the Knockers' rage. Insult them, and they could damage you for life.

It is a commanding cluster of images: lightlessness, the spirits of the underworld, the hope for treasure and happiness, wounding, cures, the half-glimpsed, the dreaded, a realm of pain and power. This is the dark basement of the Achilles world, the place that metal came from, emerging through processes that were unknown and unintelligible to most of the population, but somehow providing the power-soaked tools with which the killer-chiefs dominated the landscape.

It is at least a possibility that Homer's Hades is a nightmare fantasy fueled by the Bronze Age experience of the mine: a place in which spirits are clearly present but not to be grasped; where life has sunk away from the sunlight to the mute and the insubstantial; to beings that are only half there, regretting the absence of the vivid sunlight above; where a mysterious sense of power lurks in the dark. "When it comes to excavated ground, dreams have no limit," Gaston Bachelard wrote in *The Poetics of Space*. When you are underground, "darkness prevails both day and night, and even when we are carrying a lighted candle, we see shadows standing on the dark walls . . . The cellar is buried madness."

There is a sense of transgression at Chinflón, a feeling that this place was once alive and that the miners hacked at its life, as if they were hunting it, digging out its goodness, a form of rough and intemperate grasping, the masculine dragging of value from a subterranean womb. No one could be in the high, lonely mine at Chinflón, with its rock walls pressing in around them, and an almost oppressive silence filling the gaps between the stones, and not sense the reality of Hades as the house of sorrows, a toxic pit where the price of glory is buried suffering.

———

To the north, beyond the Sierra de Aracena, a ridge of dry, flaky schists on the frontier of Andalusia and Extremadura, another dimension of the Homeric world makes itself known. Distributed across a wide province stretching over southern Portugal and southwestern Spain are some of the most vivid memorials of the warrior world Homer's poems describe. They are stone stelae, or slabs, cut in the Late Bronze Age, from about 1250 to 750 BC, designed to show the nature of a hero's life. Other stone stelae, many shaped to look like people, can be found all over the Bronze Age world, but these are among the most articulate. None of them remains where it was found, and Richard Harrison, the Bristol archaeologist, in his catalog of the hundred or so that survive, lists their modern locations: one is in a bar in the Plaza de España in the village of San Martín de Trevejo on the Portuguese border north of Badajoz; others are in Madrid, Porto, in many local museums, in a school, in a town hall, in people's gardens and houses, one used as a seat at the entrance to an estate, another as a lintel over a window. A couple were reused as gravestones in Roman antiquity, with the name of the buried men cut across the Bronze Age designs. Many are beautifully exhibited in the museum in Badajoz. No doubt there are more still lurking unseen in walls or foundations.

The beautiful, hard landscape of Extremadura is natural horse and cattle country. Long, brown distances extend in all directions. Stone corrals are topped and mended with thorns—as they are in the *Odyssey*—and little mustard-yellow damselflies dance through the grasses. The pale roads wind over the hills, tracing the contours between the olives and the cork oaks, with the *tung tung tunk tunk* of the sheep bells a constant metal music beside them. Oaks that have been stripped of their cork are now date-black, as crusty as the blood on a cut. Grasshoppers flash their amber-ocher underwings. Cattle gather in the shade. Lizards seem to be the only liquid. It is above all a stony place: whitewashed upright flakes of schist marking the boundary between estates; bushily pruned olives peering out above stone walls; stones gathered in the dry scratched fields into big cairns, little round fortresses of solid cobble.

None of this is different from the state it was in three or four thousand years ago. Stock were raised then on the wooded savannas, as they are now. Cattle herding was the basis for all wealth. A low understory of grass sustained the herds under the evergreen oaks. Nothing would have been more nutritious for the autumn-fattening pigs than the fall of acorns.

Wheat, barley and beans were grown then in small patches of dry farming, as they are now.

In this big, open, manly environment, the stelae were often placed at significant points, where herders' roads met or forked on a hillside, where they crested a pass or came down to a river crossing. Some commanded wide panoramas. They were meant to be seen. You were meant to encounter them as you crossed the country. They were created for public display. Some were attached to graves, but not a majority. These were miniature, highly individual monuments intended to mark the presence—and dominance—of great men in their place.

The stelae are, in another medium, the *Iliad* of Iberia: heroic, human, repetitive but individualized. They mark the shift away from the communal values of the Stone Age, when joint graves gathered the ancestors in a community of the dead, to a time that valued more than anything else the display of the glorious man. None is more than six or seven feet high—these aren't great communal menhirs; they are on the scale of gravestones—but they are not recumbent. There is no knightly sinking into death here. Each is a standing monument to the vigor of a person. Gods do not appear; men dominate. The man himself is often shown as a kind of stick figure, pecked into the surface of the slab, probably with a bronze chisel, and around him are his accoutrements, the things that made him the warrior hero he knew himself to be. And the catalog of those heroic objects is a pointer to the values of the warrior world he wanted to record. To see these images is the strangest of sensations; it is, suddenly, Homer, 1,800 miles from Ithaca, more than two thousand from Troy, drawn in pictures on Spanish stone.

First there are the astonishing shields, dominating one stele after another. In the very early examples, the shield even takes the place of the man himself and stands there for him and his world. The shields are huge, as big as a man, round but notched at the top, made of many concentric rings, the symbol of resistance and resilience, usually shown with the handle visible in the center. In other words, they are seen from within the world that is protected by them. These are our shields, including us. They are the shelter for the life this man dominates, and in their massive, cosmic, many-ringed roundness they symbolize the universe of wholeness that the warrior protects. They are, in other words, the simple graphical equivalent of the great Shield of Achilles, which Hephaestus the smith god creates for the grieving warrior chief in book 18 of the *Iliad*.

Only because Homer survives can you understand entirely what the Iberian symbols hint at. Like the many-ringed shields of Extremadura, Achilles's shield has a threefold rim, and there are five layers to the shield, all constructed within its governing circularity: the earth and heaven, sea, sun and moon at the full, all the famous stars, marriages and feasts, dancing men, with flutes and lyres playing, an argument over the blood-price payable for the victim of a murder, with wives and little children standing on the walls of a besieged city. Fate herself appears here in a robe that is "red with the blood of men," but this is neither a sentimental nor a tragic vision of the world: everything is here, plowlands and cornlands, harvest and sacrifice, "fruit in wicker baskets" and a dancing floor, like the one at Knossos in Crete, with young men and women together. In bronze, tin, silver and gold Hephaestus made a depiction of the whole world of sorrow and happiness, of justice and injustice, fertility and pain, war and peace. Many shields in Homer are described as "the perfect circle"—a visual signal which confronts the sharp, narrow insertion of the blade. Even the Greek word for a shield, *aspis*, means the smooth thing, the thing from which roughness has been smoothed away. Achilles's shield is only the most perfect. In Homer, as in Extremadura, the shield is the encompassing symbol of the warrior king.

Then come the weapons: sword, spear, dagger, bow and arrow, very occasionally a quiver and almost invariably a chariot, with the horses attached, their bodies shown in profile, the chariot in plan, drawn like this in Portugal and Spain, but also, extraordinarily, appearing in the same way on the Bronze Age rock carvings of southern Sweden.

The weapons are the necessary instruments of the martial life, the tools for establishing central aspects of the hero complex: maleness, heroic individuality and dominance. It is what comes next that reorientates any flat-footed view of Bronze Age warrior heroism. These killer chieftains were obsessed with male beauty. The great Greek heroes all have blond hair (unlike the Trojans, who are dark-haired), and they have lots of it, lustrous, thick hair being an essential quality of the hero. Achilles had hair long enough for Athene to grab him by it when she wanted him to stop attacking Agamemnon. Hector's hair, after his death, lay spread around him in the dust. Paris, the most beautiful of all warriors in the *Iliad*—too beautiful—so rich and thick was his hair that he looked like a horse, "who held his head high and his mane streamed round his shoulders." The male gods are just as thickly maned. And the beauty of the warrior chiefs is inseparable from their power as men.

All of this appears on the stelae of the Iberian chiefs. Beyond their weaponry, carefully picked out on their memorial slabs, appears all the necessary grooming and beauty equipment: mirrors, combs, razors, twee-zers, brooches, earrings, finger rings and bracelets. These accessories of male beauty are not consigned to some private preparatory ritual. Making the Bronze Age warrior beautiful is central to the idea he had of himself. Here is the handsome gang leader, made more handsome by what he wears and how his body is prepared for its appearance among men. None of this culture would be possible without the bronze blades, but those blades are not its destination; they are the means to reach what these other precious objects describe: the mirror for a powerfully present idea of the self; the comb for grooming the beautiful hair; tweezers more likely to pluck an eyebrow than to take a splinter from flesh; brooches, earrings, rings and bracelets to adorn the beautiful man. When the river gods of the Trojan plain wish to attack and destroy Achilles as he is on his ram-page, clogging their streams with the slaughtered dead, one says to the other in encouragement: "His strength can do nothing for him, nor his beauty, nor his wonderful armor." Beauty is one of the elements that make him the most terrifying of men. The mirror, the comb and the tweezers are also instruments of Bronze Age war.

There is another detail that recurs on many stones, almost the only exception to the otherwise crude depiction of the heroes' bodies. Time and again, the fingers of the warrior-hero's hands are shown outstretched, explicit and bigger than-life-size. His hands seem to matter more than any other part of his body, perhaps because they were the part of him with which he imposed his power on the world around him. The hand is the agent of the burning warrior self, the essential instrument of the weapon-wielding man. That is also the role played by hands in the Homeric epics. Both Hector and Achilles have "manslaughtering hands," and it is Odysseus's hands that are steeped in blood as he exacts his final revenge on the suitors. It is as if the hands had concentrated in them all the destructive power of the warrior-hero. And when, in the *Iliad*'s culminating scene of mutual accommodation, Priam, the king of Troy, comes to Achilles in the Greek camp, it is through the hands that the drama is played out: "Great Priam entered in and, coming close, clasped Achilles's knees in his hands and kissed his hands, the terrible man-slaughtering hands that had slaughtered his many sons."

Homer rings those repetitions like clanging bells at moments of intensity and high purpose. And here, the word "hand" continues to boom on through the meeting. Achilles hears Priam's plea for the body of his precious son Hector to be returned to him for burial. That pleading love of the father makes him think of his own distant father in Phthia. Priam's words "roused in Achilles a desire to weep for his father; and he took the old man by the hand, and pushed him gently away. So the two of them thought of their dead and wept." And again, when they had finished weeping, Achilles "took Priam by the hand" and spoke to him words of pity and shared understanding of the pain men suffer in a careless world. The outstretched fingers of the Iberian warriors also carry all that love and violence within them.

There is one further object that binds Homer and the Extremaduran stelae. On one stone after another, alongside the killing equipment and the beauty equipment, is something at the heart of the Bronze Age warrior world: the lyre. Some lyres are drawn many-stringed; a few are as large as the giant universe-shields; on many stelae, the lyre is shown as no more than a simple frame with two or three strings across it. But all of them signify the same thing: here is the instrument with which this warrior can sing heroic songs of deathless glory. The weapon, the beauty equipment and the lyre are all integral to his world. He exists in memory; in some ways he exists *for* memory. Just as Odysseus sings the tale of his own adventures when he finds himself at dinner with the king and queen of the Phaeacians, Achilles is a man who sings heroic songs of deathless glory. That is how the other heroes find him when in book 9 of the *Iliad* they come to his shelter, hoping to persuade him to rejoin the battle.

> And they come to the huts and the ships of the Myrmidons [Achilles's men] and they find. Achilles delighting his mind with a clear-toned lyre, fair and elaborate, and on it is a bridge of silver; this he took from the spoil when he destroyed the city of Eëtion. With it he is delighting his heart, and he sings of the glorious deeds of men; and Patroclus alone sits

opposite him in silence, waiting until Aeacus's grandson should cease from singing.

Like Glaucus's account of generations of men following each other, just as spring leaves follow the leaves that had fallen in the autumn before, this is a moment when the passage of Homeric time stops for a second and when, in its privacy and lovingness, the world of brutality withdraws with the help of a lyre. That is what the presence of the lyres on the Spanish stelae says: not only is Homer *about* the heroic world; Homer *is* the heroic world. It is the realm of gang violence, in which pity and poetry have a central place.

If there were any doubt that song was a central part of the warrior complex, a discovery in one of the remotest parts of northwest Europe in the summer of 2012 changed all that. Archaeologists working in the High Pasture Cave on Skye found the burned and broken remains of the bridge from a late Bronze Age lyre. Homer—or at least the forms of warrior song on which the deepest elements of Homer draw—was a universal presence across the whole of Bronze Age Europe.

The Iberian stones might be seen as a kind of heraldry, the symbol-cluster for an armed knight. But they are also the first European biographies: he drove a chariot, strung a bow and killed with it, wielded spear and sword, held the shield, was beautiful and generous, lived here, sang his song. It seems from the distribution of the stelae that each warrior territory was no more than about twenty-five miles across. Seen as a kingdom, that is exceptionally small. But seen as an assertion over the landscape by a single powerful individual controlling about 270,000 acres, it is impressive. These are not petty empires but great estates. They are gang territories, equivalent to the "kingdoms" described in the Homeric catalog of ships. Nowhere are there any great buildings or constructions. All focus is on the power-body of the chieftain. His men cluster around him. His individual destiny is bound up with theirs and with the fate of the kingdom. It seems unlikely that many of these "kingdoms" outlasted the life of the man who made them. It is a place of endless, repetitive violence and competition, in which "who your father was" is important, but not enough. Honor must be revalidated in each generation. An unused sword rusts in the scabbard, and, as Glaucus said, each life can only follow the ones that came before, like the generations of the leaves.

Some of the stelae show that story. One of the richest is now in the Museo Arqueologico Provincial in Córdoba. It was found in April 1968 by some farmworkers at the foot of an ancient wall, a good block nearly six feet high and about thirty inches wide. They hauled it onto their tractor, carelessly smashing the sides and scratching the face of the stele, and took it to the nearby estate of Gamarrillas, thinking it might be good for building stone. But they noticed the engravings on one of its faces. By chance some archaeologists working nearby saw it for what it was and saved it.

A huge warrior figure dominates the scene, with outstretched hands and his penis hanging beneath him. He has a bracelet on one arm, and his whole torso is decorated with what might be a patterned cloth, his armor or maybe a whole-body tattoo. Even like this, scratched into limestone, he radiates significance. Of his chieftainliness there is no doubt. There is a little brooch next to his head, and his fighting equipment is gathered in the spaces around him: a spear, a shield, and a sword in his right hand, still in its scabbard. Beneath him is a comb, a shield and what may be a woven carpet. This is how he was in the glory of his life. But this stone also records his death. He is accompanied by his hunting dogs, both visibly male, and by his chariot. Around them groups of mourners hold hands, maybe dancing. There are no faces. All is in the body. This is a life that was lived and is now over. But for all that, an atmosphere of Homeric transience is soaked deeply into these little figures. Like the epic poems, this stone is a regretful glance back to a wonderful past, which, like the man, is gone.

Most of the stelae were thrown down, taken away and dumped after they were set up. Others were deliberately effaced. But that should come as no surprise in a world of constantly shifting chiefdoms, a power-churn where no glory lasted more than a generation or two. The same circumstances that gave rise to the stelae, to the warrior complex of which they are such vivid testimony, would also guarantee their destruction. Like the weaponry, the killing, the grooming, the insistent body-focus and the presence of the lyres, this delight in the destruction of the enemy is everywhere in Homer too, above all in the exulting over the corpse of a defeated enemy.

When one hero kills another in Homer, there is no grief or sympathy across the divide. It is a moment of triumph, when maleness achieves its undiluted self-expression. In book 11 of the *Iliad*, as one example,

Odysseus is on his destruction-drive and fixes his spear into the back of a Trojan called Sokos, thrusting it straight in between the shoulder blades, so that the point comes out of Sokos's chest. The Trojan then thumps to the ground—*doupeo*—and Odysseus stands over the dead body.

> Ah Sokos, son of battle-minded Hippasos, breaker of horses, death has been too quick for you and ran you down; you couldn't avoid it, could you, poor wretch? Your father and oh-so elegant mother will not close your eyes in death now, but the birds that eat raw flesh will tear you in strips, beating their wings thick and fast about you; but to me, if I die, the brilliant Achaeans will bury me in honor.

There is no pity in this. The destruction Odysseus celebrates is wonderful to him. Nothing is more beautiful than the sight of Sokos's dead eyes staring at the sky. Odysseus is happy at the dreadfulness he has done to that man and his now-grieving family. He has destroyed the power of that dynasty and enhanced his own. There is no sense of tragedy. He has merely defaced their memory. Their stone is down and gone; his remains upright, triumphant, crowing.

Richard Harrison has emphasized the loneliness which this ideology imposed on the warrior hero. "He is a unique and isolated figure," Harrison has written,

> whose arm is strong and deadly; he is devoted to combat, which he actively seeks out; he is detached from ordinary social space and so is shown to be tremendously swift, able to cross time or distance between worlds; and he is a very dangerous person in society and is therefore much better detached from it and sent away on a quest where he cannot harm ordinary mortals.

That loneliness clearly attached to Hector; to Agamemnon in his pomposity, his distance from love; to Odysseus on his journeying; even to Paris, the loathed creator of the war. Heroism disconnects. And the loneliness applies to no one more than to Achilles, as profoundly isolated as any figure in world literature. In his great and terrible confrontation with Hector in book 22 of the *Iliad*, after Hector has killed Achilles's great friend Patroclus, Achilles makes the ultimate statement of heroic loneliness, the isolation of the warrior which is also the dominant image on the Iberian stelae: a big man surrounded by his things, very occasionally by some mourners or even cowarriors, but essentially alone, trapped in the glory of his violence. "Hector, you, the unforgivable, talk not to me of agreements," he says, using the word *agoreue* for "talk," the word used in the *agora*, the meeting place where citizens come to mutual accommodation. Achilles does not belong there; he belongs in the wild.

There are no oaths sworn between lions and men, nor do wolves and lambs come to some arrangement in their hearts. They are filled with endless, repetitive hate for each other. Just so, it is impossible for you and me to be friends, nor will there be any oaths between us till one or other is dead, and has glutted Ares, the god of war, who carries his tough leather shield, with his blood.

In Celtic Ireland, on the far western edge of this hero world, where round, ridged leather shields have been dug from Bronze Age bogs, stories from the heroic age have been recorded in which "the heroes gave orders that they should be buried standing upright, fully armed on a prominent hill, where they could face their enemy, awaiting the moment of resurrection when they would fight again and by this means continue to protect their people." Those same upright warriors, continuing to haunt the living world, as enraged and violent as they were in life, also appear in the Icelandic sagas. Perhaps these are stories of the ultimate, cosmic loneliness, a measure of the inadequacy of the heroic idea, which only that weaponless, hand-connecting moment between Priam and Achilles could hope to assuage.

9 · HOMER ON THE STEPPES

The origins of the Greeks—or at least those people who would in time become the Greeks—were not in the Mediterranean. At some point they moved south and west in search of lands they wanted to claim as theirs, but at the deepest levels they were strangers in the southern sea. Fundamentally they were northerners, their roots in the steppelands of Eurasia, the oceanic river of grass, five thousand miles long and up to a thousand wide, that runs from Hungary to Manchuria.

Homer is full of half-buried memories of that northern past, and his recollections hint at another non-Mediterranean world, far from water, far from cities, landlocked, dominated by an enormous sky, horse-rich, focused on flocks and herds and the meat they provide, violent, mobile and heroic. This steppe-world is the place from which Achilles comes. It is not the Homeric foreground, because Homer is inconceivable without sailing ships, cities and the sea—without everything bound up in the name of "Troy": civilization, the seaborne raid, the connection to the East—but that other northern place lurks as a kind of murmured, ancestral layer, a subconscious.

The dates are hazy, but the Greeks may have come to Greece at some time between about 2200 and 1700 BC. Their origins are obscure. It is possible that the last move was south from Albania. There are early graves both there and in northwest Greece that look as if they might record the movement of people who would soon be in the Peloponnese. In the way the graves are built, and from the objects they contain, they seem to be the precursors of the Shaft Graves at Mycenae. Before that, the Greeks, or the pre-Greeks, may have lived on the banks of the Danube or elsewhere in the Balkans. And before that they almost certainly lived farther to the east, perhaps in the steppe between the Black Sea and the Caspian, in what is now Ukraine and southern Russia.

Nothing is certain, and the hints are fragmentary at best. But if you withdraw a little, and look not for exactness but for the broad northern culture-world out of which the Greeks emerged into Europe, perhaps at some time around 3000 BC, things become paradoxically clearer. Clues are everywhere: in the language itself, in archaeology, in the words of the Homeric poems and in the echoes of those poems that can be found all across the Eurasian world.

Right in the middle of the *Odyssey*, when Odysseus has penetrated to the depths of Hades and is talking there, anxiously and intently, to the blind seer Tiresias, long dead, he asks him about his own future, what will become of him. Tiresias knows that Odysseus is longing for nothing more than "a sweet smooth journey home," but, instead of guidance, he tells him the story of the books of the *Odyssey* still to come, the sufferings and anxieties he will undergo, the "world of pain" he will find in Ithaca. And then the old seer says something else, strange for classical Greeks, enigmatic today.

Once Odysseus has killed the suitors in his palace, Tiresias says, he will not yet have arrived home. For his true homecoming, he must leave Ithaca again and begin a second odyssey, not a sea journey this time but on land, another voyage in search of peace.

> You must go out one more time.
> Carry your well-planed oar until you come
> To a race of people who know nothing of the sea,
> Whose food is never seasoned with salt, strangers
> To ships with their crimson prows and long slim oars,
> The wings that make ships fly. And here is your sign—
> Unmistakable, clear, so clear you cannot miss it:
> When another traveller falls in with you and calls
> That weight across your shoulder a fan to winnow grain,

Then plant your bladed, balanced oar in the earth
And sacrifice fine beasts to the lord god of the sea,
Poseidon.

Only then, in that sea-free place, will Odysseus's demons be stilled and the uncertainties that have haunted his life laid to rest. That northern winnowing scene is a dream of home.

Tiresias goes on: once Odysseus has appeased the power of Poseidon, he should turn to the immortal gods, "who hold broad heaven in their hands." He should relinquish sea for sky. And only after that sky world has embraced him will Odysseus be able to die "in the ebbing time of a sleek old age," as Richmond Lattimore translated Homer's phrases, the world of the sea eased from his mind, his soul now as calm and reflective as a dark, northern, freshwater pool.

Image-ideas cluster around Tiresias's gnomic instruction. The oar becomes the winnowing fan, the sea becomes the earth, the wind, which would have driven Odysseus's ship across the sea or nearly destroyed him on his raft, becomes the breeze that sorts the grain from the chaff, as each fanful is thrown up and the lighter dust blown away. The Greek word for the winnowing fan is *athereloigos*, meaning the "destroyer of bristles" (*athēr*, plural *atheres*), the husky sheaths of the grain. But *athēr* can also mean anything difficult or prickly: the spines of a fish or the barbs of a weapon. So the winnowing fan is also a smoother of barbs, a spike remover, the tailor of life. The grains will emerge clean and pure, and the jagged world of hostility will float off on the breeze. Only here, deep in the land, will certainty be recovered. Poseidon, the god of wrongness whose origins, at least in part, are Mediterranean, as the great defender of Troy and enemy of Odysseus, the presider over storms and earthquakes, who has dominated the poems and been at the heart of their sufferings, will at last be put in his place.

Is there some historical root to this moment? Are Tiresias's words a form of archaic memory, fueled by the idea that somewhere in the world, a long way from Greece, is a place where the troubles that afflict Odysseus and the Greeks do not obtain? Where there is no sea, nor even any hint of the sea, and which is not subject to the near constant sequence of earthquakes and tempests that besiege and break on Greece and Anatolia? Is

Tiresias reaching far back to a time when the Greeks did not yet know Greece but were living the life of seminomadic pastoralists, planting their grains, tending their flocks, ignorant of salt and ships? Is this, in other words, a kind of retrospective pastoral, a Greek vision of an abandoned Eden? Did life to the Greeks, at some half-acknowledged level, seem better before all the temptations and threats of the Mediterranean life disturbed their certainties? Was the movement south a transition into risk? If it was, Homer is the record of what happened when that risk was taken.

There is another remembered story of Odysseus, not in Homer, but recorded from Sophocles in some rough Latin notes of plays and myths which have otherwise disappeared. Telemachus, Odysseus's son, is one month old when Palamēdēs, a messenger arrives from Agamemnon, instructing Odysseus to come to the war against Troy. Odysseus reacts as Achilles might, skeptically, reluctantly, and to escape the summons pretends to be mad. He takes a donkey and an ox, yokes them together on the same plow, as no man ever has or would, and when he has cut the first furrow he sows it not with seeds but with salt. Palamēdēs doubts Odysseus, and to test him takes the baby Telemachus and puts him down on the unbroken grass in the path of the plow.

As Odysseus approaches his son he turns the plow aside, bending the furrow away from his baby's flesh, and by that swerve shows he is sane. He loves his son more than he loves himself, and so has no choice but to go and suffer at Troy. He takes with him a murderous loathing for Palamēdēs, the clever diplomat. In time Odysseus concocts accusations against him, that he is secretly colluding with the Trojans against the Greeks, and finally stones him to death as a liar and traitor.

It is a suggestive enmity, a twin of Tiresias's promise of a final ease in the distant north. The southerner brings only years of pain. Faced with his invitation, Odysseus sows antiseeds, not fruitful but toxic, not land riches but sea poison, not fecundity but sterility, not northern contentment but southern trouble. Palamēdēs is Mediterranean man, the inventor of counting, money, weights and measures, jokes, dice, military ranks, the letters of the alphabet and the making of wine. He represents everything the south has to offer, including submission to an overall king in Agamemnon. He is, in his slickness, the enemy. Tiresias holds out the possibility of comfort in the north; Palamēdēs promises only southern suffering.

No two worlds could be more different than the grasslands of the steppes north of the Black Sea and the craggy broken boundaries of the Mediterranean. In Greece every view is contained and defined by its mountains. Every place is a shard, sharp-edged, hardened and definite. Boot leather is torn into shreds there. "Our land, compared with what it was," Plato wrote famously of the Greece he knew, "is like the skeleton of a body wasted by disease. The fat soft parts have gone, and all that remains are the bones." On the steppe, the bones remain invisible, coated in a pelt of grasses on the high plateaus between the river valleys, thickening into forest and marsh where those rivers make their way to the south. The Mediterranean landscape is fiercely located, subdivided by its mountain ridges, every corner separate from every other. But look across the steppe, and you see only more of what is already at your feet.

Everything is continuous there. The air you breathe is the air of the universe. Horizontality is all, and this is the continental-oceanic, a place that cares less about fixity than movement, less about detail than about the endlessness of things. And if landscapes can create mentalities as well as reflect them, it is possible to think that the steppelands lie at the root of the Achilles frame of mind: long-horizoned; looking for the profound and the eternal; attuned to the cosmic; indifferent to possessions; passionate, totalizing; vertigo-inducing in its relationship to death and fate; both giving and denying significance to human desires and triumphs.

It is possible to think that in the *Iliad* Achilles speaks for that deep northern past. He comes from somewhere else. He is half divine, has no identifiable city and was brought up by a centaur in the mountains. His homeland is farther north than anyone else's in Homer. His story is strangely disconnected from everything else in the *Iliad*; he will be killed before the sack of Troy, he goes off on plundering expeditions all around western Anatolia, and the whole account of recovering Helen would be complete without him.

Achilles does not fit with the world in which he finds himself. He holds himself physically and psychologically removed from the rest of the Greeks. He speaks the truth to them in a way no one else can. He is dense with both love and violence, the two bound together in his heart, his greatest love (for his friend Patroclus) summoning his greatest violence (for his enemy Hector). Those who are close to him adore him; those at a distance both fear and despise him. But his central quality is an inability to conform to what the world around him accepts as real.

In all these ways, Achilles confronts the forces of the sophisticated south and sets himself against them: he cannot tolerate the overarching kingliness of Agamemnon, he scorns the political sophistication and smooth-talking of Odysseus, he despises Hector, and like all warriors he wants to destroy the city. Homer calls him (as he does both Arēs, the great northern god of war, and Odysseus) "the city destroyer." And when Achilles attacks the bodies of the Trojans and their horses, the image that Homer brings to mind is not individual death but "the smoke ascending into the wide sky/from a burning city with the anger of the gods let loose upon it."

Achilles carries a presouthern, preurban, precomplicated world of purity and integrity within him.

He first appears most fully himself—before the lunacy of grief over Patroclus's death transforms him—in the speech he makes to Odysseus in book 9 of the *Iliad*. For days the war has gone badly for the Greeks. Agamemnon has stolen Briseis from Achilles. She is the girl he loves, the "bed-girl of his heart" as he calls her, and because of that theft, imposed by Agamemnon's assumption of greater authority over him, Achilles has withdrawn from the battle, has wished death and violence on the Greeks and has witnessed their catastrophic failure in the war. Now Agamemnon, desperate with the successes of the Trojans, wants to make amends, to offer Achilles not only the return of Briseis but shiploads of prizes and treasures. He sends Odysseus to make the offer, and in reply Achilles states his magnificent, troubling credo.

Just before Odysseus comes to his shelter, Achilles has been singing to Patroclus of the glorious deeds of men, of the heroic past. When he arrives, Achilles does what the hero should, and provides for his guests the meat from fat sheep and fat goats and the meaty backcuts of a great pig "rich with fat." All is ritualized and made proper, and the scene is one that would have occurred in thousands of chieftains' huts over thousands of years in the grasslands of Eurasia.

Odysseus then lists to Achilles the wonderful things that Agamemnon wants to give him: seven tripods that the fire has not touched; ten talents of gold; twenty shining cauldrons; strong horses, winners in races, that have won prizes for their swiftness; seven women skilled in noble handiwork from Lesbos, including Briseis herself, the girl Achilles loves. And there is the promise of much more, options on the future: things from Troy; more women from Troy; one of Agamemnon's own daughters as a bride; cities in Greece with lovely meadows outside them, grass as high as a horse's eye, places where men can live rich in cattle and flocks of sheep.

But Odysseus is slippery, and although most of his speech to Achilles repeats exactly what Agamemnon had said to him, he does not repeat the high king's final riling words: "Let him submit himself to me, since I am so much more kingly." Odysseus suppresses those phrases, knowing that the steppe consciousness of Achilles will not accept an overking. Nevertheless, that subtext persists in the proposal he makes. There is something nauseating in the accumulated enticements Agamemnon offers. They miss the point. Long, long ago, in the first lines of the poem, Achilles called Agamemnon "the greediest, most possession-loving of men," and this list of offered possessions is a pollution of the air he breathes. He knows Odysseus is there to lie to him. He calls him "many-wiled," the trickster. "As I detest the doorways of Death, I detest that man who hides one thing in the depths of his heart, and speaks another." Instead of that clever, southern talk, he will "speak what I want to speak."

That relentless focus on his own individuality drives the lines forward. Achilles cannot escape from the idea that Agamemnon has been sleeping with Briseis. That vision, in the present tense, haunts him. Agamemnon *has* her. He has his way with her, still, now, "the bed partner of my heart." The overking's cumulative greed has taken even her. He has made her an object too. Agamemnon does not know the meaning of love. All he can imagine is ownership, and all Achilles can think of is Agamemnon's repeated, horrible owning of his girl.

It is the most passionate speech in Homer, confused, proud, enraged, Achilles seeming not to know that Agamemnon has offered to give Briseis back. Instead, Agamemnon the criminal persists in his mind in an eternal present of wrongness, shameless as a deceiver, a man whose honor is rusted and corrupt. "Hateful in my eyes are his gifts. His gifts are my enemy. I count them at a hair's worth." Then Achilles lists the cities of the south, the great riches of Orchomenos and Thebes, and Troy itself, "where treasures in greatest store are laid up in men's houses." (These phrases, in one of the ironies of Homeric archaeology, led Heinrich Schliemann to dig at Orchomenos in search of the gold Achilles despised.) But Achilles will have none of it. Gifts that numbered as many as the grains of dust and sand in the world would not persuade him to change his mind until Agamemnon "has paid him back the pain he has done to him." That is something which by definition Agamemnon could never do. "All the wealth of Troy is not worth what my life is worth."

These are great statements. They rage at the triviality of ownership. They are unforgiving in their contempt for the greedy, Christlike in their abrasive, revelatory scouring of the facts and desires of power. Achilles speaks again of possessions, this time not the blandishments of cities but things that would have been familiar in the steppeland of the north.

> Cattle and fat sheep are things to be had for the lifting,
> and tripods can be won, and the tawny high heads of horses,
> but a man's life cannot come back again, it cannot be lifted
> Nor captured again by force, once it has crossed the teeth's barrier.

Death overwhelms every other meaning. What can matter in the face of mortality? Agamemnon is puerile and disgusting, Odysseus is a liar, Hector is pathetic; only by stepping outside the value system of the world can you find any value. It is one of the riches of Homer's characterization of Achilles that what he says is not consistent. He toys with the idea that he might go home and marry a lovely girl, settle down and enjoy the possessions his father had won. But alongside that he recognizes that we are all vagabonds on earth, nothing belongs to us, our lives have no consequence and our possessions are dross. We are wanderers, place shifters, the cosmic homeless. This is not a modern truth, and Achilles is not some new kind of existentialist hero. It is the oldest truth of all, surviving uncomfortably into the modern world of cities and overkings, diplomacy and accommodation, the power structures and the proliferation of stuff which the Mediterranean world provides, all of it more modern than Achilles can allow himself to be. He is the voice of the northern, shiftless past, asserting the claims of a higher steppeland purity against the material greed and ignobility of the fixed and southern present.

The power of the poem lies in the understanding that these things cannot be reconciled. The *Iliad*'s subject is not war or its wickedness but a crisis in how to be. Do you, like Agamemnon, attempt to dominate your world? Do you, like Odysseus, manipulate it? Do you, like Hector, think of your family above all and weaken your resolve by doing that? Or do you, like Achilles, believe in the dignity of love and the purity of honor as the only things that matter in the face of death? These questions are urgent for Homer because the arrival of a steppe culture at the gates of a city made them urgent. There is more to the Achilles story than this: in the course of the poem he suffers, grows, loses himself in the violence of grief and finally comes to a new and deeper understanding, but in this great speech of steppeland consciousness, Homer bequeathed to us the first unforgiving idealist of our civilization.

Greek is part of the Indo-European language family that stretches from Ireland to remote valleys in the deserts of western China, from Sweden to India, from Spain to Lithuania. It has been known since the late eighteenth century that the languages in this family are each other's siblings. In every one of them, common roots can be found in both vocabulary and grammar. Those connections can only mean that each of the daughter languages descended from a mother language spoken somewhere in the distant past before its speakers moved off into the many corners of the continent. So a man who is my *brathair* in old Irish is my *frater* in Latin, my *broðor* in Old English, my *broterèlis* in Lithuanian, my *bratrŭ* in Old Church Slavonic, my *phrater* in Greek, my *bhrátar* in Sanskrit and my *procer* in a dead language called Tocharian B, once spoken in the desiccated valleys of Chinese Turkestan, eight thousand miles from the Irish monks and their brethren on the shores of the Atlantic. Languages that can have had no chance of having borrowed words directly from each other nevertheless demonstrate intimate family connections. They carry the marks of their own inheritance; like verbal tumuli, these words enshrine their own history.

Linguists have long realized that if they could establish the words that were shared across these vast distances—particularly by now well-separated languages—they might be able to reconstruct the world in which the original Proto-Indo-European language was spoken. This is the great paradox of language: words are the least substantial medium in which meaning can be formed, but they can preserve hints and suggestions of the ancient past when material remains scarcely can. Of course languages evolve, but words that have been transmitted only in speech can nevertheless retain something in their core that is resistant to the erosions of time.

Working over two centuries, linguists have been able to create an astonishingly detailed shared word-picture of the Proto-Indo-European world of about five thousand years ago, the world from which Achilles came. It sounds, first, like a dream environment, teeming with life; wolves, lynxes, elk and red deer, hares, hedgehogs, geese and cranes, eagles and bees, beavers and otters (their name the same word at root as both "water" and "hydro") have cognates in all of the Indo-European languages. There are no shared words for laurel, cypress or olive: this cannot have been a Mediterranean place. But cattle and sheep are both there. This is a milky, yogurty existence, with words for butter, cheese, meat, marrow and manure, for steer, calf, ox, cow and bull. These people were lactose-tolerant, feeding off the all-important transfer of nutrients (via hay and cheese) from summer grass to winter food. A verb for the driving of cattle, and a word for a large cow-sacrifice, are spread across the whole Indo-European language-world. The original word for a dog is closely bound up with the word for sheep: the first Indo-European dogs look as if they were sheepdogs, and the word for sheep, with the root *pec-* (as in "pecorino," the Italian sheep cheese) is related to the word for wealth (as in "pecuniary"). It seems as if the riches of these people might have been in the animals they kept.

The language does not describe a completely mobile world. Its inhabitants had pigs, which are no good for nomadic pastoralists (both "swine" and "pork" are Proto-Indo-European words), because pigs refuse to be driven in the way sheep and cattle happily will be, and so the Proto-Indo-European people must have been at least partly settled, with places in which the words for grain, sowing, quern, plow, sickle, yoke and oxen all had a part to play. So their world oscillates between the mobile and the fixed, the rooted and the rootless, the raid or the drive away from home and the companion sense of home and hearth.

The language family to the north of Proto-Indo-European, Proto-Uralic, spoken by the hunter-gatherers in the forests of northern Eurasia, has no words for any buildings beyond their tents. But Proto-Indo-European is not quite like that. These people had words for house, hearth, post, door, doorpost, hurdle, wattle, wall and clay. Their buildings were clearly substantial, wooden, closable. They also had a word for refuge or fort, but no word for city. Nor is there any hint in the language of anything resembling public architecture: no temple, no palace, no public square.

Their villages were clusters of houses, and the word for a village was the same as the word for a clan. The language makes the point clearly enough: what mattered about these places was not the buildings but the people within them. This is not a monumental world, but one centered on the lives of clannish groups of families. They had metals. They spun thread, wove cloth and sewed. And they had wheeled vehicles, and boats for crossing rivers and lakes, with oars but no sails.

This reimagining of a distant world is one of the triumphs of linguistics. None of these claims about the Proto-Indo-European way of life is a guess; all are founded on a careful analysis of the inherited languages. And the reconstruction has penetrated beyond the physical. It is clear that the culture was male-dominated, that individuals considered themselves heirs of their fathers and that girls left their native homes to live in the houses of their husbands and their husbands' families. The word for marry—when applied to men—is intimately connected with the word for lead. Men "led" women to the marriage bed.

It seems likely that young men in the Proto-Indo-European world were organized into warrior bands, perhaps raiding parties, and they used bows, arrows, clubs, cudgels and swords. Society may have been organized into three ranks: farmers, priests and a warrior elite, out of which the chieftains and even kings emerged. The word for king embodies the principle of order, a meaning still implicit in the English word "rule," with a connection between "rex" and "right," between ordaining the world and possessing it, but there is also evidence in the inherited languages of a powerful sense of hospitality and its duties. "Guest" and "host" are different descendants of the same root, a measure of the mutuality buried within them. The mutual giving of gifts, the swearing of oaths and the expectations of loyalty from that behavior are all evident in the descendant languages. Trust was part of the Proto-Indo-European moral consciousness.

It is possible to push farther in, beyond their external lives. Linguists can reconstruct a Proto-Indo-European word for belief, *kred-dhehl*, whose descendants have reached us in the form of "creed" and "credo." That original compound word seems to have meant "heart-put/place," so that belief is the place where you put what matters most to you. There is, in other words, clear linguistic evidence of a commitment to otherness, a mental life beyond the self. But not much of a pantheon can be reestablished. Nearly all the gods of Olympus in Homer are Mediterranean borrowings; the only undoubted exception is Zeus, the male sky god, whose name means "the sky," with a further derivation buried within that, as the word for sky comes from a root that means "the shining." God is the shining father, life is lived in his light, and when the great heroes are described in Homer either as "brilliant" or as "godlike," the connection is the same: they are glowing in a light derived from the power of that shining sky. The sky is the great permanence. In its divine brilliance, there is no change.

Beneath that steppe-sense of the governing sky there is a parallel and contradictory aspect of the Indo-European mind. In every daughter language from Iranian to Hindi, to Hittite, Greek and Roman, all the Romance, Slavic and Germanic languages, Irish and the other Celtic languages, finite verbs are forced into a precise tense. Nothing in Indo-European can escape being located in the time at which it occurred. In other languages, such as the Chinese language family, there are no tenses, and it is possible to blur those distinctions, for actions to be described without it being clear when they happened. Not in the Indo-European languages; this particular form of consciousness is trapped in an awareness of time passing. Homer's and Achilles's agonies over the transience of glory; the very fact of epic poetry as a way of denying the effects of time; even the creation of the tens of thousands of Bronze Age tumuli marking the landscapes of Eurasia from Bahrain to County Clare—all are products of that time-dominated frame of mind, the awareness of the passing of things which lies at the deepest levels of the way we think. It is the governing polarity: the sky persists in a way that is outside time; nothing that is done on earth shares that eternity. Homer is framed around that recognition, and it is one in which, for example, the idea of a Messiah could never have originated. There is no closing the gap between the eternal and the transitory. Gods and goddesses might sleep with men and women, and have children with them, but those heroic children can only ever be mortal.

Grief and triumph; a sense of irony and even tragedy; an overwhelming and dominant masculinity, thick with competitive violence; a small but hierarchical society, strung between a seminomadic way of life and one that was settled in small wooden houses; a vivid background in the natural world; a valuing of cattle and meat; in love with horses; no understanding of the city or of any relationship to the sea—all of that is implicit in the shape of this reconstructed language, and all of it looks very like the background to the world of the Greeks in their camp on the Trojan shore.

But where and when can this world be located? That question is still far from being answered. There is plenty of evidence, but none of it adds up. Language cannot be attached to preliterate archaeological remains, and modern genetic evidence is still too confused for any clear outline to be derived from it.

Nevertheless, it seems clear from the memories embedded in the daughter languages that the Proto-Indo-Europeans came from a place where they could grow crops (or at least harvest wild ones) and maintain herds of grazing animals on extensive pastures. They could not have been desert, mountain or forest people. They did not live in the arid south or the frozen north. There is a word in the original language that might mean beech tree, birch tree or oak tree. And another that might mean salmon, or maybe sea trout, or maybe trout. This looks like a temperate, river-valley existence. But the grazing animals would have required expansive grasslands too. These people have a word for bee, but there are no bees east of the Urals, so they can only have been on the western, European side of those mountains. The presence of many farming words means that they must have been farming before about 2500 BC, which is thought to be the last possible moment before the original group broke up and scattered across Europe and north Asia.

These clues scarcely pinpoint a region, and people's idea of the ancient homeland of the Proto-Indo-Europeans, their *Urheimat*, has wandered all over Eurasia. Originally it was thought to be in Afghanistan, but it has migrated from Bactria to the Baltic, to the Pripiat marshes in Poland, to Hungary and the Carpathians in general. The Nazis, identifying their race-vision with this linguistic category, and preferring the term "Aryan" (the name of an Indo-European people in Iran) to "Indo-European," located the homeland in Germany. Some still favor Armenia in northwest Anatolia, but a modern consensus has for the time being settled on the steppes between the Black and Caspian Seas.

For the purposes of understanding the roots of the Homeric vision, it doesn't much matter where this notional homeland was. The elements of a river-valley-plus-grazing landscape extend across the whole of the western steppe, from the Danube to the Caucasus and beyond. And fascinatingly, there, in the remains of settlements, and in the burial mounds, or kurgans as they are called in Russia, which decorate the landscape, archaeologists have discovered many objects and signs of life that look distinctly as if Achilles had passed that way.

Of all the steppe-Homer linkages, the most powerful is the horse. It was probably domesticated on the steppe in about 4200 BC, first as food and then to be ridden. A man on foot in the modern Eurasian steppe can shepherd no more than two hundred sheep; one on a horse can manage a flock of five hundred. It was a revolutionary difference. This early riding was not yet the militarized pastoral nomadism associated with the Scythians or the Mongols. Nothing of that kind would emerge until after 800 BC, but the speed of the horse, the invention of the bit and the bridle, the control they gave to a rider, the ability to accumulate great reservoirs of meat, to raid and withdraw from pedestrian settlements—all of it changed people's lives and would change history.

The great grasslands of the steppe were now available to a mobile, horse-mounted people in a way no one could have attempted before. Giant flocks were grazed on the giant grasslands. The men who could control them became leaders and chieftains. Mobility and glamor had arrived, and the horse was a version of power that the great men tamed and dominated (both descended from the same Proto-Indo-European root, *demha*). The careful husbandry of the Neolithic farmers was now overlaid with the rush and glamor of horse-based life. The human steppe cultures began to revere the power of the horse, fusing their visions of human power with equine beauty. The word at the root of "equine" means "quick" in Indo-European languages, and the horse and its speed, the ripple and sheen of horse muscle, became central to these people's idea of greatness.

The disconnected limbs of the horses that appear all over later prehistoric Europe, on coins or in hill figures, are the horses seen in this magic, dematerialized way. They are more spirit than body, often with huge, disproportionately alert eyes, their whole being prancing, all curve in their haunches, all muscle in their neck and back, the tension in them

A first-century BC gold coin or "stater" of the Celtic Parisii tribe, near Paris.

not unlike the tension in a ship under sail at sea. Tautness, urgency and stretch are their governing qualities. Here the horse is something like the wind, not dominated by man but coexisting with him, an extension of the possibilities of life.

Some clues to this world of the horse can be found at a timber town, not that large, about 150 yards across, at a place called Sintashta, on the banks of the wide, gravelly Sintashta River, sweeping down through the grasslands east of the Urals and on the borders of Kazakhstan. A timber-reinforced wall with gates and towers surrounded the buildings, with a V-shaped ditch outside it. Inside there were about fifty houses (some have since been eroded away by the river), and in all of them people had been making bronze and copper swords, knives and axes.

It was clearly a violent, warrior society, with the need for weaponry and a defensive enclosure. In the nearby cemetery, more than half of all the people were buried with weapons, including nearly all the men, but

The Bronze Age White Horse at Uffington, Oxfordshire, England.

some were also buried alongside something else, quite new: war chariots with light, spoked wheels. They are the oldest chariots to have been discovered, dating from about 2100–1800 BC, precisely the same moment as this book has been arguing for the genesis of the *Iliad*. The Sintashta people cannot be the ancestors of the Greeks—who must already have been far to the southwest of there—but to archaeologists it looks as if they might have been the ancestors of those Indo-European-speaking people who were making their way east of the Urals and on to northern India.

Sintashta—and some twenty equivalent settlements have now been found—is a cousin to the Homeric world. Here, as in Patroclus's tomb in the *Iliad*, whole horses were sacrificed at the burials. Drivers were buried with bone, disk-shaped cheekpieces, critical elements in the kind of bridle needed for tight control of chariot horses. There are some flint blades in the graves, which are thought to have been made for javelins—those light spears that can be thrown by a warrior on the ground or from a chariot. The chariots themselves are clearly fast, light war machines, quite different from the heavy transport wagons that had been around on the steppe for a thousand years. These have spoked not solid wheels about three feet in diameter and are designed to be driven at a gallop. The chariot itself would have been skeletal, consisting of little more than a few struts. In the *Iliad* it is possible for one man to pick up a chariot to move it out of the way.

This combination of things is deeply Homeric; chariot races fill the penultimate book of the *Iliad*, at the funeral games Achilles stages for Patroclus, where skill in driving, in turning corners, could only have been achieved with the new cheekpiece bridles. At the same time, it is clear from the funerals of both Hector and Patroclus that these were giant communal events, great crowds of people attending the funerary rites of the heroes. Here too at Sintashta, one burial has the bones of six horses, four cows and two rams killed for the death of the great man. Archaeologists calculated that those animals would have provided two pounds of meat for each of three thousand participants. It so happens that the giant kurgan near this animal feast would have taken, it is thought, three thousand man-days to build, just as in Homer the people of Troy and the men of the Greek camp build for many days the funeral pyres for their fallen heroes. Horses, chariots, bronze weaponry, multiple animal sacrifices, massive meat feasts, chiefdoms, wall-defended camps, huge funeral rituals, spectacular communal displays—the *Iliad* and Sintashta belong to one culture world, and that world is the Indo-European steppe.

One last intriguing element appeared at Sintashta: some great men were clearly celebrated in death and their fame consolidated by a great communal outpouring of love and grief. Glory gathers around these funerals. But in life there is no such distinction visible in the wooden houses at Sintashta, no palaces, no apparent grandeur, no hierarchy in the buildings. Here, then, in Sintashta, were warrior chiefs who loved speed, who loved horses, who loved fame but who were not focused on the riches or comfort of the places in which they lived. They were, in other words, not Agamemnon but Achilles, the choosers of glory in battle, not men who were greedy for possessions. Here in Sintashta were not only the cousins of the Greeks but the world from which Achilles came.

Horses mattered to the Homeric Greeks: both Poseidon and Athene were horse gods, drawing on the power of unpredictability, the horse's muscled body, the possibility they always seem to harbor of violence and suddenness, the fire in the eye. This deep Indo-European horse-experience explains its prominence in Homer. It is an inheritance from the steppelands, which can otherwise seem a little mysterious. No fighting happens on horseback in Homer. It is ships, not horses, that have brought the Greeks to Troy. Chariots are used in battle as little more than taxis. The Trojans are city people on the shores of a strategic waterway from the Aegean to the Black Sea; horse mobility is not at the practical heart of their lives. And yet horses rule in Homer.

Achilles, Nestor and even Odysseus are deeply connected with them. Achilles has a herd with him at Troy. His horses speak and weep. He is at times, in the speed of his running, compared to "a prize-winning horse" himself. And it is one of his own horses, Xanthos, who tells him of his death to come. But it is the Trojans and their allies whose lives are drenched in the image and potency of the horse. The Trojans were Indo-Europeans too, having arrived in Anatolia earlier than the Greeks, and despite their city existence they continued to practice some of the habits of the steppe world from which they had come. They are, as fellow descendants of the steppe, the great horse people of Homer. The finest horses of all belong to the Trojan allies from Thrace, a region which for Homer stretches north from the Aegean with no boundary. Those horses are in effect the spirit of the north, whiter than snow, as fast as the wind, terrible, shining like the sun.

"Breaker of horses" is one of the Trojan epithets. Hector, in one of the most beautiful of all warrior similes in the *Iliad*, is

> like a horse that has fed his fill at the manger, who breaks his halter and runs over the plain, wanting to bathe in the fair-flowing river, and feels exultation in his limbs, holding his head high while his mane floats streaming around his shoulders and he glories in his own splendor as he runs to the pastures and the dwelling places of the mares.

The horse is what the hero might dream of being. Aeneas has horses that come from a line bred by Zeus, the great sky god of the north. The Trojans sacrifice live horses in the river Scamander that flows past their walls. And the horse dominates the names of Trojan warriors. Quick Horse, Raid Horse, War Horse, Black Horse and Good Horse all go out to battle for Troy, sounding like a band of Comanches.

This is the shared horse-matrix out of the north that allowed the Greeks to imagine the best thing they could give the Trojans, the one irresistible gift which that city could not refuse. The Trojans would surely see it as a gift from Poseidon Hippios, their great horse-god protector, the wall maker: a wooden horse that looked like a fortress itself. It took one to know one; the great unifying and shared belief of these two cultures was the giant creature they both feared and revered. It does not appear in the *Iliad*; Homer's great war poem stops short of that moment. Only in the *Odyssey*, in retrospect, is the tale told, twice, each time slightly different, each immersed in tenderness and sorrow.

First Menelaus, the husband of Helen, the aggrieved man from whom Paris stole his wife and thus began the war, tells Telemachus, Odysseus's son, what happened. It was a trick, a hollow ambush, a mark of Odysseus's cleverness, the product of his "dear, steadfast heart." But as Menelaus tells the tale, he remembers only his wife's enigmatic and mysteriously intimate behavior. The Trojans have hauled the horse into the city, and at night Helen walks around it. It is a thickly sexualized moment; she is close up to the body of the horse, touching it with the tips of her fingers, murmuring gently through the timbers to what she guesses must be the Greeks inside, speaking to each of them in the voice of the wives they have left behind, like a sorceress becoming one by one their loved and longed-for women away in Greece. What multiple treachery is this? The Greeks are there to cheat the Trojans. Only for Menelaus is the voice truly of his wife, but she is the wife who betrayed him. Is this intimacy now an attempt to betray them all again?

Nor is Helen alone. She is accompanied by a Trojan, Deïphobus. He is the brother of Hector and Paris, and is now Helen's latest husband, with whom she sleeps reluctantly and whom she is now also longing to betray. Violence and desire, treachery and strangeness, the threatening closeness of the horse, one of the gods of trouble, fills this scene like an acid fog.

The second time we hear the story, Odysseus is with the Phaeacians, who are the epitome of civilization and wholeness, at a dinner lit with braziers, where a bard is ready to tell any tale the stranger wants to hear. Odysseus asks him to tell the story of the building of the Trojan Horse. The bard obliges but goes on to describe the horror of the sacking of Troy, when Odysseus, accompanied by Menelaus, goes looking for Deïphobus. When they find him they cut him horribly, as Virgil described it in the *Aeneid*: "his whole body mutilated, his face brutally torn, his face and hands, the ears ripped from his ruined head, his nostrils sheared by a hideous wound."

Odysseus cannot bear the tale he now hears. As he listens, "he melt[s]," Homer says, in a word used for snow in heat, sugar in water, a cloud giving up its rain, flesh falling from a long-dead body, or of a creature that pines away for a companion it has lost. Homer does not stint in describing the depth of Odysseus's grief.

> As a woman weeps, lying on the body
> Of her dear husband, who died fighting for his city and his people,
> As he tried to beat off the day of pitilessness,
> And as she sees him lying and gasping for breath
> And winding her body around him
> She cries high and piercing while the men behind her
> hit her with the butts of their spears
> and lead her away to captivity to work and sorrow
> and her cheeks are hollow with her grief.
> Such are the tears that Odysseus lets fall from his eyes.

Nowhere in Homer is the harrowing of war seen more entirely. The horse has summoned the deepest of encounters with the nature of reality. Odysseus is the sacker of cities, the mutilating criminal himself, over whose crimes he now weeps like the victims whose life he has destroyed. Every person here—the bard, the king, the warrior, the weeping widow, the traveler—is understood.

Homer then has the bard—a blind man whose name is Demodocus, which means "popular with the people"—say something that drives far into the center of what Homer means and why Homer matters: "The gods did this and spun the destruction of people / For the sake of the singing of men hereafter." The song, this poem, this story, is the divine purpose of the war. The war happened so that the poem could happen.

It is the deepest Homeric wink. The Phaeacians are enjoying this, it says, and you are enjoying it too, aren't you? Despite yourself, you love this account of grief, and that pleasure in tragedy is the purpose of the Homeric poems. The poems recognize the dreadfulness of the events they describe; they also understand the pleasure to be derived from hearing of those events. Nothing is theorized, nor is that contradiction resolved, but from these words we understand that the beauty of the poems depends on the horror of what they say.

This is the flagstaff statement in the very first paragraph of Simone Weil's great 1939 essay on the *Iliad*, "The Poem of Force":

> Those who had dreamed that force, thanks to progress, belonged only to the past, have been able to see in the *Iliad* a historical document; those who know how to see force, today as yesterday, at the centre of all human history, can find there the most beautiful, the purest of mirrors.

"Le plus beau, le plus pur des miroirs" is what the Phaeacian bard was saying. There is no hiding in the *Iliad*, no deceit, no flinching from the view of horror, no reluctance to record the bitter jokes in the face of blood, no sweetening of dismemberment, no pretense that, when the stomach wall is cut, innards do not lurch out onto knees and laps, no forgetting that brains spatter from a spear-mangled head, nor the way wounded, dying men scratch and jerk their life out as they scrabble uselessly at their killers' feet—the word Homer uses means "to clutch at," "to gather like men picking up the harvested grains"—no screen to shield you from the fire, no euphemism to pretend this isn't the way that men behave, no glaze to cloud "the purest and most beautiful of mirrors." It is clarity, summoned here by the great horse, that makes the words of the *Iliad* the most disturbing ever written.

Achilles inherited his life from the steppe. Inflation, scale, ambition had come with the horse and its breaking. It was the archaic companionship on which the steppe cultures were built. Equipped with horses and with their carts and heavy wagons, the steppe people could move. They were perhaps driven west by an increasing aridity on the steppe, which reached a peak of dryness in about 2000 BC, perhaps drawn by the richness of European soils. Wherever they went, they made their burial mounds, which are now to be found all over the steppe and beyond, at Marathon and Troy, on Salisbury Plain and in Denmark, all over Germany, and in Greece, and were probably once above the Shaft Graves at Mycenae, which were flattened only late in antiquity.

Those burial mounds, or kurgans, are houses for the greater dead, the articulate if silent earth equivalents of epic poetry, the memory capsules of giant lives lived in giant landscapes. They first started to appear on the southern steppelands of Eurasia in about 3800 BC and contain the tutelary objects ancestral to the equipment of the Greek heroes: copper spirals, often in pairs, to hold the braided hair of a single man, the glamor trappings of the decorated body, imported copper beads, almost certainly sewn to clothes that have now disappeared, along with thin sheets of metal like foil armor, and equally thin, insubstantial tubes of copper rolled into cylinders. They had axes with them and copper pendants made in the shape of beautiful freshwater mussel shells. Other shells were carved out of alabaster, and some of the steppeland heroes wore belts of freshwater mussels themselves, each shell carefully perforated where a thread joined it to the others.

In northern Ukraine, at a place called Karagod a few miles short of the border with Belarus, just in the fringe-zone where the southern steppe merges into the coniferous forest of the taiga, there is a small Bronze Age tumulus. The afternoon I was there, a blanket of silence hung in the sunshine. The sandy soil was rutted and dug up by wild boar into raw scrapes. But they were only minor interruptions. The continuous grasslands stretched away in front of me, just as Tolstoy said, the same on the horizon as they were at my feet, full of small, undemonstrative flowers: creamy white scabious, lady's bedstraw, mauve-blue campanulas, the dots of brighter paint in the endless, blond, receding grass.

As I walked through them, green grasshoppers danced up like the bubbles off a newly poured glass of champagne. In the binoculars there was nothing but glow and haze, a slow motility in the distant air, as if the world itself were simmering. I have never been anywhere filled with such languorous, labile beauty. Bugs skittered over the puddles, but everything else slowed in the heat. Cattle grazed in the distance, their legs dipped and narrowing into the pool of haze, while the swallows and sand martins wove in and out of them as if pursuing some hidden, threaded path. A kind of vanilla sweetness wafted from the lime trees, and wild raspberries grew and fruited beneath them. There were patches of lily-of-the-valley in the shade of young oaks. A wide, slow river came sliding out of the north, as unconcerned as a cow at its cud, and by the reedy riverbanks the damselflies performed and danced, pairs of dark wings on electric bodies. The breeze blew up the underside of the willow leaves, silvering them, and in the wind the edges of the water lilies curled up too, lifting one lip away from the water.

Is there anywhere as seductive, as reflective, as this glow-thick grass-land? It seems on these continental afternoons as if this might be the remembered nature of the Homeric world, the place to which Tiresias's deep memory was returning. On the evening I was at the kurgan near Karagod, a small posse of horses, roans and grays, ten or eleven of them, their manes and tails swinging in the breeze, came down through the willows and alders in front of me. They were not large animals but independent, swaggering, ganglike, uncowed by work, brushing through the reed bed at the fringe of the river and on through the grass, which like their manes and tails was being stirred by the wind from the east.

They stood half-turned in front of me, a hundred yards away. I don't know if these were wild horses, but the gap between us was electric, its charge full of suggestion and threat. It reminded me of the moment in Edwin Muir's famous 1950s post-nuclear-war vision when late in the summer strange horses came into his collapsed world. These animal companions had returned to join the human beings.

> We did not dare go near them. Yet they waited,
> Stubborn and shy, as if they had been sent
> By an old command to find our whereabouts
> And that long-lost archaic companionship.

That remembered paradise appears again and again in Homer, not as part of the present scene of war and trouble, but as the ground against which that grief-ridden existence is compared. War occupies the raging present at Troy, the violence of the sea fills the *Odyssey*, but peace lies in the back of the mind and constantly breaks through into the surface of the poetry. Sleep sits in a pine tree in the likeness of a singing bird. Hector looks down at his baby son and thinks he is as beautiful as a star. Nature is often violent in these comparisons too, filled with wolves, lions, eagles, hawks and vultures, troubled by ferocious rivers and gales over the sea, but throughout Homer the world of peace consistently resurfaces as a place of reproach and yearning, both memory and possibility.

In one comparison after another, windows are cut through the war into that calm-drenched past. The chariot horses of Achilles trample the dead like cattle stepping on the threshing floor, crushing the barley.

Menelaus and Agamemnon work their way through the Trojan ranks side by side like a pair of oxen struggling hard as they plow a fallow field. Homer is so in love with this idea of nature as a giant reservoir of stability that at one point in the *Iliad*, midbattle and midcrisis, he describes Hector, just at the point he is charging, armed and shouting, at the Greek enemy, as "a snowy mountain." Some critics have thought Homer might have meant an avalanche by this, but there is nothing in the Greek to justify that. It can only be that the horror of war summoned, as a kind of longing, an image of nature, vast, still and beautiful, in which violence had no part to play.

It was an Edenic afternoon as I sat on the kurgan and listened to the corncrakes and the quails. The kurgan itself is on a little rise overlooking its shallow valley, a small act of local domination. It is filled no doubt with a warrior and his few possessions. No one has ever excavated this mound, but if it follows the usual pattern, his relatives and descendants are pushed in at the side, over the generations, not disturbing him, but clustering around him, borrowing his significance, some perhaps placed here as human sacrifice around the great man, just as the twelve Trojan boys are sacrificed by Achilles at the grave of Patroclus.

Foxes and badgers have made their home in that kurgan now, and beside a small thorn tree its anciently stored earth pours out of the lip of their dusty entrances. Here, or at Troy, or in Epirus in northwest Greece, or on the downs in England, in Denmark, or on the chalk hills above Dover, every tumulus hints at the same story. These tombs are tattoos, or, more, scarifications, permanent marks, intended to make the skin of the planet meaningful. As epic poetry in turf, their aim is to deny time, making something lasting and resonant in a world that otherwise promises only transience. Every tumulus carries within it the memory of the songs sung when it was made. They are mourning mounds. Every one is invested with that moment of grief. Richness is buried there, because richness is what has died with the great person they contain. And if the earth can say nothing, poetry will remember what was said in these places.

The words for tomb, womb and cave all stem from the same Proto-Indo-European root, and so the tumulus can be seen as a kind of earth home, a womb for a birth into an otherworld, one of the dark places where the barriers are down between this world and the next. To put the body in the earth is to lead it toward that other world, closing it off from the present and the living with stone slabs or balks of timber. It both connects and separates the living and the dead.

The inside of the tumulus is both homely and strange. The body is laid out on its back, sometimes with its knees raised, sometimes in a crouched or fetal position. Powdered ocher covers the bones. Outlines of men's feet and other signs are painted in ocher on the tomb floors. Under the body a blanket made of reeds, or woven fabrics, skins or felted wool is laid. This is a bed; death is a little sleep.

The tumulus cemetery and settlement at Usatovo, near Odessa on the northwest coast of the Black Sea, from the years around 3000 BC, looks as if it might have been made by the deep ancestors of the Greeks. These people were still herders and horseback pastoralists of the coastal steppes but in touch with other worlds in Europe to the west and the Caucasus to the east, perhaps paddling along the Black Sea coast in sailless dugouts or trading and warring with the neighbors on long horseback journeys across the grasslands. Beads and buttons of Baltic amber accompanied them in death, alongside Anatolian silver and Near Eastern antimony. The great men were buried with axes, adzes and chisels. Others had their copper thrusting-daggers with them, many of the blades with a stiffening central rib to strengthen the weapon as it entered the flesh, that ancestral gesture which lies at the heart of the *Iliad*. And these are not utilitarian objects; some of the daggers are silver-plated. Already there was glory in violence.

These tumuli entombing the proto-heroes spread west along the coast of the Black Sea as far as the Danube delta, many of them heaped up over small stone houses for the dead. Those around the river Ingul, in southern Ukraine, northeast of Odessa, some of which are as late as 1900 BC, look increasingly like predecessors of the Greeks.

In those Ingul tumuli, the dead, like the Greeks at Mycenae, were laid in their tombs wearing masks. Some are full reconstructions of the face, some no more than coverlets for the eyes, all made not of gold, as those of their Mycenaean descendants would be, but of unfired clay, colored with ocher, or with ash or finely powdered bone to whiten the fabric, to make flesh of the clay. From the smooth form of their underside, it is clear that the clay of these masks was put on the flesh of the dead face before it had rotted. Through this colored earth, in the few days after death, the person was made permanent. That must have been the hope or the assumption. Mouths and eyes are modeled in the clay. Some of the heads have skull-caps of tar molded onto the hair.

If there can be any doubt that this culture was already focused on the individual and his destiny, or that the Homeric agonies over human transience were already present in these ancient steppeland lives, here is undeniable evidence of it. But, just as in Mycenae, this attitude toward death, the person and his preservation was not addressed merely to the warrior himself. There are women and children in these tombs, also masked like their men, treated with respect, considered significant. And so the vision of heroism here is not exclusively male but more broadly genetic. It is the transmission of meaning across the generations that guaranteed value in their world. Women and children were core components of an understanding of life that depended on breeding and inheritance. Perhaps that was only to be expected in people whose wealth was measured in the size and well-being of their herds, but this is the matrix from which one important part of the Homeric worldview emerged: it is a world not of palaces and institutions but of warriors and their families. It is at least possible that in these graves the Russian archaeologists also found the spiritual and mental predecessors of Achilles.

Poetry itself supports that idea. Across the whole of the Indo-European world, echoes and repetitions of shared attitudes and phrases continually resurface. Scholars have pursued Homeric phrases through an entire continent of poetry and have come up with a set of attributes that seem to stem from those early beginnings.

Homer's idea that poetry brings "undying fame" to the hero is not his at all. It appears in exactly that formula in Iranian and northern Indian epics. Heroes with *kleos* or *klutos*, the words for fame or glory, built into their names are known in Greek (Hera*kles* means "the fame of Hera," the goddess of marriage and women) but also in Indo-Iranian, Slavic, Norse, Frankish and Celtic (including *Cluto*rix—whose name, like a wrestler's, means the "King of Fame"—a fifth-century AD chieftain known only from his tombstone now built into the wall of the church in the little village of Llandissilio in the middle of Pembrokeshire).

Poetry and war are joined in this; both are fame businesses. The same epithets are attached to these fame-seeking heroes across the whole enormous continent: he was "man-slaying" in Ireland and Iran, and "of the famous spear" in Greece and India. He stood as firm and immovable in battle as a mighty tree in Homer, Russian and Welsh. Like the Greeks, Irish heroes raged like a fire. In Anglo-Saxon, Greek, Vedic and Irish, that rage could emerge as a flame flaring from the hero's head. Proto-Indo-Europeans saw the great man as a torch. Across the whole of Eurasia his weapons longed for blood, even while this blood-seeking vengeance wreaker was to his own family and clan, wherever they might be, the "herdsman of his people" and their protective enclosure. There were no city walls in this world; the hero himself was their protection and their strength.

From one end of Eurasia to another, men stand like trees, but enemies are also felled like trees, in the way a carpenter or woodsmen would fell them. When death arrives, a darkness comes on the hero. Life itself for the Proto-Indo-European consciousness is inseparable from light, especially the light of the sun, and that is the energy the heroes share with the universe. For all of them, courage is not something that appears casually in everyday life. Only when battle summons them, and when the noise of battle reaches up to heaven, as it does in all these daughter traditions, does courage appear and the hero find himself "clothed in valor."

These phrases, which are shared between Homer and the poets who sang to their man-lords across the widths of Eurasia from the Atlantic to the Himalayas, are the creases in the mind of the Proto-Indo-European people from whom we are all descended. They are the oldest of the ancestral thoughts to which we can have access. We are their heirs, just as Homer was their heir, a descendant of the steppelands.

Memories of this pre-Greek world lingered on for the Greeks, first in the knowledge that they were not one people but an agglomeration of families and their leaders, speaking something like the same language but never unified. Homer thinks of the Greeks as a gang of bees, alive, investigative, aggressive, buzzing with their needs and desires but never one unitary mass. This is not the army of a single nation. They are, as Nestor tells Agamemnon, different tribes and gangs, who must be organized clan by clan, people by people, listening to their leaders, scarcely integrated, resistant to overall kingship. These are in origin the groups of steppeland warriors who have come south to the more tightly organized world of the centrally ordained city.

More intriguing still is the geographic residue in Homer's language.

The sea has no place in the most ancient layers of Greek. There is no Proto-Indo-European word for the sea, beyond a root that means something like "pond" or "lake." *Thalassa*, the Greek word for sea, has no reliable etymology. It may have come from the language spoken in Greece before the Greeks arrived there. The sea was an alien environment, and when Homer speaks of it the only way he can treat it is as a steppeland. The phrase that recurs repeatedly in both Homeric poems, neatly filling the second half of a hexameter, is *ep' eurea nota thalasses*, meaning "on the broad backs of the sea" or "on the sea's broad ridges." Warriors set out across the sea's broad ridges for battle or for home. The ships drive like horses across them. Poseidon, the sea god who is also the horse god, finds his own horses stabled in his extraordinary palace deep in the sea, glittering with gold, "imperishable for ever," unlike the world over which he presides. He drives them across his own wet steppeland.

> He harnessed to the chariot his bronze-shod horses
> Flying footed, with long gold manes streaming behind them,
> and he put on clothing of gold about his own body
> and took up the golden lash, carefully constructed,
> and climbed into his chariot and drove it across the waves
> And about him the sea beasts came up from their deep places
> and played in his path
> And acknowledged their master as the sea stood apart before him rejoic-
>   ing. The horses flew on with all care
> and the bronze axle beneath was not wetted
> until they carried him fast to the ships of the Achaeans.

That glorious drive of the sea-horse god, a baroque ceiling waiting to be painted, is a gilded stampede across the sea as if across the endless grasslands of the north. *Nota* could mean "the backs of men or animals, of boars, of horses and eagles," but also "the great wide surface of the land." It is the word for that steppe continuousness, the only model on which the early Greeks could base their understanding of the sea.

The sea-as-land penetrates far into the poems. When Aeneas is remembering the time before there was even a city at Troy, he thinks of it as a place where great fortunes were made in the raising of horses. So beautiful were they that the north wind—that essence of mobility from the distant north, gusty, with the cold of the north at the back of it—fell in love with them, disguised himself as a black stallion, coupled with them, and the Trojan mares gave birth to twelve magical young horses. Not only could they run along the top of the ears of the ripened corn, miraculously not breaking the grains from their stems, but then beautifully "They would play across the sea's wide ridges/Running the edge of the wave where it breaks on the grey salt sea."

Land and sea are continuous in this imagery. Blowing ears of corn and the curling break of a swell coming ashore are the same thing. When Nestor gives advice to his son on the driving of chariots, the relationship to the horse and to the ship effortlessly coalesces.

> It is by cunning and craft that the helmsman holds his swift ship
> On its track, though buffeted by winds, over the wine-dark sea.
> By cunning and craft the charioteer beats charioteer . . .
> And holds his horses steady in his hand, watching the lead horse.

What the wind does for the ship at sea, the horses do for the chariot on the plain. It is Penelope who says that fast-running ships serve as horses for men on the salt sea.

And when Odysseus is finally on his way back to Ithaca, not only is the ship taking him there as fast as a chariot at full speed; it mimics one: "Just as in a field four stallions drawing a chariot all break together at the stroke of the whip, and lifting high their feet lightly beat out their path, so the stern of the ship would lift and the creaming wave behind her boiled in the thunderous crash of the sea."

There is an overbrimming technological energy in those lines. It is the sensation you get whenever a boat accelerates at sea—imagine Homer's delight at a RIB (Rigid Inflatable Boat) with a pair of 200-horsepower Yamahas on the back—its sudden, gut-felt harnessing of liquid power. In the centuries after 2000 BC, the speed of the chariot and the ship were transforming men's experience of the world. And there are signs in Homer of a real excitement at the idea of machinery. In the *Odyssey* the ideal king Alcinous has beautiful metal dogs—made by Hephaestus, the smith god—guarding the entrance to his palace, dogs which will live and bark forever. When Hephaestus is making Achilles's wonderful new armor, he has magical-mechanical robotic golden girls to help him, automata that can carry and talk and think, as well as automatic tripod tables which under their own power wheel in and out of the dining room of the gods.

The myth of Daedalus and Icarus, dazzling inventors of hubristic, dangerous machines, labyrinth-traps and wings that melt in the heat of the sun, are probably associated with this arrival of the new technology in the Aegean world. This is the first moment of European entrancement with the life-expanding potential of technology, but anxiety over the new machinery surfaces in the *Iliad* too. In book 5, in the first great battle of the poem, the Greek warrior Meriones pursues a Trojan called Phereclus. He strikes him in the right buttock

> and the spearhead drives straight on
> passing under the pelvis, jabbing at and piercing the bladder.
> He drops, screaming, to his knees, and the death-mist swirls about him.

This one grievous ending, like all the others at Troy, is due to what Phereclus learned. Without him, Paris would never have been able to go to Greece to steal Helen, nor the Greeks come to claim her from Troy, as Phereclus is the great shipwright

> Who understands how to make with his hand all intricate
> Things, since above all others Pallas Athene loved him.
> He it is who built for Paris the steady, balanced
> Ships, trim launchers of death, freighted with death
> For all of Troy and now for him too.

The synchronicity is revolutionary: the technology of the new chariots, probably from the north, and the technology of the sailing ship, certainly from the south, seem to have arrived in the Greek world at about the same time, perhaps at around 1800 BC. That is also a likely moment for the Greek arrival in the Mediterranean. High-speed chariots, high-speed sailing ships and a warrior culture from the north all come together in the Aegean at the same moment, which is also the moment the Homeric poems are born. This newly energized world is the meeting of cultures that Homer records.

There are some intriguing linguistic linkages. A whole range of Indo-European languages have a word for the pole at the front of a wagon or chariot to which the horses are attached (it is a "thill" in English), which becomes the Greek word for the rudder post of a ship. The word for the tiller or the helm of a boat is also at root the same word as the rings on a yoke. The word for the loops attached to the yoke through which the beasts' heads are put is also the word for the crossbar connecting the double steering-oars at the stern of a ship. The Greek word for rudder can also be applied to reins. At this most fundamental level, the sailing ship is the sea chariot for the Greeks, and the sea is the liquid steppe. And all of them become intimate with heroism.

There had been sea craft long before in the eastern Mediterranean, of astonishing antiquity. There were people on Crete, which has been separate from the mainland for at least five million years, making hand axes and stone scrapers 130,000 years ago. They can only have arrived by boat or raft, probably from Anatolia. The whole civilization of the Cyclades was created and connected by straight-hulled, low-freeboard, paddled canoes, of which the earliest representation that survives was made in about 2800 BC. No sail appeared in the Mediterranean until about 2500 BC (it had probably been invented in the Indian Ocean), when sailing ships started to travel along the coast between Egypt and the Levant, bringing raw materials into what the archaeologist Cyprian Broodbank called "the colossal vortex of consumption" of the Egyptian state.

Judging by depictions on Minoan seals from Crete, and also by the increasing spread of luxury Egyptian and Near Eastern objects into Crete and Cyprus, these sailing ships were pushing up toward the Aegean by about 1950 BC. They were quite different from the old paddled canoes, with a deep, curving plank-built hull, a tall mast, held in place with rigging, as well as a sail and a steering oar. They were the most complicated and sophisticated constructions the Aegean world would ever have seen. And above all, they brought speed and power to the sea world. A hand-paddled canoe had been able to cover perhaps ten to twenty miles in a good day. A sailing ship might go a hundred. On a beam reach, the fastest point of sailing for a ship of this kind, the leading edge of its sail hauled far forward, it might achieve seven or eight knots. The sailing ship could carry tons of cargo, where a canoe could have taken little more than the

The battle face of the *Iliad*: brutal, excluding, potent.
One of the golden masks discovered by Heinrich Schliemann
in the Shaft Graves at Mycenae in 1876.

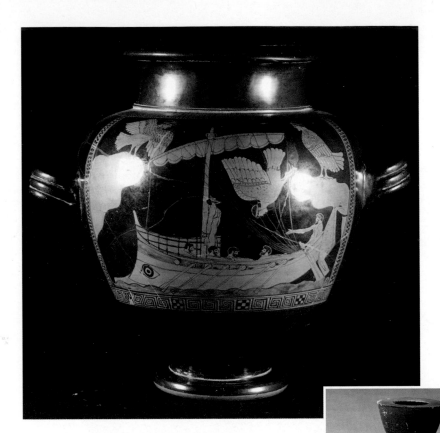

Throbbing with desire for the Sirens, Odysseus, bound to his ship, resists the illusions of nostalgia. From a storage jar made in Athens in about 480 BC.

A 6th-century BC *lekythos* shows the tiny mosquito of a dead man's soul half-hovering above his head. For Homer, life itself was rich, life-after-death terminally diminished.

"Battle was sweeter to them than the land of their fathers." The sword-bearing charioteer, hunched over in his war-lust, drives against an enemy. A limestone stele from the Shaft Graves at Mycenae, ca. 1600 BC.

A gold drinking cup covered in the interlaced, bind-and-release spirals which entranced Homer's world.

Scales in the Shaft Graves, made of gold so thin they could only have weighed the butterfly souls impressed on them.

His father's son: tiny, dead Mycenaean princelings went to their graves encased in gold, front and back, a habit of reverencing the children of the great which goes back to the steppes.

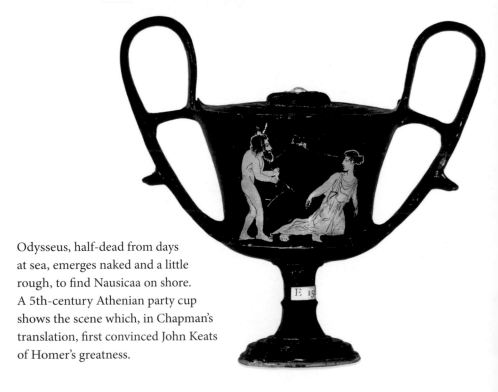

Odysseus, half-dead from days at sea, emerges naked and a little rough, to find Nausicaa on shore. A 5th-century Athenian party cup shows the scene which, in Chapman's translation, first convinced John Keats of Homer's greatness.

The *Iliad* in Extremadura: a Late Bronze Age stele now in Badajoz shows a warrior, his sword and the giant shield marked with the concentric rings of the cosmos.

Metal heroes: Extremaduran figures with shield, swords, bow, spear and two objects central to the hero-complex: a bubble-handled mirror, for beauty, and a musical instrument, for epic song. Both men have large, "man-slaughtering-hands."

Southern storytelling: the multiple scenes on silver gilt bowls produced in the Near East (this one from Cyprus ca. 725–675 BC but showing Egyptian, Assyrian and Phoenician stories of battle and triumph) provide a possible model for Homer's description of the Shield of Achilles.

The shape of the south:
fluency and fragility in
a Kamares eggshell-ware
cup from the temple-palace at
Phaistos on Crete, ca. 1900 BC, just
as the Greeks were entering the
Mediterranean world.

A golden libation bowl
from Olympia, now in
Boston. Only when
Odysseus on the shores
of Hades pours all the
good juices of the earth
on to the ground can
the dead re-acquire the
ability to speak.

The luxurious world of Sinuhe: an Egyptian ivory cosmetics container in
the shape of a duck with fish on her back.

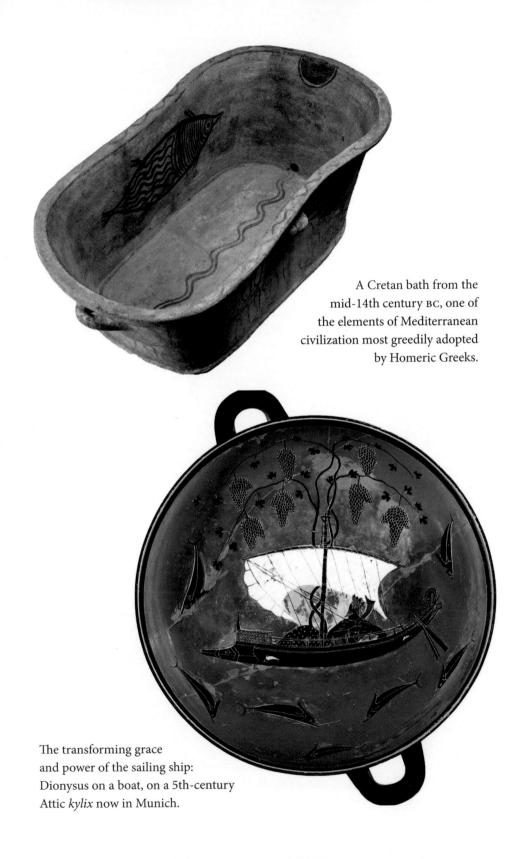

A Cretan bath from the mid-14th century BC, one of the elements of Mediterranean civilization most greedily adopted by Homeric Greeks.

The transforming grace and power of the sailing ship: Dionysus on a boat, on a 5th-century Attic *kylix* now in Munich.

men needed to paddle it. A high-hulled sailing ship could live in the kind of waves that would swamp a canoe. For the first time people could experience storms at sea and survive to tell the tale.

Nowhere in Homer is this amazement with the ship more overwhelming than when Odysseus finds himself washed up in book 6 of the *Odyssey* on the shore of Scheria, the island of the Phaeacians. Scheria is the Homeric equivalent of Southern California, or at least the urbanized, enriched, technological world of the Near East, filled with people who are living the enviable life: a city with beautiful harbors, wonderful gardens, orchards surrounding their palaces, no suffering or grief in their lives, playfulness, elegance, riches, the presence of power buried under a coat of luxuries and ease.

The north meets the south here: Odysseus is never more ragged, never treated more as a wanderer from God-knows-where, and his hosts are never more beautifully organized, more integrated as a single contented orderly world. These are the polarities of the Homeric experience. The Phaeacians are what the Greek wanderers dream of being. Homer introduces a stream of them to Odysseus (whom they consider a pirate and a drifter), and just as the Trojans are alive in their horse names, the Phaeacians can scarcely be distinguished from their ships and the sea. Odysseus stands there encountering (in Robert Fagles's translations) a stream of muscled young men: Topsail, Riptide, Rowhard, Seaman and Sternman, Surf-at-the-Beach, Stroke-Oar, Breaker and Bowsprit, Racing-the-Wind, Swing-Aboard, Shipwrightson, Seagirt the son of Greatfleet and Broadsea the son of Launcher. The king's own sons are called Ship-Famous, People-Dominator and simply Sea.

Could Homer have made it any clearer? Here, in the sea-based city, the delight and riches of an urban life are derived from the magic of the sailing ship. And the heart of the Phaeacian ships' excellence, to an open-mouthed Greek, hopelessly provincial in these upholstered surroundings, is their ability to sail *on thought alone*. Alcinous, the king, explains how it works in this floating, gravity-free world.

> Our ships can sail you home.
> They have no rudders as those of other nations do,
> but can understand our thoughts and our desires; they know all the
>   cities and countries of the world,

and can cross the sea through mist and cloud,
never any danger of wreck or harm with them.

The ships are as miraculous as Achilles's weeping-talking horses. They are "as quick as a bird, as quick as a darting thought." But perhaps embedded here is a memory of the ignorant northerners' first encounter with the miracle of the sailing ship. No need to paddle it to make it travel across the sea. Just arrange its parts as they need to be arranged, make a libation to the right goddesses, and on thought alone the ship will sail to the ends of the earth and back.

These rocket ships, as Cyprian Broodbank has said, "drastically shrunk maritime space." They were adventure machines. Egypt could be reached from Greece in four days. Sudden arrival and sudden violence were now possibilities. They could sail to windward, or at least within fifty degrees of the wind, in a way paddlers would find difficult and exhausting. Life had speeded up. The whole geography of the sea and its surrounding lands had changed. It was as transforming as the invention of the steam engine. And that excitement and amazement at the wonder of the sailing ship and its effects on the dynamics of life soaked deep into the fabric of the Homeric poems. In Homer's hands, sailing ships became the vehicles of heroes.

It is never quite said explicitly in Homer, but it is assumed that this sense of boat-perfection has become for the Greeks one of the joys of life. Ships are always fast or well-balanced or well-made. The word usually translated as "well-balanced," *eisos*, has a moral and psychological dimension to it and means "equal," "properly shared like a feast," or "well-balanced in mind." The wisdom of Odysseus is described as *eisos*, his wholeness and beauty as self-sufficiently itself as a well-made ship. The adjectives—"fast," "well-balanced" and "well-made"—contribute formulas that slip the sea craft into the verse form, but they are also a kind of repetitive admiration for the wonder of ships. Menelaus remembers how fast they were when at last, at the end of the war, the Greeks left Troy for home. It was fast ships that repeatedly brought wine from Greece to the warriors in their foreign camp. Homer recounts the variety and strength of the different bands of men that went to Troy by remembering the numbers of ships in which they traveled. It is the ships, as Ajax reminds them, that are their only guarantee of getting home dryshod. It is the ships they must defend, and around the ships is where the fiercest fighting rages. The sea might be salt and bitter, so wide in places that even seabirds cannot cross it, but the well-benched ships, the hollow ships, the ships whose hulls are black with waterproofing tar, the ships equipped with all the gear that strong-benched ships carry—these are the foundations of their lives in the southern sea.

So now, each time the wind fills in, and you roll the headsails out and get the main up, and you feel the boat starting to gather way, to pick up its skirts, unable to resist the pull of the wind, you will know something essential of the Homeric world. Here under the bow you can listen, like the Phaeacians carrying Odysseus home, to the water surge and fall, that repeated *hoosssh-hoosssh* of a hull at speed. And here, as you make your way between the blue islands, the boat heeled far over and the curves of the headsails bellied out to leeward, you can begin to know and sense the power of possibility in the well-balanced, well-benched ship, equipped with all it needs, acquiring the world, stretching the idea of what it means to be alive, leading men to adventure, home or war.

10 · THE GANG AND THE CITY

The Greeks are camped on the edge of the beach, a gang of men divided among themselves, with no secure leadership, the atmosphere angry and uncertain, no constancy in their arguments or their dealings with each other, no faith in their purpose, no substance in their loyalties and no women with any significance beyond their sex. They are living in rough sheds built against their ships. The rigging has rotted. They are surrounded by loot but sleep on the skins of wild animals. Dogs eat the dead. Dogs are everywhere on the battlefield. They chew at the genitals of the corpses, and birds clap their wings over the remains. If you walk across that realm of death at night, you must pick your way through "the abandoned weapons and the black blood." The Greeks confront the realities of life and death with unadorned directness. No family, no safety, no home, no sense that virtue is rewarded or frailty sheltered. No prospect of dignity in old age or security when weak. No meaning beyond the presence of force.

They have been here too long, and the language vibrates with its own violence. The burningly angry killer-chief Achilles says that Agamemnon, his nominal leader, is dog-eyed, dog-faced, shameless, greedy, a wine drinker, with his heart as flaky as a deer's. Agamemnon calls Achilles "the most savage man alive, violence itself, beyond all feeling." Anger and disgust ripple through their "shaggy breasts," in the roughness of their hearts. In private they are tender about themselves and their girls, but here they overbrim with hate, each longing for the other's "black blood to come pumping out on to my blade." They stand nostril to nostril in mutual loathing. This is a gang world, marginal, desperate and tragic, a place of outsiders. Civilization it is not. Like all gangs, they have their meetings and their discussions, their insistence on hierarchy and obedience. And this fight between the leaders feels ugly and unwelcome, deplored by the old men. Nevertheless, it is an organic part of who the Greeks are, one aspect of the anarchy and violence that crouches just beneath the surface of every interaction between them. The Greeks are the barbarians in this story.

Across the plain, Troy is different. Here are the people of a city, full of conviction, with well-ordered relations, allies who remain true to each other, a king to whom all give respect, brothers, sisters, wives, parents and children all living in a mutually dependent, interlocked system, with institutions that seem permanent. Noble women lead graceful lives. There are arguments within the family, there are hints of luxury and softness, but this is a place where not merely the bodies of slaughtered animals but woven and embroidered cloth, the flexible and intricately constructed thing, is the offering they make to the gods.

The Trojans are at home, and the web of their connections is wound closely around them. When Hector, their young war leader, midbattle, returns to the gates of the city, "the wives and daughters of Troy come crowding up around him, asking for their sons, brothers, friends and husbands." (This is the network the Trojans are embedded in.) Hector goes into the city, to the palace of Priam, his father, and enters

> that most beautiful house
> Built with polished colonnades –and deep within its walls
> are fifty chambers of polished stone, built close to one another;
> in them the sons of Priam sleep beside their wedded wives;
> and for his daughters on the other side, inside the court,
> are twelve roofed chambers of polished stone, built close to one another;
> in them the old king's sons-in-law sleep beside their respected wives.

It is the geometry of coherence—of repetition and continuity—of people understanding and responding to the virtues of mutual accommodation, the opposite of the shiftless place of the Greeks outside. So this is the confrontation: gang against city, individual violence against domestic order.

The wind blows unbroken across the plain, and among the Greeks unbridled maleness meets in erect competition or tensed standoff. The sexuality is inescapable. It takes the old Greek war-leader Nestor to say it. When persuading doubters not to return to Greece before Troy falls, he gives them the plain invitation: "Let no man hurry to sail for home, not yet . . . Not until he has slept with the wife of some Trojan." Only sex with the enslaved wife of a dead enemy could justify the grief and trouble they have endured over Helen. The symbols at the heart of the city of Troy are those elegant, well-swept corridors of polished stone and the beautiful woven cloth its people give their gods; for the Greek camp it is edge-sharpened bronze and the unsheathed phallus.

The *Iliad* is not shut into the Trojan plain; it loves mobility; its gods and goddesses fly across the islanded world of the Aegean with effortless fluency and a wide surveying sense of its geography. The poem often travels away to Olympus, the home of the gods, to Africa and to other mountains where the gods take up temporary residence. Minor deities are sometimes caught between flights, rushed off their feet, in transit from Anatolia to Egypt, or to a dinner party in the house of the west wind. But the poem *never* goes to Greece. No scene is set in a Greek house. Greek places are referred to with formulaic adjectives—"rocky," "with-many-ridges," "sheepy"—but with none of the overwhelming sense of reality that clusters around Troy and its rivers, its woods, springs, washing places and even individual trees and burial mounds. In that poetic sense, at one of the deepest levels of the poem, the *Iliad* portrays the Greeks as a long way from home.

It is true that they occasionally refer to the places they come from, but the psychological weight in those references is not to buildings or cities. The Greeks look back with longing and a sense of loss to their families, their distant fathers and their fathers' fathers, their wives and children, the brotherhood of their clans, the hearths which are defined by the people who gather around them, not to any palaces. They love their land, which gives them food and sustenance, its wheat-bearing fields and lovely orchards, but not the kind of deeply instituted fixity and built wealth they have come to get their hands on at Troy. What they miss, in a phrase that is repeated again and again, is "the loved earth of their fathers." But in Greek there is no distinction between "fatherhood" and "fatherland." The word for them both is *patra*, and it can apply in Homer to a shared descent, a cousinage, a sense of family or clan. Fatherhood is fatherland, and blood and heart are home.

Even the loved earth of the fathers is trumped by something else in the Greek mind. When the great owl-eyed goddess Athene, terrifying in her power, carrying her magic *aegis*, or breastplate, moves through the Greek army, putting a deep hunger for violence in their hearts, allowing them to fight without rest, home itself drops into insignificance.

> And now sweeter to them than any return
> In their hollow ships to the loved earth of their fathers
> > Was battle.

The word Homer uses for the deliciousness of that violence in battle is *glukus*, "sugary," even "sickly," used of nectar and sweet wine, of the people you love. Battle, in many ways, is the Greek home. As the agents of severance, they are themselves severed from home. The most delicious thing they can imagine is a world of unrelenting violence.

"Beware the toils of war," Sarpedon the Lycian hero says to Hector, "the mesh of the huge dragnet sweeping up the world." Buried inside that terrifying image of war trawling for the lives of men, its net stretched from one horizon to the other, ushering the mortals into the cod end, is the Greek word for flax, the thread that the Fates use at the beginning of each of our lives to spin our destinies. And so the metaphor makes an assumption: war is part of destiny. It is not an aberration or a strangeness. It is, for Homer, a theater in which the structure of reality is revealed.

Simone Weil and many others have read the *Iliad* as an antiwar poem. But to see it as a polemic in that sense is to reduce it. Homer knows about the reality of suffering but never thinks of a world without conflict. On the shield of Achilles, the smith god Hephaestus creates dazzlingly opposed images of the good world and the bad, set against each other. But even in the good world of justice there is still murder and violence. We might long for peace, but we live in war, and the *Iliad* is a poem about the inescapability of it.

All of that lies behind the *Iliad*'s massive oversupply of suffering. The poet's conception that the Greeks have been on this beach for nine long, dreadful years—a historical absurdity—stands in for eternity. This is how things are. This is how things have always been. This is how things are going to continue to be. War is the air a warrior society must breathe. And alongside that everlastingness of grief, its repetitive return, is a deeply absorbed knowledge that suffering can only be told in detail. No counting of casualties will do; no strategic overview will understand the reality; only the intimate engagement with the intimacy of pain and sorrow can ever be good enough for the enlightenment that is Homer's purpose.

Scholars have worked out that 264 people die in the course of the *Iliad*. It doesn't seem enough. One atrocity in some villages on the northern borders of Syria, one nighttime drowning of African refugees in the Mediterranean, one week of car bombs in Baghdad—any of them can outdo it. Only the epic engagement with Atē, the blind goddess of ruin, whose name means both "wrongness" and "wickedness," can tell what those figures conceal. People are pitiably weak in the face of ruin, pathetically hoping that their prayers for happiness might prevail. That is why the goddesses of prayer in the Homeric universe are broken, tragic figures:

> they limp and halt,
> they're all wrinkled, drawn, they squint to the side,
> can't look you in the eye, and always bent on duty,
> trudging after Ruin, maddening, blinding Ruin.
> But Ruin is strong and swift—She outstrips them all,
> loping a march, skipping across the whole wide earth
> to bring mankind to grief.
> And the Prayers trail after, trying to heal the wounds.

Christians might think of prayer as something that can summon divine power; Homer knows different. "Of all that breathe and crawl across the earth," Zeus himself says, "There is nothing alive more agonized than man." The term the great god uses is *oïzuroteros*, "more miserable," from the word for a wailing lament, the unbroken, everlasting, ululating cry that echoes from one end of the *Iliad* to the other.

When the poet is reaching for a comparison that will sharpen the pity of life and the futility of killing, it is fish that repeatedly drift into his consciousness. Perhaps because they are so disgusting, nibbling at the bodies of the dead; perhaps because a fish is so unable to look after itself when caught on a hook, in a net or on a spear, both fish and fishermen are for Homer absurd.

Fish gasping for the sea are not simply poignant in their hopelessness. In the *Iliad* fishing is the source of some of Homer's bitterest and jokiest comparisons. When Patroclus, the friend and childhood companion of Achilles, his great intimate in a world where no one else seems to love him, borrows Achilles's armor at a moment of great crisis for the Greeks in the war at Troy, and strides out into the mass of the Trojans, he pins them against the ships drawn up on the sand. This is his *aristeia*, his moment of greatness, his time of horror. Patroclus rampages through the Trojan bodies, repetitively and brutally: "Patroclus keeps on sweeping, hacking them down, / making them pay the price for Argives slaughtered."

One poor Trojan, Cebriones, a bastard son of Priam, the king of Troy, is killed by Patroclus with a stone smashed into the front of his skull. Both Cebriones's eyes fall out into the dust at his feet, and the body, jerked into death, somehow dives out of the chariot to join them. The beautiful, elegant, much-loved Patroclus mocks the corpse: "Hah! look at you! Agile! How athletic is that, as if you were diving into the sea. You could satisfy an army if you were diving for oysters, plunging overboard even into rough seas as nimbly as that." Corpse as oyster diver; ridiculous victim, vaunting killer. At one point, in describing Patroclus's safari, Homer sinks to nothing but a list of the names of those he destroys: "Erymas and Amphoterus and Epaltes and Tlepolemus son of Damastor and Echius and Pyris and Ipheus and Euippus and Polymelus, son of Argeas: corpse on corpse he piles on the all-nourishing earth."

Patroclus moves on, as Robert Fagles translated Homer's phrase for the unstoppability of this, "in a blur of kills." But then the rapidity, the appetite for more, stops and stills for a moment, and dwells on the detail of one particular death, one moment of heroic prowess.

Next he goes for Thestor the son of Enops
cowering, crouched in his beautiful polished chariot,
crazed with fear, and the reins jump from his grip—
Patroclus rising beside him stabs his right jawbone,
ramming the spearhead square between his teeth so hard
he hooks him by that spearhead over the chariot rail,
hoists and drags the Trojan out as an angler perched

on a jutting rock ledge drags some fish from the sea,
some precious catch, with line and glittering bronze hook.
So with the spear Patroclus gaffs him off his car,
his mouth gaping round the glittering point
And flips him down facefirst,
dead as he falls, his life breath blown away.

Man as fish, body as rag doll, killing as a form of acrobatics, the absurdity of the slaughtered corpse—this is vertigo-inducing, a plunge into the black hole of reality, fueled by the mismatch of sea-angling with war.

Christopher Logue, the most brilliant of all modern interpreters of Homer, drove these lines farther into domestic savagery.

Ahead, Patroclus braked a shade, and then and gracefully
As patient men cast fake insects over trout,
He speared the boy, and with his hip as pivot
Prised Thestor out of the chariot's basket
As easily as lesser men
Detach a sardine from an opened tin.

The first fighting does not begin until 2,380 lines into the *Iliad*, but thereafter the blood flows, increasingly, with an increasing intensity and savagery, until the climax comes in the crazed berserker frenzy of Achilles's grief-fueled rampage through the Trojans. The culmination is in the death of Hector, when steppe-man finally meets and kills the man of the city. The Greeks might think battle sweet, their warriors might see battle not as a burden but a cause for rejoicing, but Homer does not.

Now the sun of a new day falls on the ploughlands, rising
Out of the quiet water and the deep stream of the ocean
To climb the sky. The Trojans assemble together. They find
It hard to recognize each individual dead man;
But with water they wash away the blood that is on them
And as they weep warm tears they lift them on to the wagons.
Great Priam does not let them cry out; and in silence
They pile the bodies on the pyre, and when they have burned them
    go back to sacred Ilion.

The Greek words translated here by Richmond Lattimore as "hard to recognize" carry multiple meanings. *Chalepos* (hard) means both "emotionally painful" and "difficult to do"; it is a word that can be applied either to grieving or to rough ground over which you cannot help but stumble as you walk. *Diagnonai* (to recognize, like diagnosis) means "to distinguish or discern," to sort out a single important thing from a confused mass, to find individuality amid the blood and muck of the heaped-up bodies. So the phrase can mean either that it was physically difficult in the mounded carnage to make out who it was that was dead; or that finding your own dead amid the mass of others was the most harrowing of experiences. Or both. Those hot, silent Trojan tears, *dákrua thermà*, allied in these lines with the deep calm of the ocean and the water that washes the blood away, are among Homer's greatest legacies to us, the persistent belief, amid all this damage, that there is value and beauty in human ties.

Homer's portrait of the Greeks at Troy fits the historical situation in the centuries after 2000 BC, when newly empowered northern warriors, equipped with sailing ships and chariots, could batten on the walls of a rich trading city in northwest Anatolia, clamoring to get at its women and its goods. But it is also a portrait of something more enduring: a well-set-up, well-defended establishment is under attack from outsiders who long for, envy and wish to destroy it. The siege at Troy, often seen as a kind of war, as if these were two states battling with each other, is in fact more like a gang from the ghetto confronting the urban rich. Outsiders and insiders, nomadic and settled, the needy and the leisured, the enraged and the offended—the hero complex of the Greek warriors is simply gang mentality writ large.

Iliadic behavior echoes through modern urban America. As the criminologists Bruce Jacobs and Richard Wright documented from the streets of St. Louis, Missouri, American gang members talk about themselves, their lives, their ambitions, their idea of fate, the role of violence and revenge, in ways that are strangely like the Greeks in the *Iliad*.

Revenge is at the heart of their moral world, a repeated, angry and violent answer to injustice, to being treated in a way that does not respect them as people. There appears to be no overriding authority or legitimacy on the streets of St. Louis. Authority resides in the men themselves and their ability to dominate others. "This desire for payback," Jacobs and Wright say, "is as human and as inevitable as hunger or thirst." Crime itself on these streets becomes moral, and revenge a form of justice.

Like the Greeks, these gangsters are "urban nomads," not set up in their elaborate houses, but living nowhere in particular, "staying" or "resting their head" in different places according to mood or what is going on. They are rootless, dependent on themselves, displaying their glory on their bodies, in their handsomeness, their jewelry and in the sexiness of the women on their arms and in their beds.

They can only rely on themselves: "maintaining a reputation for toughness dominates day-to-day interaction." And because any act of revenge has to deter the enemy from taking revenge in his turn, there is an accelerator built into the process. Any insult, any slight, any suggestion that you are not a man worthy of respect summons severe, intense and punitive retaliatory violence. Achilles longs to kill Agamemnon after he has humiliated him in public over a slave girl he loves. The St. Louis gangsters take revenge without a thought.

One evening a man called Red knocks into a stranger at a bar by mistake and spills his glass of cognac on him. In response, the stranger "bitch-slaps" him, not with a closed fist but with an open hand, usually reserved for women. "Everyone was watching," Red says, "so it made me look bad." Red leaves the bar and waits in the dark in the parking lot. When the man comes out he shoots him, not once but several times. This is the only way in a warrior society that you can be yourself or protect the fragile boundaries of the self, forever under attack from those around you who are all feeling the same.

Homer usually talks with a mysterious decorum about acts of extreme and horrifying violence, perhaps as a product of the poem evolving over generations, so that a kind of linguistic dignity is laid over the top of the violence itself; but have no doubt, the words of the gangsters reflect a Homeric reality, nowhere more than in book 10 of the *Iliad*. The behavior that book describes is peculiarly horrible, a stripping away of any skin of dignity and nobility. Like "two lions into the black night/Through the carnage and through the corpses, the war gear and the dark blood," Odysseus and Diomedes slink off toward the Trojan line.

They come across a young Trojan, Dolōn, out in the night and set off to chase him, "like two rip-fanged hounds that have sighted a wild beast, a young deer or a hare." They catch him, and he stands in front of them in terror, gibbering and in tears. The two Greeks interrogate him, smiling, getting out of him any information they can, but he knows what is to come. He begs for his life, reaching up to the chin of Diomedes, asking for mercy, but Diomedes

> strikes the middle of his neck
> With a sweep of the sword, and slashes clean through both tendons,
> And Dolōn's head—still speaking—drops in the dust.

This is the most shocking moment in Homer, part of a hideous murder-run in the dark, with many dead, and booty taken, including wonderful horses and chariots, at the end of which Odysseus laughs aloud, has a swim in the sea and then a beautiful bath. Its amusement and delight at violence leaves a hollow in the reader's heart, which is scarcely filled by the way the Greeks "vaunt" over the bodies of the people they have killed, calling them fools, telling the world of their own excellence, their right to stand over the dead and damaged body of the rival. This is also how gangsters "trash talk." "I got your punk ass," Bobcat tells one of his victims, "and now look at you . . . Now if you'd paid this cheese [money], you'd have been all right, but now you fucked up, you bleeding and shit . . . you talking about your ribs broke. Now what the fuck?"

Words are a way of making it hurt. This is the hero delivering justice, telling his victim, and his audience around him, just how powerful he is in the world. "Catching and punishing those who have wronged them makes offenders feel mighty," Jacobs and Wright say, "while at the same time it masks their objective impotence." "I had an adrenaline rush," one of their informants told them about a particularly horrible piece of violence, "like I was the shit, like I was in control." "I felt like I was in some pussy," another said after using a baseball bat to break the legs of a man who had vandalized his car. "You know [like I] busted [a] nut"—or ejaculated.

This elision of self-enlargement, sexual gratification and extreme violence to other men's bodies lurks in the subtext of Homer. A theater of sex and violence is at the heart of both the *Iliad* and the *Odyssey*: the stolen woman Helen; the twice stolen woman Briseis (once from her family, all of whom Achilles has murdered, once from Achilles, who comes to love her); the recurrent boast that the Greeks will kill the Trojan men and take their women, as they have taken other women from other cities; the sexual battening on Penelope by the suitors; the savage retribution exacted by Odysseus on those who have wanted to have sex with Penelope, and then on the women of his own household who had had sex with those suitors. This is a core reality in Homer, which finds its explicit echoes in gangland.

Colton Simpson, from South Central Los Angeles, was fourteen in 1980. His mentor Smiley, his "road dog," his running mate, glows to him like a hero, just as Achilles and every Indo-European hero has always glowed: "When he smiles it's as if the light, the sun behind him, fills me, fills each and every one of us standing there before him."

When the law is no good, the only justice that makes sense is retaliatory, and that is the governing ethic of the Greeks in the *Iliad*. It is the dark heart of the gang on the beach, where *personal affronts attack identity*, where *counterstrikes tend to be excessive*, where *minor slights are interpreted as major blows to character*, where warriors *rely on the honor that accrues to those who demonstrate prowess in disputes*, where *honor is accumulated much like real capital and bringing someone down for what he did to you raises your worth in the eyes of your peers*, where *intolerance earns respect* and *strength is protective*. Every one of those phrases in italics is used by Jacobs and Wright to describe life in the murderous slums of St. Louis, Missouri; every one also describes the world of the *Iliad*.

The city itself floats in the half distance, a dream world of order, where the warrior is not constantly under test, where he can rely on those who are around him and who love him. The marginalized gang members, shut out beyond its walls, can only look on with envy and loathing.

Violence in the warrior gang is a means to survive and prosper. Without violence they would shrivel and fade, beaten by the city, by the pointy heads and the Brahmins. Violence is only doing what justice requires them to do. Violence is their destiny. And it should come as no surprise that these gangs must also have their epics. "No one forgets who was killed where and for what purpose," the Berkeley sociologist Martín Sánchez-Jankowski wrote. "Some Chicano gang members can tell you who was killed twenty years ago, before they were born, because this history has been passed down to them, these members have attained a degree of immortality, which mutes the fear of death and much of its inhibiting power." The gangs treasure *kleos aphthiton*, deathless glory, because in their vulnerability and their transience, the way in which there is nothing beyond their bodies and the memory of their actions, they need it more than anyone who is lucky enough to live in the law-shaped, law-embraced, wall-girdled city.

There is a code of conduct within the gang, as there is among the Greeks. Neither rape nor fighting with weapons was allowable within any of the thirty-eight gangs studied by Sánchez-Jankowski. The same kind of sanction exists within the Greek camp, although the natural fissiveness of all gang life is reflected there too. Achilles and his men come within a whisker of leaving Agamemnon's coalition. Nevertheless, there is a rawness in modern gang life and their talk—the gang term for a gaping wound is "a pussy"—from which Homer holds back. The LA gang world takes delight in the explicit elision of sex and violence, dominance and abuse, in a way that Homer buries and dignifies. The latent sexuality that is threaded through the poems never quite breaks the surface. Homer can be horrifyingly direct and concrete but is never ugly, as if the language has been washed and cleansed in the centuries over which the poems evolved. The trash talk of the Greeks on the beach is conveyed in terms that could be heard in the halls at Pylos. The words of the desperate men in South Central LA and East St. Louis perform some archaeology on that Homeric language, stripping away its civility, exposing the body and the suffering beneath; but that should not be seen as some kind of return to truth. Homeric truth, the meaning of Homer, is about the integration and fusion of qualities, the acquired wisdom of Homer knowing warrior rage intimately but seeing and hearing it through the words of the city.

For the Greeks, the great urban civilizations of the Mediterranean lay temptingly and glitteringly to the south, and you might wonder why, of all the places they might have chosen for their encounter with the city, Troy became Homer's focus. Is there any evidence that in the years of the Greek arrival, in the centuries around 2000 BC, Troy was the site worth sacking?

It was certainly not the richest, biggest or most powerful city of the Near East. Seen from the churning dynamos of money and power in Egypt and Mesopotamia, or from the great port cities of the Levant, Troy, on the far northwestern corner of Anatolia, can have looked like little more than a regional outpost of the urban world, a place that did indeed have a citadel and a lower city, but which was nevertheless on the very margins of the urban universe. But seen from the other direction, "in the eyes of its northern neighbours," as the Oxford and Sheffield archaeologists Andrew and Susan Sherratt memorably put it, "Troy must have been the brightest light on the horizon." It sat at one of the great crossroads of antiquity, performing the role later filled by Byzantium-Constantinople-Istanbul, controlling the routes between both the Aegean and the Black Sea and Anatolia and southeast Europe. The persistent north winds that blow across windy Troy, and a steady north–south current through the Dardanelles, meant that no sail-driven ship could make its way north there. Every cargo had to be landed. Every precious object coming west from Anatolia of necessity passed through this four-point pivot. Every movement from the north into the Mediterranean, and every Mediterranean desire to reach the Danube, the gold of Transylvania, the great rivers of the Pontic steppe and the copper mines that lay beyond them, or the metals coming from the Caucasus—all had to come through Troy.

The great Trojan treasures found by Heinrich Schliemann are now in Russia, where they were taken by the Soviets at the end of World War II. The silver and gold vessels, the bronze, the jewelry and the astonishing carved stone axes were buried in Troy perhaps as early as 2400 BC or as late as 1800 BC. Schliemann named what he found "Priam's Treasure," and from the very beginning was ridiculed for imagining that the levels of the city in whose ashes they emerged, Early Bronze Age Troy II, a thousand years or more before the conventional date of the Trojan War, could have had anything to do with Homer's Trojan king.

But just as at Mycenae, Schliemann's suggestion is worth considering. He had found a burned layer along with a gate and a tower, and considered them "the ruins and red ashes of Troy." In just the same way, his assistant Wilhelm Dörpfeld later settled on Troy VI, destroyed in about 1300 BC, and the Cincinnati archaeologist Carl Blegen came down in favor of Troy VIIa, which came to an end soon after 1200 BC. That remained the modern consensus under the huge German excavations from 1988 to 2003 led by Manfred Korfmann. But, as the British archaeologist Donald Easton has written, these were "three different sets of material evidence all supposed to prove the same identification and authenticate the same

Sophia Schliemann, aged twenty-two, wearing
"The Jewels of Helen," Athens 1874.

event." There is nothing to associate Homer with any archaeological remains at Troy. The only pointer toward a date around 1200 BC is the guess made by Herodotus in his history. But his guesses, and those of other classical Greeks, were stabs in the dark at a time when no one knew how to date the distant past. There is certainly no better reason to associate Homer with the Troy of about 1200 BC than with a city a millennium earlier. And if finds are anything to judge by, the later Troys seem to have been poorer than the city Schliemann identified as Priam's. Just as it is possible to imagine that the warriors in the Shaft Graves at Mycenae are themselves not the ancestors of the Homeric heroes but their sons and grandsons, there is nothing inherently unlikely in Schliemann's suggestion that the Trojans of about 2000 BC were living in the city to which the Greeks laid siege.

Nothing found in later levels of Troy can in any way match what Schliemann found here. It was a mass of gold and silver: six gold bracelets, two gold headdresses, one gold diadem, four golden basket-earrings, fifty-six golden shell-earrings, and 8,750 gold beads, sequins and studs. The jewelry was probably made in Troy. A great deal of evidence for smelting and casting has been found in the city. But these treasures are also signs of Troy's connections north and south. The tin the Trojans used for their bronzes probably came from Afghanistan. The beautiful golden basket-shaped earrings which Schliemann found are identical to others that have been found in Ur in Mesopotamia. There is amber here from Scandinavia, even a bossed bone plaque of a kind found at Castelluccio in Bronze Age Sicily.

Troy was the great entrepôt at the interface of the northern and southern Bronze Age worlds. The only way that Afghan tin and the Mesopotamian ways of working gold could have made their way to Bronze Age Transylvania and Hungary was through the Trojan gateway. No equivalent of Troy existed farther north or west. Only the palace center at Knossos in Crete could rival the extent of Troy in the centuries after 2000 BC. Just as the Vikings and the Crusaders would later lust after the riches of Byzantium and Constantinople, the Greeks longed for Troy.

Another treasure, now in the Boston Museum of Fine Arts, and with an obscure history, provides yet more spectacular hints at what any Greeks, or proto-Greeks, might have found at Troy if they had arrived there in the centuries around 2000 BC. The Boston treasure seems to have come from "northwest coastal Turkey," the province of Troy itself. It was made in about 2300 BC and consists of the gold ornaments to be buried with a noble woman: heavy lion-headed gold bangles, sun and moon disks to decorate a dress or headdress, golden pins, hair rings and diadems, finger-rings and gold ribbons.

These objects add to the reality of early Trojan glamour, but the most intriguing aspect of them is that they are probably Egyptian or made by an Egyptian craftsman who had come to Troy, perhaps bringing Egyptian gold, to decorate a queen of Troy in a way she knew she deserved. He brought with him the motifs of the crouching lions and the lotus flower which were familiar at home in the Egyptian Old Kingdom, and which came north trailing clouds of imperial glory.

Of all the objects that might be thought contemporary with the arrival of the Greeks in the world of cities, none can match the dazzling, hieratic power of the four Trojan hammer-axes that are now in Moscow. They are wonderful, high-polish, metal-mimicking, power-concentrating objects, three in a kind of jade, one in beautiful, gold-flecked Afghan lazurite.

They were stolen by Schliemann in 1890, the last year of his life, from the part of the site at Hisarlik that belonged to his rival and enemy, the English diplomat and antiquarian Frank Calvert.

But the squalor of that recent history is somehow appropriate. Schliemann named his son Agamemnon and in that choice declared himself the heir of "the greediest, most possession-loving of men." You only have to look at these hammer-axes to feel some kind of desire to own them. Their smooth, cool solidity, the creamiest of surfaces in the hardest of materials, was surely designed for display and allure, even for envy. The beauty of violence is embedded in the ritual of their presence. Look at them with any kind of object-lust, and you will find yourself looking through the eyes of Agamemnon.

Here in these objects, smuggled out of Turkey by Schliemann, legitimately wanted by the Turks, held on to by the Germans, hidden by the Nazis, taken by the Russians, then hidden again for almost fifty years, now also claimed by the distant heirs of Frank Calvert, you can see, far more than in the dusty, abused walls of Hisarlik, exactly what the marauding Greeks were after. Everything here concentrates a power which it then emanates. This is beauty and exoticism as instruments of control, embodying the core function of a great city, drawing in the rich and strange, then displaying it as a sign of dominance.

If the plain on which the Greeks are camped is the zone of severance and "the pitiless bronze," the city is the realm of jointness and connection, a place for weaving. In Troy, woven cloth becomes the medium for Homer's story. And in that detail there is an astonishing linkage between the archaeology of Troy and the city portrayed in the *Iliad*. From Schliemann onward, archaeologists have found powerful evidence of an almost unparalleled scale of cloth-making in the city, at all levels of Trojan society. In the ashes of Troy II, which Schliemann identifed as Priam's city, he found a small round clay box and in it the remains of a linen fabric decorated with tiny blue-green faience beads and a spindle full of thread. Carl Blegen in the 1930s found hundreds of tiny gold beads around the remains of a loom that had been set up with a half-finished cloth on it. And in Troy as a whole, these early levels of the city have produced over ten thousand clay spindle whorls, small weights attached to a spindle, whose momentum helped the process of spinning. It is a historical truth that Troy spun and wove.

When Helen first appears—the woman at the heart of the story, the Greek who was stolen by Paris the Trojan prince, whose infidelity began the war, who has come to love the Trojans but still longs for her homeland, who feels guilt and passionate desire for Paris but regret for the home and family in Greece she lost, who is in other words an amalgam of severance and connection—she is in the hall of her house weaving.

On her loom is "a great cloth" that is called *marmareën* in some versions, in others *porphyreën*. These are powerful, laden words, both intimately connected with her history and with the sea. *Marmareos* can mean "gleaming or twinkling like sunlit, wind-stirred water;" *porphyreos* "heaving," "surging like a sea swell," "gushing like blood," "pouring in like death in battle," "lurid like a rainbow," which for the Greeks was a portent of bad things to come, or "purple like the ink of the cuttlefish." It is as if Homer concentrated in those phrases the whole sea-tragic story of the war, and Helen's own catastrophe within it. Into the weft of her cloth, of a double fold, she is working many woven images "of the endless bloody struggles/the horse-taming Trojans and the bronze-armed Greeks/had suffered for her sake at the god of battle's hands."

Helen, even as she remembers the source of her grief, becomes like Homer the weaver of the tale. As he tells it, she is weaving it. Dressed in shimmering linen, with two of her attendant girls beside her, she goes to the ramparts of the city, where the old men, singing like cicadas in the treetops, look at her and see in her face "how terribly like the immortal goddesses she is to look on," that pun on the destruction that beauty can bring embedded in the Greek. Then, amid the horror of war, looking down from the closed ramparts at the armies drawn up below them on the open geometries of the battlefield, Priam, the king of Troy, does the beautiful thing, drawing Helen near to him, binding her in, weaving the reassurances of civility around her.

> Come over here, where I am, dear child, and sit down beside me,
> To look at your husband of time past, your friends and your people.
> I am not blaming you: to me the gods are blameworthy
> Who drove upon me this sorrowful war against the Achaians.

This is love as a kind of weaving, a bringing together of the things that war has separated. The shuttle of the weaver travels to and fro, but the blade merely plunges in. The making and maintaining of a city is a multiple act, reflexive and responsive, in the way that the killing of an enemy, the one-way journey of a soul out through the teeth and down to Hades, could never be. That is why the offering that the Trojans make to the great goddess Athene is made of cloth.

> The queen herself goes down to the vaulted treasure chamber where her robes are, richly embroidered, the handwork of women from Sidon, on the far eastern shores of the sea, whom Paris himself has brought from Sidon, as he sailed over the wide sea on that journey on which he brought back high-born Helen . . . The best and the thickest with the finest embroideries, which shine like a star, gleaming and brilliant, they take as an offering to Athene.

These are the treasures of the innermost place in Troy, the *thalamos*. These are its essential materials. It is a place of women and children, rich with fineness brought from the east, from the great urban civilizations of which Troy was the farthest outpost, far to the northwest, of their heartland in West Asia and Egypt. Here too, Homer is describing the meeting of worlds. This is what lies at the heart of the distant towers seen from the Greek camp on the shore, and it is here that the poem demonstrates its love and admiration for the marvelousness of women and womanliness.

In the Greek camp, women are traded as commodities. A woman and a tripod are put up in one lot as a prize for a chariot race, where a tripod is thought to be worth twelve oxen and a good serviceable maid-of-all-work four. That is not the atmosphere in Troy or in the most erotic scene in the *Iliad*, where Hera, the queen of the gods, prepares herself for love. Troy is much closer than the Greeks to the gods. There is a shared atmosphere between the city and Olympus, and the beauty of cloth, the essentially Trojan material, slides easily over into heaven. Alongside the delicious ointments with which Hera burnishes her body, she dresses slowly, seductively. It all happens inside her private chamber on Olympus, the doors closed with a secret bar, a female inwardness. She smoothes her body with exotic oils, the perfume drifting down from heaven in a mist of scented rain over the surface of the earth, while around her shoulders she wraps the "ambrosial robes" that Athene has made for her. They are smooth and satiny, with many figures embroidered on them, and she pins them across her breast with a golden brooch, circling her waist with a sash, before borrowing from Aphrodite, the goddess of love, the magic breastband which has woven into it all the hidden powers of longing and desire, "the whispered words that can steal the heart from any man." Weaving knows secrets which the heartless bronze could never hope to grasp.

There is a wariness in Homer about these delicious feminized delights of the city. They are not from the world of the warrior on the plain. When Nastes of the Karians, one of the Trojan allies from elsewhere in Anatolia, turns up for battle like a girl for a party, in golden clothes, "poor fool," he is soon dead: "He goes down under the hands of the swift-running Ajax and fiery Achilles strips him of his gold in the river." It is a wet, messy killing as Achilles, the agent of nature, takes his revenge.

Alongside pathetic Nastes is Paris, whose lust was the cause of the war, and who is now an empty urban fop, a pretty boy, beautiful, woman-crazed, a Hollywoodized warrior, happier in scented rooms, in bed with his beauty, than out fighting where his city might need him to be. His helmet is embellished with a richly embroidered chin strap, with which he is very nearly choked to death by a Greek, before a god rescues him and whisks him away to his boudoir. Homeric distrust of the potential for unmanliness in the city, whose beauties and order are nevertheless deeply desirable, is never far beneath the surface.

These polarities sharpen as the war deepens. The Greeks become increasingly animalistic. The Trojans are increasingly identified with the great walls that will save them from the savages at their gates. Group battle scenes give way to a sequence of individual tragedies. The shedding of blood is now close-focus. Dark underlayers bloom, and a persistent suggestion heaves up, just beneath the surface, that these men are cannibals.

Something of this has been there from the start. Agamemnon has said that the Greeks should not hesitate to kill Trojan babies. Zeus accused Hera of wanting to walk in through the gates of Troy and eat Priam and his children and the other people there, to take them raw, to glut her anger. But by the middle of the poem, the levels of body-abuse have steepened and animality has entered the battle.

Idomeneus stabs Erymas straight through the mouth with the pitiless
bronze, so that the metal spearhead smashes its way clean up through
the brain, and the white bones splinter,
And the teeth are shaken out as he hits him and both eyes fill up
With blood, and as he gapes he spurts blood through his nostrils
And his mouth, and death's dark cloud closes in about him.

The Myrmidons, the men Achilles has brought here from Phthia, are

like wolves, who tear at raw flesh,
in whose hearts battle-rage knows no end,
who have brought down a great antlered stag in the mountains,
and then feed on him, till their lips and cheeks are running with blood,
and who then move off in a pack, the crowd of them,
to drink from a spring of dark water,
lapping with their narrow tongues along the black edge of the water,
belching up the clotted blood, their bellies full and their hearts unshaken.

The Greeks begin to lose the fight. Achilles refuses to stir from his
tent. His beloved Patroclus takes his armor and wears it so that the Trojans might think Achilles himself has returned to the battle. The trick
works, the Trojans take fright and Patroclus starts to push them back
from the ships. But he goes too far; Hector kills him, and he lies dead in
the dust. Standing over his body, in the midst of battle, Hector makes the
great statement of the city against the plain.

Patroclus, you have thought perhaps of devastating our city,
Of stripping from the Trojan women their day of freedom
and dragging them off in ships to the beloved land of your fathers.
Pea-brain! . . . Now vultures will eat your body raw.
Idiot! Not even Achilles can save you now.

The armies fight over the body of Patroclus with a new and horrible
intensity, a struggle that lasts for hundreds of lines. In the fight, the beautiful Trojan Euphorbus is killed by Menelaus, and his lovely hair, braided
with gold and silver, like the body of a beautiful wasp, is soaked and clotted

with blood, civilization drenched in war. Menelaus now, with the battle frenzy in him, is like a mountain lion that has caught a delicious cow, the best cow, and is "mauling the kill, gulping down the guts that are inward." Hector strips the armor from Patroclus, the glorious armor which Achilles had lent him, and drags at the body, meaning to cut the head from the shoulders "and give the rest to the dogs of Troy." He promises huge rewards to those who can drag back to the city the now naked body of Patroclus, who has become nothing but flesh, stripped of meaning, meat for the dogs and birds.

The Trojan warrior Hippothoos—the name means "Quickhorse"— tries to get the straps of his shield around the tendons in Patroclus's ankle so that he can pull him back to the dog-feast in the city, but Ajax shafts him in the head, and Quickhorse's brain "oozes out from the wound along the socket of the spear, all mingled with blood." In this horror flensing-yard scene, a Greek dies with a spear under the collarbone, a Trojan with a sword in the guts "so that he claws at the dust with his fingers," and another Greek with a spear in the liver under the midriff.

The desperate struggle is for the flesh of Patroclus, simply to possess his physical remains, the grisliest possible tug-of-war, stretching the body in the way people pull and stretch at an ox hide to make usable leather of it,

> with so many pulling, until the bull's hide is stretched out smooth,
> so the men of both sides in a cramped space tug at the body
> in both directions; and the hearts of the Trojans are hopeful
> to drag him away to Ilion, those of the Achaeans
> to get him back to the hollow ships.

On different warriors, the blood runs from their hands and feet, "as on some lion who has eaten a bullock." Menelaus is like a mosquito "who though it is slapped away from a man's skin, even / so, for the taste of human blood, persists in biting him." Hector, hanging on to the body of Patroclus like "a tawny lion who cannot be frightened away from a carcass he has in his claws," is desperate to pull the body back to Troy so that he can "cut the head from the soft neck and set it on sharp stakes." This is not your elegant, noble, neoclassical Homer. This is rawness itself. Bloodthirsty Arēs, the god of war, the metaphor not yet dead, has become the governing force in a battlefield that wants more than anything else to drink human blood.

This is the environment into which Achilles now drives, grief-mad from the death of Patroclus. He will not eat, as civilized men sit down and eat, but wants to feast on the body of Hector. Like a man with a rifle at a fairground booth, he pops out death to twenty-three Trojans in a row: a spear in the middle of the head, a spear through the side of the helmet, another in the head, one in the back, one in the back and out through the navel, one in the neck, one in the knees with a spear and then finishing him off with a sword, one with a spear, another with a sword, one with a sword in the liver, a pike in one ear and out the other ear, a sword in the head, a sword in the arm then a spear in the arm, beheading with a sword "and the marrow gushes from the neckbone," a spear in the belly and a spear in the back, and then seven men whose deaths are remembered only in their names.

As he wearies momentarily of killing, he takes twelve young men alive, to sacrifice on the pyre of Patroclus.

> These bewildered boys, dazed like fawns, he drags away
> And lashes their hands behind them with well cut straps,
> the very belts they wear around their tunics,
> And gives them to his companions to take to the hollow ships.
> Then straight off in, raging to kill again.

He is beyond humanity now and has become "an unlooked for evil." His sweetness and capacity for love have left him. To the pitiable Lycaon he talks with all the reason of a madman.

> Now there is not one who can escape death, if the gods send
> Him against my hand in front of Ilion, not one
> Of all the Trojans and above all the children of Priam.
> So, friend, you die too. Why moan about it?
> Patroclus is dead, who was better by far than you are.
> Do you not see what a man I am, how huge, how splendid
> And born of a great father, and the mother who bore me immortal?

Everyone has to die, so why don't you? "Die on, all of you," he tells the Trojans, "till we come to the sacred city of Ilion, you in flight, and me killing you from behind."

Even as the universe of the battlefield becomes a careless and pitiless place, the allure and goodness of the besieged city become ever more precious. This is where the grand spatial geometry of the poem comes to its sharpest point. Achilles is the untrammeled world of the plain. "I will not leave off my killing of the proud Trojans," he says, "until I have penned them in their city." He is polarizing the world he controls until they are indeed all running and shuffling toward the high, wide walls Poseidon built for them—all except Hector, their champion, who must remain out on the plain with his killer.

Homer binds the Trojans to the physical facts of their city. Priam, Hector's father, the human embodiment of Troy's virtues, becomes coterminous with the city's walls and gates.

> The aged Priam takes his place on the god-built bastion,
> And looks out and sees, gigantic Achilles, where before him
> The Trojans run in their hurry and confusion, no war strength
> In them. He groans and descends to the ground from the bastion
> And beside the wall sets to work the glorious guards of the gateway:
> "Hold the gates wide open in your hands, so that our people
> in their flight can get into the city, for here is Achilles
> close by stampeding them."

This is the Iliadic confrontation at its sharpest. The city gates must close the Trojans in while Achilles is out in the plain, "fierce with the spear, strong madness in his heart and violent after glory." Everything in the *Iliad* comes into pincer-intimacy in these lines. The warriors join their "beloved parents, wives and children" inside the gates, "For they dare wait no longer outside the walls and the city" because on the plain Achilles is running free and dangerous across the open ground. Only Hector, the isolated Trojan, remains outside the walls, "shackled by destiny," awaiting the climactic meeting with the inhuman violence of the gang-man Achilles.

Metaphorical geography has the poem in its grip here. This is not the meeting of Achilles and Hector; it is the deathly confrontation of two ways of understanding the world. The key words clang through the poetry:

"city," "battlements," "walls," "Ilion," "gates," "crowded," "city," "wall" and "city" again, all within twenty lines of the beginning of book 22, and all set against that other world, the flatlands, the open plain, the *pedion*, over which Achilles runs like a prizewinning chariot horse, half-human, gleaming, looking like the Dog Star, a beacon of hate, sheathed in metal, the bronze in which he seems to be made shining brighter than any other star, a being radiant with horror, bringing evil and pain to men.

Homer never seems more real or more terrible than when Priam stands on his walls and talks pleadingly down to his son Hector standing outside the gates below him. Hector is terrifyingly alone, when the understanding of Trojans is that community is safety. "Come into the walls, my child," Priam says to him, "so that you might save Trojan men and Trojan women."

And then the old king makes a speech of Shakespearean poignancy and power.

> I have looked upon evils
> And seen my sons destroyed and my daughters dragged away captive
> And the chambers of marriage wrecked and the innocent children taken
> And dashed to the ground in the hatefulness of war, and the wives
> Of my sons dragged off by the accursed hands of the Achaians
> And myself last of all, my dogs in front of my doorway
> Will rip me raw, after some man with a blow of the sharp bronze
> Spear, or with spearcast, has torn the life out of my body;
> Those dogs I raised in my halls to be at my table, to guard my
> Gates, who will lap my blood in their savagery and anger
> And then will lie down in my courts. For a young man all is decorous
> When he is cut down in battle and torn with the sharp bronze, and lies
> Dead, and though dead all that shows about him is beautiful; but when
> an old man is dead and down, and the dogs mutilate
> The grey head and the grey beard and the parts that are secret,
> This for all sad mortality is the sight most pitiful.

The dogs eating his genitals, like blood on the gold-laced hair, is Priam's vision of the triumph of Achilles, the triumph of the gang over the city, the anarchy of violence over the generations of people and the bonds which tie them. Hector's mother, Hecabē, from the parapet above, holds out her breasts to him, bared and open. "Sweet branch," she calls to him, "child of my bearing," "look upon these and obey. From inside the wall beat off this grim man."

Hector's sense of honor, his debt to his city, will not allow him to go inside "the lovely citadel," and the fatal race begins. He and Achilles run round and round the walls, Hector in flight, Achilles in pursuit. It is like a dream, Homer says, when your running brings you no closer to your prey, nor takes you farther from your terror-pursuer; and it is a dream hell out on the plain, where there can only ever be one destiny. Sometimes Hector shelters under the walls, but Achilles gets between him and the wall "and forces him to turn back into the plain."

With unrelenting consistency, Homer applies his geography: city is goodness and connection, plain is horror and terror; city is Hector's weakness, plain Achilles's strength; city is the realm of the Trojan families, their women and children, while the plain belongs to Achilles alone—during this climax of grief the other Greeks have disappeared from view.

When finally Hector pauses, tricked by Athene, Achilles catches up with him and they talk. Achilles plunges for cannibalism. I want, he says, "to hack your meat away and eat it raw for the things that you have done to me." There can be no surprise. Achilles spears Hector in the soft part of the neck, just where the armor opens a little white mouth of skin, "and clean out through the tender neck goes the point." After killing him, he abuses Hector's body by dragging it *fast* behind his chariot. Hector's hair and head are tumbled and wrecked in the dust, and this physical action is the emblem of the gang-man's triumph, the imposition on the man of the city of the dirt of the plain.

With Hector's death the city's fabric is irreparably torn. Hector's mother casts aside her "shining veil." His wife, Andromachē, does not at first hear the news. She is weaving a cloth in the inner room of her high house, a red folding robe with figures embroidered on it, not unlike the cloth Helen had been working so many thousands of lines ago. Andromachē calls out to her handmaidens to prepare a bath for Hector, for when he comes back from the fighting. Then she hears the mourning and wailing of the other women, and the shuttle with which she had been weaving drops from her hand. Running to the ramparts, she sees Hector's body dragged around the city walls, his head in the dirt, Achilles triumphant. She collapses, "gasping the life breath out of her," while all the woven things fall from her, the circlets around her head and breast, the cap she is wearing, even as the threads of

Troy tighten around her and "her husband's sisters and the wives of his brothers hold her up among them." In their house, she then remembers, there are all kinds of clothing, "fine-textured and pleasant, wrought by the hands of women," ready for Hector. "All of these I will burn up in the fire's blazing," Andromachē says. "They are no use to you." The woven and the severed; the heart of Homer's meaning.

The *Iliad* might have ended there, with the victory of the plain over the city, but it doesn't. Troy is about love, children and home. Its lifeblood is in the virtues of human community, of not claiming the ultimate against your enemy but finding it in you to say that, whatever he has done, humanity is shared. Troy is a desire for wholeness, a desire that wholeness might survive the necessary violence, that there is no "tragedy of necessity."

The poem ends before Troy falls, but Homer orchestrates something subtler and richer than the hideousness of any military triumph. After Achilles kills Hector, the whole of the city goes into horrified despair and mourning. The women wail, the men cover themselves with dung scraped up from the streets. This moment of hopelessness is the pit of the poem. Achilles is still threatening to eat Hector's body raw. It looks as if everything the city enshrines means nothing in the teeth of the Greeks' triumph. Priam resolves to go to their camp across the plain to find Achilles and beg him for the body of his son.

The old king slowly prepares and gathers carts full of the best that Troy can offer, including beautiful cloths: robes, mantles, blankets, cloaks and tunics, as if wanting to drown Achilles in the woven. But that is the point. Priam is going to take the city out into the plain. That has been the place where in book after book, death after death, the wrong thing has been done. Priam's journey is a kind of healing laid across that theater of horror. He travels slowly, at night, with his mule carts; no heroic northern chariots here. He comes at last into the shelter of Achilles's camp, and without announcement the old king kneels down next to Achilles, clasps his knees and "kisses his hands, the terrible man-slaughtering hands, the hands that have shed so much blood, the blood of his sons." That old man's kiss is the moment of arrival. Achilles thinks of his own father in Phthia and comes to understand something beyond the world he has so far inhabited. Both men give way to grief.

> Priam weeps freely
> For man-killing Hector, throbbing, crouching
> Before Achilles's feet as Achilles weeps himself
> Now for his father, now for Patroclus
> And their sobbing rises and falls in the house.
>
> Food is cooked for them, mutton souvlaki.
>
> They reach down for the good things that lie at hand
> And when they have put aside desire for food and drink
> Priam gazes at Achilles marvelling now how tall he is,
> And how beautiful
> And Achilles looks at the nobility of the old king
> And listens to his words.

They gaze at each other in silence, and that exchange of admiring looks is the *Iliad*'s triumph. Priam has brought the virtues of the city into Achilles's heart. Hector will now be returned to his father and will be buried with dignity outside the city. In that way, Troy has won the war. Achilles, the man from the plains, has absorbed the beauty of Priam's wisdom, of his superhuman ability to admire the man who has killed his sons, and from the mutuality and courage of that wisdom, its blending of city and plain, a vision of the future might flower. Achilles will soon be dead, Troy will soon be broken, the Trojan men will soon be slaughtered, Priam among them, horribly murdered by Achilles's own son, their women abused and enslaved, but here, in poetry, in passing, a better world is momentarily—or in fact everlastingly—seen.

11 · HOMER'S MIRROR

It is possible—just—to look at Homer the other way around, and to hear the story of the Greeks arriving in the Mediterranean not as the Greeks told it in Homer but as the inhabitants of the literate, bureaucratic, authoritarian civilizations of the Mediterranean littoral told it themselves.

Nothing survives that describes Achilles or Odysseus directly, but there is a handful of Egyptian, Hittite and Hebrew texts that deal with people and habits occupying precisely the culture space of Homer's Greeks: northern Indo-European warriors arriving in a world where they do not belong, where they seem like barbarians, people who don't quite know how to behave. These unsympathetic versions of the Homeric story are strangely unsettling. Suddenly here is Achilles as his enemies might have seen him; Odysseus described by the smart, rich, complacent city-folk; Greek heroism as gang hooliganism; the Greek habit of woman-theft as nothing but rape; the beautiful volubility of the Homeric warrior looking pompous and absurd. Here, in this new light, are the Homeric tales with "Homer"—the dignity, understanding and tragic beauty of the poems—stripped out of them.

The Tale of Sinuhe is a short poetic biography of an Egyptian civil servant. It is a miraculous survival, the oldest version preserved on a reused roll of papyrus, buried in the tomb of a government official in the Egyptian city of Thebes on the west bank of the Nile in about 1800 BC. Probably looted from the tomb, it found its way to a London auction room in AD 1843, and versions of it are now preserved on fragments of papyrus in the British Museum and in Berlin. It had been popular in Egypt up to about 1000 BC, but until the Victorian Egyptologists deciphered it, no one had read Sinuhe's story for three thousand years.

It is from almost exactly the moment the Greeks were arriving in the Mediterranean, piratical, violent men, hungry for the gold that soon enough would appear on the bodies and in the graves at Mycenae, but comes from a frame of mind perfectly opposed to theirs. This elegant, melancholic verse novel from the richest culture in the ancient world may be the contemporary of the first versions of the *Iliad* and the *Odyssey*, but it loves nothing about them.

Sinuhe's Egypt is a huge state structure. He is part of the great service industry attending to the god-pharaoh's well-being, a court official—"a writing-man" is the Egyptian term—and a bureaucrat. It was the best possible job he could have. "Be a scribe," a contemporary papyrus instructed its young readers. "Your limbs will be sleek, your hands will grow soft. You will go forth in white clothes, honoured, with courtiers saluting you."

The Homeric assumption that suffering and conflict lie at the heart of existence, that life is essentially uncomfortable, is simply absent from Sinuhe's world. His life is framed around repetitiveness, stability, normality, precision and security. Everything is measured and known. His tale begins on "the 7th Day of the 3rd Month of the Nile Flood Season, in the 20th year of the Pharaoh's reign." The rough estimates of Homeric time, the wide, veering guesses at the date of the Homeric stories, the generations that pass unrecorded—all that belongs to a different conceptual universe. For Sinuhe—whatever the historical truth—the pharaohs had ruled as far back in time as it was possible to imagine. Peace had prevailed, one pharaoh had succeeded another, cosmically great, unaddressably powerful, each handing the throne to his successor in a single direct linear sequence. The heart of happiness for these Egyptians was submission to that authority. The pharaoh "makes those born with him plentiful," Sinuhe says. "He is unique, god-given. How joyful this land, since he has ruled. He extends his borders. He is the lord of kindness, great of sweetness. Through love he has conquered. His city loves him more than its own members." Set that alongside the description of Agamemnon and his gift-giving in the *Iliad*, and you suddenly see him as a would-be pharaoh, a provincial satrap with ambitions beyond his reach, vulgarly attempting pharaonic status in the face of Achillean integrity.

The life of the Egyptian poor was miserable. They could expect to die when they were thirty-five, thousands lived in workhouses, obliged to sweat out their days in forced labor camps for the pharaonic regime and its monumental ambitions. But above them a bureaucratic middle class, Sinuhe's class—perhaps 1 percent of the population was literate— managed the culture of continuity. In their linen-dressed elegance, the sense of overwhelming crisis and disruption that colors the deepest levels of the Homeric world was not even considered. Life was continuity. There was no need to be heroic, nor did the Greek hunger for honor play any part. For the ancient Egyptians, goodness consisted of service to pharaonic authority. As there was no distinction between that authority and the government of the universe, this life could be considered a kind of anteroom to heaven. The more silent and stable it could be made, the better.

Sinuhe loves the white linen he wears every day, and all the order in the Residence where he works. He is no self-sufficient hero. No existential crisis or anxiety about his individual identity or destiny ever pursues him. Sinuhe is a "Follower" and "True Acquaintance" of the pharaoh. His life is defined by the authority he serves. One of his tasks is to look after the pharaoh's children, but at the moment his story begins, this steady, beautifully organized life is destroyed by a flash of panic. He hears something, a report of the old pharaoh's murder in the palace. He thinks he should not have heard it, and worried in this totalitarian state that he might somehow be caught up in the repercussions, or even held responsible, he runs for his life, away from Egypt, north to the borders of Syria, and on across them, traveling at night, hiding at the edges of fields until at last he comes to a part of the world called Upper Retjenu.

It is the Egyptian name for Lebanon and maybe for the places beyond it. But Retjenu as a word is not a Semitic form; it does not belong in the Near East. It is Indo-European, probably from the language spoken by the Lycians, warrior inhabitants of southwest Anatolia, known to Homer as allies of the Trojans. Sinuhe, in other words, has found himself far out in the wilds surrounded by the warrior culture of the north. He has arrived in the land described by Homer. It is not the sort of world he is used to. It is a good country, he says, with figs and grapes, more wine than water, honey and oil, with all kinds of fruit on its trees. Barley is there, and emmer-wheat, and "numberless are its cattle of all kinds." It is called Iaa, the "rushy place," damp, fertile, rich in pastures, a million miles from the Egypt into which he was born.

The experience is horrifying at first. "This is the taste of death," Sinuhe says, panicking at the disorder around him. All the calm of Egypt was gone. But then Sinuhe falls in with a chieftain, a warrior prince, a Diomedes or Sarpedon, and the chieftain does what heroes do in these circumstances: gives him plenty of cooked meat and wine, and delicious roast birds. They go hunting together, and from the great herds of cattle without which the Indo-European chieftains felt naked he gives Sinuhe "milk in every cooked dish." The mark of Homeric civilization: beef in white sauce.

And so Sinuhe goes native. He abandons his white linen for armor. He turns warrior. His children become heroes, "each man subjugating his tribe." Battle, which was absent from the life of an Egyptian bureaucrat, something that happened out here in the rawness of life on the frontiers, away from the deep calm of the central Egyptian state, now becomes the norm. He plunders cattle and carries off men and women as slaves. He kills again and again, as the Indo-European hero must do, and he attains "high regard" in the heart of his lord and chieftain, who loves him, knowing his valor.

Then the crisis: the naturally fissive atmosphere of the Indo-European warrior band breaks into the open, and a situation not unlike the opening scenes of the *Iliad* suddenly erupts. As Sinuhe latter recalls:

> A hero of Retjenu came to provoke me in my tent;
> he was an unmatched champion who had conquered all the land.
> He said he would fight me, he planned to rob me, and had a mind to
>   plunder my cattle, on the advice of his tribe.

Honor, rivalry, dignity, the brutally assertive self, the demands of violence, the contempt for communality—suddenly you are in the world of the Greeks outside Troy, but portrayed in an Egyptian tale. It doesn't take much to imagine the shudder of anxiety in listeners at a party in Thebes one balmy evening in 1850 BC, just as the sun was setting over the western desert and the shadows were lengthening over the Nile. Did people out there really behave like this?

Sinuhe accepts the challenge, triumphs over the nameless hero, shooting him in the neck with an arrow and then killing him with his own ax, shouting his own vaunting war cry over the fallen hero's back. But he is still an Egyptian, asking, in one of the most resonant questions for this moment in human history: "What can establish the papyrus on the mountain?" That is also the great Homeric question. What place can civilization have in a world dominated by the brute geological facts of violence and dominance? How fragile are the fibers of papyrus when set against the great rock-thrusts of the heroic world? Could these two ways of being ever be compatible?

Sinuhe is so successful as an Indo-European warrior that he ends up with more cows than he knows what to do with. Even so, an everlasting longing for Egypt lingers in his heart. "What matters more than my being buried in the land where I was born?" he asks. Somehow, the new pharaoh hears of Sinuhe's longing, and soon enough an invitation arrives from him for Sinuhe to return to Egypt, where he will be honored and forgiven. Sinuhe gives his property in Retjenu to his eldest son and returns to Egypt, where he "touches the ground between the sphinxes" and comes face to face with the god-king he reveres.

"Act against yourself no more," the pharaoh tells him, and as he hears the words, Sinuhe feels himself reabsorbed into the fabric of Egyptian society. The king says "he shall not fear," and Sinuhe is re-created as a courtier. He abandons himself to the happiness of the king's grace, prostrating himself before the pharaoh. Here in "the enduring security of the state" is the beauty of order to which he is at last allowed to return. He is rewarded with the things he has been dreaming of all the years he was away in the Homeric world.

> I was appointed to the house of a prince
> And costly things in it, with a bathroom in it,
> And mirrors,
> Clothes of royal linen
> Myrrh and kingly fine oil
> With officials whom the king loved in every room
> And every serving man at his duty.
>
> The years were made to pass from my limbs
> I became clean shaven and my hair was combed

I was clad in fine linen
I was anointed with fine oil
I slept in a bed.

It is his majesty who has caused this to be done.
There is no other lowly man for whom the like was done.
I was in the favours of the king's giving
Until the day of landing came.

The "day of landing" was the Egyptian phrase for the moment of death, the time when a human being at last achieves the goal of a perfect life, and Sinuhe's return to Egypt is like a return to heaven. For all his adventuring, Egypt had originally made him what he was. Only there could he be himself again, and only by submitting to the Egyptian powers could his day of landing be good.

Our Odyssean frame of mind looks on that scene of Sinuhe's reabsorption into his native world as a moment not of triumph but of diminution, a surrender of the vital if agonized self to the emasculated certainties of a beautifully bathed, shaved, linen-coated "Follower." Was it really worth exchanging his florid Indo-European hair and beard, that fullness of self-assertion, for the bland comfort-soup of a happy "landing"? Or are we, as Homer's heirs, merely addicted to crisis? Why not accept with Sinuhe, and the profoundly impressive longevity of Egyptian civilization, that the world of white linen and pharaonic tyranny is a better place than the discomforts of Retjenu and the threatening behavior of "heroes"? Are those heroes not in the end exactly as the Egyptians saw them, little better than human hyenas, repetitively needing to establish their sexual, genetic dominance of the pack? Surely human life has more to it than the Homeric tragedy of necessity? Or to put it in a more Sinuhesque way: is that necessity really necessary? Why not accept the virtues of modesty and the realities of power?

No Homeric character could ever have behaved like Sinuhe or have thought that his destiny was so bound up with the blessing the pharaoh and his court could bestow on him. Sinuhe ends up with a single answer: it is better to be at home, to submit, to recognize that power is god. Across the whole of the *Iliad* and the *Odyssey*, there is nothing singular like this.

The Homeric view of the world is essentially traumatic and multiple. All is in contention; power is something to be fought for, not accepted; the gods themselves are at each other's throats; nature may stand there as a beautiful background, but it too is drenched in conflict and pain. The claims of individual triumph can never be reconciled with the claims of communal love and society. We live in the great and eternal war between those principles, *Timē* and *Aretē*, honor and virtue, self and other. Achilles sees that war as the source of human tragedy, Odysseus as the opportunity for self-advancement. And beyond them both stands Homer, the great voice of understanding, regarding us all, refusing to decide.

The Tale of Sinuhe is a mirror image of Homer, exploring the polarities of city and warrior-world from the opposite direction. But there are also parallels between them. Sinuhe could be seen as the Egyptian Odysseus, the hero thrust out into the wilds, gaining wisdom there, doing well even in his exile, finally returning, full of apprehension, to the place he longs to call home. And in one marvelous detail, they are clearly part of the same thought-world. Both, on reaching home, become themselves again by having a bath.

The bath for Homer is always a gesture of welcome, the physical metaphor for the domestic embrace. Perhaps the most famous bath in Greek antiquity is the one in which Clytemnestra murders Agamemnon on his return to Mycenae after the war. But that is not a Homeric story; it is the bleak invention of Aeschylus in the *Oresteia*. For Homer, whether it is the bathing of Odysseus after battle, or Telemachus on his visit to Nestor at Pylos, the bath is always beautiful and integrative, a moment of absorption.

Intriguingly, there is nothing uniquely Greek about this. The Homeric word for a bath, *asaminthos*, like hyacinth and labyrinth, comes from an unknown, non-Indo-European language spoken in the Mediterranean before the Greeks arrived there. It may have been the language of Minoan Crete. The unwashed Greeks coming down from the north borrowed the word as they borrowed the thing and the habit. The story of the hero returning home to the deliciousness of a bath is distributed all across the eastern Mediterranean and Mesopotamia. It is a shared symbol of homeliness and well-being. Gilgamesh, the ancient king of Uruk in south Iraq, who had also been journeying in the wilderness, in search of wisdom, cleansed its filth from his body as he came home to the city,

washing his long hair clean as snow in water . . . throwing off his furs
and letting the sea carry them away, so that his fair body could be seen.
Let the band around his head be replaced with a new one. Let him be
clad with a garment, as clothing for his nakedness. When he gets to his
city, when he finishes his journey, may his clothes show no sign of age,
but still be quite new.

When Jacob returns in Genesis to Canaan, he tells his household first
to "wash yourselves and change your clothes," because in this shared
Near Eastern culture, the thought-world to which the Homeric Greeks
were so anxious to belong, no homecoming could be complete without
the cleanness and sense of renewal that a bath can give you. Sinuhe, Gilgamesh, Jacob and Odysseus all soaked themselves in the same delicious
soapiness.

You can still find beautiful baths in the palaces on Crete and at Pylos,
Mycenae and Tiryns on the mainland. Some are adorned with fish and
the wavy lines of comforting water. Among the austere stoniness of those
excavated sites, the baths become emblems of the longing to which the
Homeric mind was prey. Nothing could be more inviting, more soaked in
the desire for peace and civilization in a troubled world. The bath stands
in opposition to Odysseus's sufferings on the open sea. Here the water
will merely lap at his limbs; the giant sea bream on the walls of the bath
are his cohabitants in their shared springwater pool, the painted sea-
waves no more than the memory of grief.

And so when Odysseus has at last made the frightening witch Circe
submit to his will, he can allow her maidservants, the "daughters of the
springs and the woods and the sacred rivers which run down to the sea,"
to prepare him a bath. One of these girls, he recalls,

brought in the water and lit a blazing fire under the big cauldron so that
the water grew hot. When the bright copper was boiling, she eased me
into the bath and washed me with water from the great cauldron, hot
and cold mixed as I desired, allowing it to run over my head and shoulders, washing the pain and weariness from my heart and limbs. When
she had washed me and rubbed me with oil, she dressed me in a warm
fleece and a shirt around my shoulders and led me to the hall, where she
had me sit on a silver-studded chair with a stool to rest my feet.

But there is this difference: lying in their baths, Sinuhe, Gilgamesh and Jacob could all know they were returning to a home they could trust. Singularity and obviousness cluster around their bathrooms. But Homer is subtler than the Egyptian, Mesopotamian or Hebrew storytellers, because complexity and multiplicity, the fusion and stirring of meanings, is central to his purpose. Odysseus, when slipping into the delicious, erotic balm of Circe's bath, is still years and miles from home, his "mind wandering, far away, lost in grim forebodings." Circe is only the illusion of home and love, the wish-fulfillment version to which the traveler will always succumb. Her bath is a taunt and a punishment. Odysseus—and his listeners—must wait for the real thing.

A sidelight equivalent to Sinuhe's is thrown on the Homeric Greeks in the astonishing archive of 30,000 cuneiform clay tablets recovered from the capital of the Hittites at Hattusa, near Bogaskale in central Anatolia. Contrasts and parallels abound here too. The Hittites were another Indo-European people who came south into Anatolia during the centuries after 2000 BC, infiltrating and then taking over the territory of the non-Indo-European Hatti, finally pushing on their southern frontier against the fringes of the great Mesopotamian powers and even the Egyptian empire.

Such close contacts with the ancient civilizations to the south meant that the Hittites adopted the literate, urbanizing habits of the Near East far earlier than the Greeks. By the time of the Shaft Graves at Mycenae, the Hittites were already running an enormous, bureaucratically organized empire, with a network of military roads strung across it, stretching from Lebanon to the shores of the Aegean.

They kept their records in both Hittite and Akkadian, the Babylonian language that had become the lingua franca of diplomacy and government across the whole region from central Anatolia to the Tigris and the mouths of the Nile. The clay cuneiform tablets found at Hattusa are the file copies retained by the Hittite foreign office after the original treaties, usually on bronze or occasionally silver or iron tablets, had been sent to the other parties.

They give glimpses of an embracing power-world which carries echoes of life in the palaces at Troy, the fifty sons and sons-in-law gathered around Priam, the overwhelming nature of inheritance and the sense of greatness rippling down from its kingly source. The quasi-medieval atmosphere at these gatherings could not be farther from the high-risk anarchy barely an inch below the surface at any meeting of the Greek chieftains. One Hittite treaty, as its tablet records, was concluded in a great and ceremonial meeting

> in the city of Urikina in the presence of Crown Prince Nerikkaili; Prince Tashmi-Sharumma; Prince Hannutti; Prince Huzziya; Ini-Teshshup, king of the land of Carchemish; Ari-Sharumma, king of the land of Isuwa; Amar-Mushen, uriyanni; Halpa-ziti, commander of the troops of the right; Prince Heshni; Prince Tattamaru; Prince Uppara-muwa, overseer of the golden grooms; Prince Uhha-ziti; Sahurunuwa, chief of the wooden-tablet scribes; Hattusa-Kurunta, general; Prince Tarhunta-piya; Lugal dLamaa, commander of the troops of the left; Ali-ziti, chief of the palace servants; Tuttu, chief of the storehouse; Palla, lord of the city of Hurma; Walwa-ziti, chief of the scribes; Alalimi, chief of the cupbearers; Kammaliya, chief of the cooks; and Mahhuzzi, chief of the offering officials.

Whether it is Victorian India, Tenochtitlan, medieval Bohemia, shogun Japan, the world of *The Leopard* or Bronze Age Anatolia, this is the air breathed in any court, dense with rank, title, glamor, precedence and surely a hint, here and there, of what is called, even now in palaces, Red Carpet Fever: excitement at being connected with the royal.

That self-importance surfaces in Homer in the overbrimming superciliousness of the Phaeacians, condescendingly welcoming the shipwrecked seafarer Odysseus to Alcinous's regal halls. The Phaeacians "never suffer strangers gladly." They don't like him much, nor he them. Even here, as he is accepting their hospitality, Homer gives him the traditional epithet he shares with Achilles and Arēs, the god of war: *ptoliporthos Odysseus* (city-ravaging Odysseus).

They guess he might be captain of a ship full of men who are *prēktēres*—an interesting word, with its origins in the verb for "to do," meaning that Odysseus comes over to the Phaeacians not as a nobleman who can play athletic games but as the leader of a band of practical, pragmatic practicers of things, merchants in other words, dealers, or as Robert Fagles translated it "profiteers," freebooters who blurred the boundary between trader and pirate. Nothing irks Odysseus more powerfully than the suggestion that he is merely a sea-robber or tradesman. Is he not a hero? Has he not fought at Troy? Has he not suffered at sea? But the suspicion won't go away. When he and his crew find themselves facing Polyphemus, the Cyclops, the same idea recurs. "Strangers, who are you?" the Cyclops asks them. "Where do you come from, sailing over the sea-ways? Are you trading? Or are you roaming wherever luck takes you over the sea? Like pirates?"

Perhaps this is a reflection in Homer of a reality that the poems do their best to conceal. Odysseus and the other Greek chieftains might think of themselves as noble kings, the fit subjects for epic. Homer does its best to portray them as that. The civilized states of the Mediterranean saw them as anything but. What were they but the "much-wandering pirates" Odysseus sometimes talks about, taking what they could from the wealth of the world around them, hugely status-rich in their own eyes, virtually status-less in the eyes of those they were coming to rob? It is exactly how Odysseus himself describes his behavior as he leaves Troy. "From Ilium the wind carried me," he tells the Phaeacians, "and brought me to the Cicones." This was a tribe, allied to the Trojans, who lived at Ismarus on the shore of the Aegean, somewhere north of Samothrace. "There I destroyed the city," he goes on quite straightforwardly, using a term to mean that nothing was left, "and killed the men. And from the city we took their wives and many possessions, and divided it among us, so that as far as I could manage, no man would be cheated of an equal share." It is one of the moments in which Homer coolly reveals the limitations of Odysseus's mind. Our hero thinks he is telling his hosts how excellently he behaved, ensuring that unlike Agamemnon he did not mistreat his men. But he is blind to the significance of the actions preceding this exemplary fairness, the piratical destruction of an entire city and the enslaving of its women.

The same uncertain status of the pirate-king lies behind one of Odysseus's most famous sleights of hand. He and his men are suffering at the hands of the Cyclops. The Cyclops wants to know who Odysseus is. In his answers, he says that his name is "Nobody." The Greek for that is either *outis*, which sounds a little like *Odysseus* if spoken by a drunk or slack-jawed giant; or *mētis*, which also sounds like the Greek word for cleverness, craftiness, skill or a plot. When Polyphemus calls for help, the other Cyclopes ask who has hurt and blinded him. "Nobody!" he answers, or "Cleverness!" and so his friends—and the audience—can only laugh.

It is a nifty trick, but the story means more. Odysseus is indeed a nobody, essentially homeless, for all the illusions of an Ithaca floating somewhere beyond the unreachable horizon. His own naming of himself as a Nobody is an oblique and dreamlike reflection of exactly what the Phaeacians think of him. He may be king of Ithaca, the son of Laertes, a man whose fame has reached the sky, but that is not how the world of the *Odyssey* treats him. Everywhere he arrives anonymous, not somebody but nobody. Even when he comes home, he is more beggar than king, unrecognized by wife, son, subject or retainer. That double status is at the heart of the *Odyssey*: it may describe a historical situation—the marginality of people who were heroes to themselves—but it also addresses a permanent human condition. My own world may cultivate me, ennoble me, even heroize me, but what possible significance beyond the confines of home can those labels have? What possible standing could Odysseus have "in the city of Urikina, in the presence of Crown Prince Nerikkaili"?

In about 1350 BC, a treaty was drawn up between the Hittite Great King and a man known as Huqqana. He was from Hayasa, a region on the frontiers of the Hittite empire, in northeastern Anatolia, in what would later become Armenia. Hayasa, in a way similar to the condition of Greece in the centuries after 2000 BC, was an agglomeration of tribal chiefs, with no overarching or supreme leader. Because of this, and because of its incipient and eruptive anarchy, it was not, as far as the Hittites were concerned, part of the civilized world. The Hittite Great King, who referred to himself as "My Majesty," had married off his sister to Huqqana in a form of political alliance, but there was anxiety in the air. How could he be sure that Huqqana, this man from beyond the borders of acceptability, would behave?

The expectations were not good. The Hittite king called his new brother-in-law "a low-born dog." Huqqana mustn't gossip, which he would be tempted to do: "Given that they now bring you up to my palace and that you hear about the customs of the palace it is important! You shall not divulge outside the palace what you know or what you hear."

More problematic was the question of sex.

> Furthermore this sister, whom I, My Majesty, have given to you as your
> wife, has many sisters from her own family as well as from her extended
> family. For us the Hittites, it is an important custom that a brother does
> not take his sister or female cousin sexually. It is not permitted. Who-
> ever does such a thing is put to death. Because your land is barbaric, it is
> in conflict [without law]. There a man quite regularly takes his sister or
> female cousin. But among the Hittites, it is not permitted.

Huqqana has to learn that he should treat women courteously and with
dignity, an instruction that brings with it echoes of the distinction in the
Iliad between Greek and Trojan treatment of women.

Then, strikingly in the middle of all this treaty language, the Great
King of the Hittites tells Huqqana a story, or at least reminds him of one,
which can't fail to drive the point home. Huqqana, when he came to the
palace, was to be careful around the women he met there. "When you see
a palace woman, jump out of the way and leave her a broad path." Did he
remember the story of Mariya, clearly someone who had once been close
to him, perhaps another chieftain from Hayasa?

> And for what reason did he die? Did not a lady's maid walk by and he
> look at her? But the father of My Majesty himself looked out of the win-
> dow and caught him in his offence, saying "You—why did you look at
> her?" So he died for that reason. The man perished just for looking from
> afar. So you beware.

Just as the *Tale of Sinuhe* reorients the Homeric vision of the hero and
allocates him effectively the role of thug, the story of Mariya, the Hayasa
warrior chief who dared look at one of the lady's maids of the Hittite
court, puts the skids under the bland assumption, underlying much of
that Iliadic world, that women were for the taking.

Other intriguing historical realities appear in these Hittite documents. They are late in this story. By the fourteenth century BC, the Mycenaean Greeks had established their palaces on the mainland, had become
at least administratively literate themselves and were now dominant in
Crete and across the Aegean. They had entered a form of existence that

had absorbed much of the organized state apparatus and mentality of the Mediterranean world. By now they were as Trojan as the Trojans.

All that, in the lightest of touches, is confirmed in the Hittite documents. In a treaty drawn up in about 1250 BC between the Great King of the Hittites and the king of Amurru, in northern Lebanon, the Great King, as ever, tells his treaty partner how to behave.

> If the King of Egypt is My Majesty's friend, he shall be your friend. But if he is My Majesty's enemy, he shall be your enemy. And the Kings who are my equals in rank are the King of Egypt, the King of Babylonia, the King of Assyria and the King of Ahhiyawa.

That last name should leap out at you. After many decades of acrimonious scholarly debate, it is now generally accepted that Ahhiyawa is the Hittite transcription of Achaea, the Homeric name for Greece, and that the king of Ahhiyawa's inclusion in this most distinguished list of the great powers of the late Bronze Age is a mark of the Mycenaean triumph. That great quasi-imperial status does not reflect the atmosphere of the *Iliad*, nor of Odysseus, the homeless, the wandering albatross of the southern sea. By the time these treaties were being drawn up, the Greeks were no longer the outsiders; they had become members of the Mediterranean power network.

Not that that peace prevailed. The margins of these states were ragged and contested, and the great kings were always planning and making moves against each other in the crush zones between their empires. On the western margins of Anatolia, where the king of Ahhiwaya could wield most power, he consistently troubled the allies of the Great King of the Hittites. At some time before 1400 BC, a Hittite ally in the far west of the Hittite zone of influence, Madduwatta, was attacked by a king of "Ahhiya" and driven out of his lands, at least until the Hittites came to his aid. When the old Hittite king died, his son wanted to remind Madduwatta of the service that had been done to him.

> The father of My Majesty saved you, together with your wives, your sons, your household servants and together with your infantry and your chariotry. Otherwise dogs would have devoured you from hunger. Even if you had escaped you would have died of hunger.

The most fascinating word in this extraordinary document is the name of the ruler of Ahhiya: he is called Attarissiya. That is not a Hittite name, nor is it exactly Greek, but it may well be what "Atreus" sounded like to a Hittite—the name in Homer of the father of Agamemnon and Menelaus, itself perhaps a derivative of *atrestos*, "the untrembling, the fearless."

From these few threads some kind of fabric can be woven, describing a tense, mutually suspicious and occasionally violent relationship between the Greeks and the Hittite empire. Attarissiya had invaded Hittite territory with foot soldiers and a hundred chariots, and had also fought along-side Madduwatta in an attack on Cyprus. Another warrior, the Greek king's brother, the Hittites called Tawagalawas or Tawakalawas, which is the way they might have heard the name of a Greek called Eteocles (which happens to be the name of Oedipus's son). A letter also survived in the foreign office archives in Hattusa, from a Greek they knew as Kagamunas or perhaps Katamunas, a name which has been interpreted as Kadmos, the greatest of the Thebans.

It is like a picture of the post-Homeric world, one that the rulers of the great Mycenaean palaces might have recognized, but surviving only in the most fragmentary and enigmatic of splinters. Part of this jagged Greek–Hittite boundary of the thirteenth century BC was a pair of places called in the documents "Taruisa" and "Wilusa." Hittite scholars are now certain that these are the names of places referred to by Homer as Troy and Ilios. They may be two places conflated in the *Iliad* or a region and its capital. In a treaty with the Great King of the Hittites, the king of Wilusa is addressed as Alaksandu. That is a Hittite version of a Greek name, Alexandros, the alternative name which the *Iliad* gives to Paris, Priam's son. By the time of these late documents, Troy had become a Greek-governed city, absorbed into the Greek world, at archaeological levels where shards of Mycenaean pottery have also been found. If there had ever been a Trojan war, it had already happened, and the Greeks had won.

The relationship remained tense between the Hittite king and the Greek prince at Troy, and the treaty includes some significant instructions sent out to this marginal kinglet from the imperial capital far to the east. The Hittite administration was keen to impose the written word as the medium of communication between them and the modern test of authenticity. "People are treacherous," the Great King told Alaksandu.

If rumours circulate, and someone comes and whispers to you "His Majesty is undertaking something to do you down, and will take the land away from you, or will mistreat you in some way," write about it to My Majesty. And if the matter is true, when I, My Majesty, write back to you, you shall not act rashly.

That sounds like an instruction from the urban to the oral world, from the literate Near East to a culture that had yet to think of writing as a central aspect of government. It is one of the great transitions of history—the Homeric horizon, caught at the very moment the Greeks were crossing it.

A third, suddenly reorienting view of these relationships appears in, of all places, the Old Testament. Just at the moment the Greek king Attarissiya was raiding Anatolia and Cyprus, in the thirteenth and twelfth centuries BC, and establishing settlements which archaeologists have been uncovering in the last few decades, the cities around Gaza in southern Canaan were taken and occupied by people whom the Jews called the Philistines. They had been drawn to the markets and the grassy downland of southern Palestine, where beautiful pear and almond orchards surround the mudbrick villages and where cattle and horses can graze on the clover and young barley of the open plains. Their lands—Philistia—are now the gentle, hilly farmland of southwestern Israel. "Philistine" in Hebrew means "the invader" or "the roller-in," and from the style of their rock-cut chamber tombs, the pottery they made once they had arrived in Canaan and from the form of their own names, it is clear that these Philistines, arriving from out of the west, were Mycenaean Greeks, cruising the Mediterranean seas, searching out new lands, ready to fight whomever they found there.

The war in Canaan between Greek and Hebrew was long and grievous, but at its symbolic climax, as depicted in the First Book of the Prophet Samuel, the readers are treated to one of the most hostile depictions of Homeric warrior culture ever written. The Philistines had taken up position on a hillside at Socoh in the rolling agricultural country of the Judean foothills, a few miles west of Bethlehem. A champion came out of the Philistine camp, a man called Goliath, to challenge the Israelites drawn up on the opposite hillside.

Goliath is a huge, clumsy, half-ludicrous, threatening and contemptible figure. He is, even in the earliest and least exaggerated manuscripts, six feet nine inches tall, wearing the full equipment of the Homeric hero: a bronze helmet on his head, bronze armor on his chest, bronze greaves on his legs and carrying a sword and dagger of bronze. Everything about him is vast. His armor weighs nearly 140 pounds, the head of his spear fifteen pounds.

Massively overequipped, a cross between Ajax and Desperate Dan, Goliath stands there shouting across the valley at his enemies:

> Why do you come out to do battle, you slaves of Saul? I am the Philistine champion; choose your man to meet me. If he can kill me in fair fight, we will become your slaves; but if I prove too strong for him and kill him, you shall be our slaves and serve us. Here and now I defy the ranks of Israel. Give me a man . . . and we will fight it out.

The stolidity of the Greek, his philistinism, his need to spell everything out, to put his own self-aggrandisement into endlessly self-elevating words—all of that comes out of Goliath like the self-proclaiming spout of a whale. But this is exactly what in the *Iliad* one Greek warrior after another liked and needed to do. Shouted aggression, the Homeric *haka*, was the first act of any Greek battle.

"When Saul and the Israelites heard what the Philistine said, they were shaken and dismayed." It was not in them to make the symmetrical response—you shout at me, I'll shout at you—which is one of the foundations of the Homeric system. And so a painful and faintly ludicrous asymmetrical situation developed. "Morning and evening for forty days the Philistine drew near and presented himself," standing there, twice a day for a month and a half, bellowing across the valley like a giant bronze cuckoo clock.

The shepherd boy David, the youngest of his family, whose brothers are in the Israelite host facing the Philistines, is told by his father, Jesse, to take some loaves and cream cheeses to their commander. He arrives there and to his amazement sees and hears Goliath shouting away. "Who is he," David asks, "an uncircumcised Philistine, to defy the army of the living god?" That is not a Greek question. A Greek would have understood what Goliath was saying, and would have responded by strapping on his armor. Defiance and the locking of horns was no more than a recognition of Homeric reality. When Saul, the king of the Jews, finally accepts that David might respond to the challenge of the Greek giant, he tries to dress him in his own armor. David accepts it meekly but then hesitates and proclaims his difference.

> "I cannot go with these because I have not tried them." So he took them off. And he picked up his stick, and chose five smooth stones out of the brook, and put them in a shepherd's bag which he had with him as a pouch. He walked out to meet the Philistine with his sling in his hand.

It is a version of the Homeric arming of the hero and the single-combat meeting of warriors, the *monomachia* between Paris and Menelaus, Hector and Ajax, Achilles and Hector, which anchors the whole of the Homeric experience. But this is more like a parody of it than a borrowing. The unprotected boy, with his shepherd's bag and stick, crouches down in the brook running between the two embattled hillsides, and with his fingers in the water, picks out the plain smoothness of five good stones. No love affair with bronze, no sharpness, no self-enlargement. In everything David does, and in every lack he suffers, there is one implied and overwhelming fact: the god of the Israelites. In his presence the difference between armor and armorlessness, bronze and flesh, is like smoke in wind.

> And the Philistine came on and drew near unto David and the man that bare the shield went before him. And when the Philistine looked about, and saw David, he disdained him; for he was but a youth, and ruddy, and of a fair countenance. "Am I a dog that you come out against me with sticks?" And he swore at him in the name of his gods. "Come on," he said, "and I will give your flesh to the birds of the air and the beasts of the field."

David told him that he would kill him and cut off his head,

> and all the world shall know there is a god in Israel. All those who are gathered here shall see that the LORD saves neither by sword nor spear; the battle is the LORD's and he will put you all into our power.

And David put his hand in his bag, and took thence a stone, and slang it, and smote the Philistine in his forehead, that the stone sunk into his forehead; and he fell upon his face to the earth.

Is there any wonder that this story has lasted as long as Homer? Those forty days of shouting, all the grandeur of bronze, the whole rhetoric of assertive Homeric heroism, is now clogged with the mud filling Goliath's mouth and nostrils. A painting by the young Caravaggio, now in the Prado, of David after the death of Goliath is, in this way, one of the most beautiful commentaries on Homer that has ever been made. It is Caravaggio's least violent and most understanding version of that subject. Michelangelo had shown David on the Sistine Chapel ceiling with his sword in midswipe over Goliath's neck. Titian had painted a butcher's view of the cut neck itself. Caravaggio himself would later paint ferocious and tragic images of David holding the severed head (a head which bears the painter's own grieving features), but this first David of his is soaked in calm. The boy looks as if he is about twelve years old. His body is wrapped in a loose white cloth. His lower legs are bare and his feet inelegant, the toes slightly misaligned, with dirt under the nails and a soreness around them. Nothing is idealized. Goliath's vast dead hand remains clenched on the ground, and blood has dried on his big severed head, around the wound left by David's slung stone, the puncture through which the heroic balloon has collapsed.

What survives in the painting is the beauty of the boy, his intentness on the knot as he ties a cord around Goliath's hair, his simplicity, his seriousness, his lack of bombast. He kneels on the giant Greek chest, from which the head was severed, as if on a workbench, blood just staining his hand, his own face in shadow, a face of humility, the heroism entirely inward. This is the view of Greek heroism given us by the Hebrew scriptures: weak and bombastic compared to the clarity and strength of the pious mind.

12 · HOMER'S ODYSSEY

Nothing can be relied on in Odysseus's world. His stories of impossible monsters—Scylla, Charybdis, the Cyclops, the Sirens—are all told as if true. Others with real places and people—Egypt, Sicily, the Cretans—are clearly Odysseus's own lying tales. Odysseus is an unblinking fraud who in the passing of a smile will slip from deceit to the defense of honor and back again. At his most soothingly and persuasively elegant, his words "fall like winter snowflakes." But he is no weakling. His grandfathers were raw and primitive men: Autolycus, whose name means "the wolf himself," and Arceisius, "Bear Man." He comes from nature but is a multiple of multiples: *polymētis*, many-skilled; *polymechanos*, very ingenious; *polytlas*, much-enduring; and best of all *poikilomētis*, dapple-skilled, with so much woven into him that he shimmers and flickers like an embroidered cloth.

So uncatchable is Odysseus that when the poem describes his state of mind, you can never be certain where to find him. When he is lying in bed, anxious and unable to sleep, Homer says he is "tossing backwards and forwards, like a sausage that a man is turning backwards and forwards above the burning coals, doing it one side, then the other, wanting it to cook quickly. So Odysseus was turning backwards and forwards, thinking what he should do." *Entha kai entha*, backwards and forwards, hither and thither, literally "there and there"; Homer repeats the phrase three times in five lines. It must be branded on his hero's heart. But is

Odysseus the cook or the sausage? Is he turning or being turned? Is he the passive victim of his life or its principal actor? Or both?

It is fitting that at the beginning of the *Odyssey*, this slippery figure is nowhere to be found. He is away, an absence, the longed-for man-not-there. Twenty years have passed since he left for the war in Troy. The other heroes have returned home. Only Odysseus remains missing. No one has seen him these last ten years. Meanwhile his queen, Penelope, is surviving surrounded by a herd of young men from Ithaca, and the rival kings of nearby islands, all of them clamoring for her hand, her body and her husband's kingdom. She keeps them at bay, flirtatiously but reservedly, while her son, Telemachus, is humiliated and reduced by these wine-swilling, pork-consuming parasites. The word for them in Greek is *mnēstēr*, which means "a man with something in mind," "a man with intentions."

With the help of Athene, Telemachus escapes their clutches for a while and goes to ask for news of his father in the great palaces of the Peloponnese, at Pylos and at Sparta, where the old heroes tell him what has happened: his father is a prisoner on the distant island of Ogygia, where the love-nymph Calypso holds him in her sway. Only after four books and 2,222 lines does Odysseus, the hidden man, first appear.

Calypso's isle of voluptuousness is the earth's navel. She promises her captive, as all lovers do, immortality and agelessness, and she presides over him as the goddess of longing. Her hair hangs about her eyes as seductively as it does around the face of the dawn. Her island is hilly and forested, and her delicious cavern, where the scents of sweet-smelling cedar fill the air, where the owls and cormorants sit chattering in the luxuriant growth at its mouth, and the vines hold out bunches of grapes that ripen as you watch—what is this but the entrancingly shaggy cavern of desire? She is Courbet's *Origine du Monde*. Fresh streams run down through her meadows starred with violets, thick with beds of what was either parsley or celery, a refuge "at which any immortal god who came there would gaze in wonder, their heart entranced with pleasure."

One spring morning, on the southeast coast of Sicily just north of Syracuse, I went somewhere which, for that day anyway, seemed to be filled with Calypso's overbrimmingly desirable spirit. It is known now as Penisola Magnisi but was called Thapsos by the ancient Greeks. A low, flat island, about a mile long, just off the coast, is joined to the mainland by a narrow sandy neck. North and south of that neck there is shelter and good holding, whatever the wind, the classic early Greek recipe of twin harbors. The rim of the mainland beside it is now a mess of modern oil refineries and tanker-loading bays, but Thapsos remains uninhabited. Walk along the sand of the tombolo toward it, keep your eyes looking out to sea, and you can find yourself in a virtually untouched Odyssean world.

This little island holds the earliest of all signs of the Greeks in the west. They were here in the sixteenth century BC, as the Shaft Graves were still being dug at Mycenae, moving out into the Mediterranean as they had already come south to the Aegean. Archaeologists have found Mycenaean, Cypriot and Maltese pottery here, mixed in with local Sicilian jars and plates. It was somewhere, I thought, where I could start to come close to Odysseus on one of his distant shores.

But coming to Thapsos that beautiful morning, with the Mediterranean glittering beside me, it was impossible to think I could be here for the Bronze Age, for Odysseus, or for anything that was not part of the astonishing present, because the island that morning was awash with flowers. The true wild sweet pea, the great-grandfather of all sweet peas grown in the world, was here, its scent mixed with the sugary wafts of the sweet alyssum that was growing in clumps among the limestone, smelling from yards away like plates of honey sandwiches.

According to the Roman historian Diodorus Siculus, Sicily smelled so powerfully of wildflowers that hounds there used to lose the scent of their prey and wander about "at a loss, sniffing the air with half-closed eyes, while the quarry grazed happily several miles off." But Thapsos looked wonderful too: wine-dark stonecrop on the edges of the limestone flakes, clouds of borage everywhere, a purple-pink haze spangled with blue stars. Spires of viper's bugloss stood among them like the banners of festival knights, and all of this surrounded by a floor of brilliant pink little Mediterranean campions, *Silene colorata*, with banks of yellow marigolds and wild tangerine chrysanthemums beyond them.

Odysseus came to hate Calypso's island. He had been there too long, and by the time the poem finds him there he is weeping on the beach, pining for home, far from floweriness and Calypso's beguilements. Out on the other side of Thapsos, facing Greece and the sparkle of the sea, is this island's own version of the landscape of regret and loss. Here on the rocky, sea-stripped and flowerless coast is where the first Greeks in Sicily buried their dead. They made small, low, rock-cut tombs, deftly slipped into the limestone, each entrance coming in from the direction of the sea, the hollow of the tomb itself cut out of the depth of the rock. There are about three hundred of them, like the burrows of small rock-dwelling creatures, and two things strike you: they imitate in form the great tholos tombs of Mycenae and Pylos, the tombs of Agamemnon and Clytemnestra, as Schliemann called them, with their giant ceremonial entrance courts, or *dromoi*, the towering portals and the huge corbeled vaults of the tombs themselves. That heroic vision of the dead was transported here to the distant west, but no grandeur came with it. These Thapsos tombs are poverty itself, desperate scrapings on a rocky shore, filled with dreams and illusions of home but little else. The walls of the *dromoi* here are often no more than eighteen inches high, the doorway accessible only if you squirm inside, the vaulted space no taller than a crouching man.

Into this island of desperate and beautiful changelessness Homer suddenly injects the opposite, the great mobilizing presence of the poem, the god who, alongside Athene, presides over Odysseus's whole being: the quicksilver dazzle of Hermes himself. He arrives as the messenger of Zeus, bringing a shock of life, "swooping down from Pieria [the home of the Muses], down from the high clear air, plunging to the sea and skimming the swells, like a shearwater who hunts along the deep and deadly ways of the barren salt sea."

Hermes does everything Odysseus might think of doing: he is the god of the thief, the shepherd, the craftsman, the herald, the musician, the athlete and the merchant. He is at home with all kinds of cunning and trickery, charms and spells. He is the god who invented music and discovered fire. Dangerous magic and a kind of phallic potency glimmer around him like static. He is at home outside the limits of normality and stability, and so he is the god of boundaries and thresholds, of roads and doors, of transitional and alien places, of mines and miners, of the ability to make and transform the fixities and prearrangements of the world. This is the god who watches over comings and goings. It is Hermes, in disguise, who leads Priam across the Trojan plain to the Greek camp and his world-altering encounter with Achilles. He is the god of politics and diplomacy, the great persuader, the maestro of difference, and all of that makes him the god of Odysseus.

Hermes delivers transformations, and so the *Odyssey* flicks to its other mode: the sea and its islands are to be not a prison but a place where movement and change are more possible than anywhere else. Hermes tells Calypso that Odysseus must leave her island and begin his journey home. And to leave, he must build himself a raft from the great trees that surround her. The very forest that made this place into a desire-trap, all that fringing luxuriance, is now seen as timber. Odysseus seeks out the deadest, driest, most juiceless trees he can find, because those are the ones that will "float lightly"—but also surely because those are the most un-Calypso-like—and they fall quickly to his ax.

Nothing in the *Odyssey* is described with more love or care than Odysseus making his raft. It comes together in parts, orderly, concrete, precise: ax, adze and augers, pegs and mortises, ribs, decks and gunwales, mast, yard and steering oar, braces, halyards and sheets. Odysseus assembles it just as Homer assembles his song, so that the ship becomes a poem of the sea. If its parts are right, and their relationship right, it will sail. Calypso provisions the raft with delicious drink and food for his journey and summons her warm and generous wind, a following wind, the only one that could take him home. He embarks—you can smell the new-cut wood—his spirits high, gripping the tiller, seated astern, his eye on the sail filling above him.

Now Odysseus enters his crowning moment. He is the master mariner, the great soul, godlike, commanding his own craft *technēentos*, a word that blurs the boundaries of "skillfully," "cunningly" and "magisterially." He steers by the stars, as Calypso had told him, keeping the Plow and the Great Bear, of which it is a part, on the left hand, to the north. For seventeen nights he sails with the west wind behind him like this. "Sleep never falls on his eyelids as he watches the stars above him," seeing the Plow wheeling around the North Star and "never bathing in the waters of the ocean," while the Plow in turn is watching Orion on the other side, the two of them circling each other in eternity, "the axis always fixed."

You only have to sail by the stars once or twice for that connection to remain with you for the rest of your life. I can never now look up at Cassiopeia, the five bright stars of her *W,* and not think of those hours in a driving and stormy night that I kept them in the shrouds of the *Auk*, as we headed north in a storm off the south of Ireland. Nor Orion without seeing him as he was when we made our way out with the tide one summer night into the Minch, and that most herolike of constellations stood as a warrior high to the right of us, his belt and sword glittering and jeweled, his bow up and arced to the southwest, the arrow aimed high at the heart of the Pleiades.

This exposure of Odysseus to the stars is the closest I ever feel to him, knowing that the experience of being out there, alone at sea at night, for all the changes in technology that three or four thousand years might have brought, with the sky arrayed above you and the sea and its threats dark and half-hidden, is materially the same for me as it was for him. It is the most cosmic experience of the world I know, when the universe seems not like a background but a reality, and when the scale of earthliness shrinks to nothing much. There is no history here. I am in the Bronze Age, and as Odysseus stays awake, keeping sleep at bay, watching the movements of craft and sea, I do the same, and he and I are momentarily and marvelously intimate.

But constancy is not the note of the *Odyssey*, and again Homer flicks the switch. Odysseus is within touching distance of Scheria, the island of the Phaeacians, who will take him home, its mountains "reaching towards him now, over the misty breakers, rising like a shield," when Poseidon spots the raft and decides to kill him. It is one of Homer's majestic aerial views, the little raft far below him in the expanse of sea, Poseidon's eye in the heaven far above, the midgelike fragility of our greatest man surrounded by the vast rolling dark expanse of ocean.

The storm that then erupts and blows through the next 160 lines is no dignified passage of heroic verse. It is vicious, almost formless, repetitively destructive. Every prop of every storm in every European imagination, from Virgil to Ovid and on through Shakespeare and the great composers, is brought into play here. Poseidon summons every contradictory wind. He stirs and grinds at the surface of the sea, brings clouds to hide the land, so that even the sea itself becomes invisible. Giant waves come bearing down on Odysseus and sweep though his whole being. His knees weaken, his heart melts, his giant and commanding spirit quakes before Poseidon's chthonic power.

Poseidon is "dark-maned," horselike, the enemy of the civility and coherence embodied in Odysseus's beautiful raft. The verse, which had been making such steady progress on Odysseus's starlit voyage, now churns with anxiety. Odysseus wishes he had died at Troy. At least then his death would have been heroic, not the pitiable ending now facing him.

The raft loses direction. Odysseus's hand slips from the steering oar as Poseidon's waves tower and break above him, spinning his raft in a circle. The hero is thrown into the sea, where the clothes that Calypso had given him grow heavy with the water and drag him under. Wave after wave drives him down. Only his mind, the great organ of Odyssean existence, stays whole in this frenzy of natural violence, and as he surfaces at last, spewing seawater from his mouth and with the sea streaming from his head like the torrents running from the boss of a fountain, he lunges after the raft, knowing it as his place of safety, the only way he can escape "death's decision." But Poseidon does not release him. Here and there, to and fro, *entha kai entha*, the sea-king drives him, urging on the south wind and the north wind, the east wind and the west wind, as each in their turn try to shake from Odysseus his last rags of coherence.

He is hanging on to life; the tightly bound raft and the woven cloth, the made things of a civilized existence, are part of the longed-for or remembered worlds. They are too fragile to last out here. He is beset with troubles, and death seems near at hand until at last, mysteriously, a sea-bird, *aithuia* in Greek, probably not a shearwater, but another fishing bird, maybe a tern or a small delicate-limbed gull like a kittiwake—no one has ever been sure—alights on the wave-swept platform of the raft and speaks to him.

It is one of the Homeric moments at which the distance between then and now shrinks away. You can imagine the listeners around the poet, fixed in their attention to this overturning crisis, with nothing in their minds but the predicament of Odysseus at sea, taken up with their anxiety for this man so helplessly exposed to Poseidon's rage, now, quite suddenly, feeling their hearts contract with love and sympathy at the arrival of the speaking bird. Here, maybe, is a moment of hope.

It is an experience all deep-sea sailors will have had. You are out in a storm, the boat rolls and pitches, thirty degrees one way then the other, the seas coming at you in a pattern you wish would end, the battering and shrieking of the wind unstoppable in your ear. Every surface is broken. The winds cannot leave the sea alone. What has already been plowed and folded is plowed and folded again. No structure in the sea remains whole. Not even a breaking wave is allowed to break, but the wind strips the spume from the wavetop and blows it in a half element, half air, half sea, wildly down and across the wind, as if the air were now clouded with cataracts or a sudden blast of winter. Inconstancy and capriciousness rule. There is no permanence. Nothing in a storm can be inherited from one moment to the next. But if there is one fact that a storm seems to impose—it is not physically or meteorologically true, but this is the experience—it is the sea's mysterious dominance from below. A storm-driven sea appears to acquire a vitality and viciousness, a desire to do damage, which has nothing to do with the wind but comes from inside its own enraged, destroying body. If you ever have that sensation, it is when you are meeting Poseidon.

Out of that turmoil and trouble, enacting the repeated Homeric principle of enlightenment through the arrival of the opposite, comes the delicacy and tailored perfection of the seabird. It is a sign of grace and goodness, never more than when one alights on the deck or boom beside you. I have had swallows do that, far from land, and once, briefly, a tiny dark storm petrel, a speck of life in the middle of death.

I cannot believe Homeric sailors did not also stand at the taffrails of their beloved ships watching the birds in their wake. Seabirds are too beautifully present in the poems for the sailors not to have seen them like that, godlike in their lightness above the rolling weight of the sea. I have watched them for days, equipped as they are with their own more perfect version of hull and sail, reaching and tacking beside you in the wind, dropping and climbing among the peaks and valleys below them, their primaries sometimes just nicking and flicking the surface of the sea, until without warning they make a decision and turn one wing up into the wind, exposing their belly to it, thrown upward like a cyclist on the steepest part of a banked track, and are pulled away, high and fast, in a rapid downwind run, which they end by curving slowly around to windward again, pure authority, taking up station, living with the fluency and command their liquid world requires.

Odysseus's visiting seabird is Leucothea, the white goddess. She was once a mortal girl from Thebes, with, as Homer says, "the most beautiful ankles," but the gods made her one of their own. She gives Odysseus a holy veil, full of the magic of the woven cloth. He is to tie it around his chest, abandon the raft and swim for shore. With those instructions she leaves him, plunging into the sea "like a diving tern, and the dark wave hid her." But Odysseus, who already refused the offer of immortality from Calypso, and whose mind is still searchingly alive, does not obey. He trusts his own raft too much to abandon it so far from shore, and with that Poseidon and the storm submit him to the next phase of horror. The earth shaker summons a killer wave, its crest overarching, vaulted, Homer using a word he uses elsewhere to describe caves and dark bowers roofed with trees, so that the wave becomes like a vast dark hall of destruction, which he then lands on Odysseus as a sledgehammer of vengeance.

The raft is smashed and Odysseus sunk, but he emerges and climbs onto one of the scattered planks, which he then rides in the sea "like a horse." Because finality dominates the *Iliad*, that poem introduces men in order to kill them, brought on one after another like the shambling line of an Aztec sacrifice; the many will always end in the same bleak place. But Odysseus meets death time and time again, and each time springs up whole and new, as if resilience were running in his veins; his central understanding, the great evolution from the *Iliad* to the *Odyssey*, is that the one needs to be many.

The storm continues for another two days. The life spirit in Odysseus is squeezed to near empty. His ability to survive has faced its greatest test. But then at last the wind drops, and calm spreads across the sea. Still, though, the groundswell is running, and Odysseus is lifted by one of those long, rolling waves high enough to see the land of Scheria and salvation within touching distance.

> Just like the kind of joy that children feel when their father has been lying ill in bed, dying, taut with pain, wasting away under the grip of some angry, powerful affliction, and at last those pains begin to ebb away and they can feel a warmth and ease come back into the air of the sick room around him, so to Odysseus that land and its trees seem welcome, swimming towards them now, hungry to plant his feet on the earth itself.

For Odysseus, the missing father, the man whose son knows he is dead and gone, land itself has become fatherly, the embrace of what feels like home reaching out to him. But here, at a moment of arrival and the promise of simplicity, Homer gives the gimbaled world of the *Odyssey* yet another spin. The poem might long for land but will always remain at sea, and as Odysseus gets as near the shore as a man's voice will carry, he hears the vast, destructive surf breaking on what he realizes is an iron coast, no harbors, no anchorages, all high headlands, reefs and cliffs. The hexameters, sounding as strange as a Hawaiian war chant, as heavy and hissing as the sea itself, play out what he hears:

> *kai dē doupon akouse*   *poti spiladessi thalassēs*
> and then the boom he heard   on the slippery reefs of the sea
> *rochthei gar mega kuma*   *poti xeron ēpeiroio*
> for roared the great wave   on the dry land of the mainland
> *deinon ereugomenon*   *eiluto de panth' halos achnē*
> terrible the deep belching   as folded up all things in sea surf

With the brightness of Athene in his mind he casts off again and finally, thankfully, finds a place where the all-male cliff gives way and a fair-flowing river, the emergent inwardness of the land, allows him entrance and he can rest at last, "Spent to all use, and down he sank to death./The sea had soak'd his heart through."

Of course he does not die, and from that masterfully orchestrated sequence of island, raft, storm, bird and shore—the realms of impotence, potency, threat, grace and survival—the great central section of the *Odyssey* floods out: Odysseus's meeting with the princess Nausicaa, his coming to the deeply Asiatic palace of Alcinous, her father, where he tells his tales to the assembled company. Together they constitute an enormous, cumulative exploration of human consciousness, island by island, point by point, each story exploring another dimension of what it is to be alive. In this world of flux, every island shapes the life that is in it. Arrive at any of them, push your dinghy ashore on the beach, and a different atmosphere obtains: welcome, comfort, strangeness, violence. The vocabulary of beach, rock and wood may be the same, but every island uses it in a different way, to seduce or dismember you, turn you into a pig or promise you immortality, devour your friends or make you forget that anywhere else ever existed.

The *Odyssey* is a drama of oscillation, between inner and outer, urbanity and wildness, enclosure and exposure, the memory of home and the rewards of distance, a life that is "heartsick on the open sea" and the mixed, erotic terror-allure of the women Odysseus finds wherever he goes, their welcome, their way with drugs and potions, the caves and grottoes of their inner selves.

When he arrives at the seductions of Circe's island—her name means "the encircler"—he finds there the poisoner-witch and the best cook in Homer. She has ever more deliciousness to offer, and with her charms seduces his men and turns them all into pigs. Odysseus knows that this is a dangerous nowhere, out in the middle of the full circle of the sea where they cannot know where the sun sets, nor where it rises, until Hermes, his great ally, the spirit of cleverness and ingenuity, gives him both an antidote to all her potions and the best possible advice: hold your sword to her throat and get her to promise that she will not make a pig of you, as she has to your men.

Odysseus arms himself with all the sharpness of Hermes, then penetrates deep inside Circe's world, in through the doors of her palace, into her beautiful rooms and her jeweled chair, only then suddenly to draw his sword "from his thigh," to dominate her as she kneels terrified before him. She must promise no spells, no enchantment, the freeing of his men, stripping their piggishness away, and with those promises, with his dominance secure, he mounts her in "her surpassingly beautiful bed of love."

The erotic vibrates as the underlayer of each encounter, the male fear of enclosure in endless dialogue with the male longing to be enclosed. In Hades, whose name means "the unlit" or "the unseen," this dance of attachment and detachment takes on its own sad colors. Everything that matters on earth, all love, life, growth and hope, is extinguished here and reduced to a gray, wraithlike half-existence, life without life. Achilles says he is surrounded there not by the dead but by the *kata-phthimenoisen*, the deader than dead, the dead's own dead. It is the darkest of all the *Odyssey's* inward places. There Odysseus watches the lightless ghosts walk by. There is no glory in them. They are too thin for that, evaporating as his arms try to close around them.

He sees his mother first, a longed-for shadow of the woman he knew and held, then a sequence of queens, all mortal and all dead, all of them beautiful and all once lovers of gods, each of them walking past him in somber parade. They are attendants on Persephone, the great queen of Hades itself, her own presence in the gloom of this dark cavern an emblem of all the heartache and the shocks that flesh is heir to: she is a vegetation goddess and she belongs in the bright lit world above, but Hades had abducted her and in that single act had brought winter to the earth.

These queens are all mothers of heroes, and one by one they remember their moments of intimacy with the gods: Tyro, thinking of when Poseidon in the shape of a giant wave took possession of her at a river's mouth; Antiopē, remembering Zeus coming to her on the vast plain where their sons would later build the city of Thebes; the mother of Heracles thinking of his conception, then his wife remembering their own moments of love together; the mother of Oedipus, grieving at having slept with her own son; and Iphimedeia, who "lay in the sea-Lord's loving waves" . . . and so on, too many for Odysseus to remember or tell, even though "his story held them spellbound down the shadowed halls."

Behind them all, not present here but looming over the whole performance, stands the one great figure of the noble and absent queen: Penelope, Odysseus's own wife, away, not dead, but waiting for him in Ithaca. Every one of these queenly wraiths is an image of the woman he longs for. She is the queen of all queens, filled with intelligence, fortitude and wit, the match for Odysseus in her greatness. Every one of these ghosts is a translation of Penelope into another form. They all speak of the moment when longing was over and intimacy was real, and every one of them now looks across the gulf of death to the time a god made love to them. Desire, longing, separation and greatness all appear in them arrayed before Odysseus like a frieze, every one the ghost of his own lost wife.

After the monstrous-beautiful Sirens, Odysseus comes to the limb-consuming Scylla and her friend the body-gulping Charybdis. Scylla is a six-headed, rock-bound, man-eating monster, with guts made of dogs' heads, who plucks you from above; Charybdis a vast-mouthed, in-sucking, whirlwater hell-fiend who will pull you down below. Veer too far from Scylla, and Charybdis will have you. Too far from Charybdis, and Scylla will pick off your sailors. Too far in or too far out, which fate will you choose? Together they are the nightmare of female threat, either picking your life away or drowning you in who they are. Everything Odysseus loved about women in Hades is here thrown into reverse. But Odysseus makes the wise man's choice: risk Scylla, because where Charybdis will swallow you whole, Scylla may eat a man or two, but the ship will survive.

This is Odysseus's virtue: in the face of life's impossible choices, he is able to navigate between the whirlpool and the rock.

His inner self reflects that outer wisdom. More than any other Homeric hero, Odysseus is not at one with himself. His mental world is storm-wrecked, and these outer landscapes are a projection of that broken core. But every arrival carries its lesson. "Many were the people whose places he saw and whose minds he learned," Homer says at the very beginning of the *Odyssey*. Odysseus may long "for his return and his woman," but the heart of the poem is this contingency, the absence of any overriding permanence. It is the first depiction we have of "the fascinating imaginative realm," as Milan Kundera called the novel, the great descendant of the *Odyssey*, "where no one owns the truth and everyone has the right to be understood." Abstract certainties do not apply here. Anything you might have thought true may well be false. Anything that might have seemed good can seem bad in another light. And of nowhere is that truer than the island that is Odysseus's destination, the dream of Ithaca, the place Odysseus would like to call home, "the sweetest place any man can imagine," but which on arrival, exactly halfway through the *Odyssey*'s twenty-four books, turns out to be its very opposite.

Ithaca is not what the phrase "Greek island" brings to mind. There is nothing of the drought-stripped bareness of the eastern Aegean, nor of the dry Asiatic pelt of the Trojan plain. Ithaca is green and wooded, more Tuscan than Greek. There are some wonderful harbors but little good grass or arable land. It largely consists of mountains dropping to the sea. Wild pear trees blossom beside the spring meadows, but it is "rocky Ithaca," the kind of island that has always thrived on trading or raiding but would be poor if reliant on its own resources. There are springs in the woodlands, where daisies grow in the stony turf. Magenta anemones spangle the meadows in May, and a little later in the year you can find the churchyards filled with white and purple irises. I have been there at the end of winter, which is when Odysseus arrives, and I have known nights as cold as the one in which he has to borrow a cloak to keep warm. Like him, I have sat late over an olive-wood fire, using the prunings from the vines as kindling, drinking glasses of deep black red Mavrodafni, huddled over the logs in a cold room, so that my face burned and my back froze. There was snow on the mountain paths that year, the wind was turning up the pale underside of the olive leaves and the air was more silver than golden, clarified, a distillate.

It's part of the geometry of the poems that Ithaca is like this. It is a northern country, on the northern and western edge of the Greek world, a long way from the cultivated, semi-Asiatic eastern Aegean heartland that Homer knew best. That exaggerated marginality fits Odysseus, the pirate-king of a country that is out on the edge of things. But it is a country he loves. The Phaeacians bring him here across the sea. He is asleep when he arrives, and they carry him ashore still sleeping. He wakes the next day and doesn't know where he is. He can't recognize Ithaca. Only at the prompting of Athene does he realize that this is home, and then, on seeing it, he "bends to kiss the life-giving soil."

The *Odyssey* throughout has taunted its listeners with images of palatial comfort and luxury. The Phaeacians are the model of a rich, successful Near Eastern kingdom. Their palaces, gardens and orchards all read like scenes from an Assyrian relief. Egypt has floated just off-stage as the reservoir of gold, the Greek dream of material well-being. The kings and queens of Pylos and Sparta live embedded in authority and sumptuousness. Even Circe seems to live in a beautifully equipped palace.

Odysseus does not arrive home to find a place like that. His kingdom is in chaos, not the lovely, sweet, green, untroubled oasis he longs for it to be. It is riven with difficulty, and that tension—between the desire and the reality, between Ithaca the beautiful and Ithaca the real—leads to the fierce conclusion of this great poem. It is no easy or sentimental reunion of the loved one and the loved place. Homer says "there is nothing sweeter to a man than his own country." That is what we want to think is true. But in Ithaca the poem enacts the opposite: nothing is more troubled than a man's own country, even if that is where the desire for sweetness is strongest.

Odysseus has repeatedly appeared as the impoverished northern wanderer not entirely at home in the Mediterranean world. Now he comes home as the broken king, the outsider with few allies. The only weapons he has are tricks of deceit and concealment, and Athene makes sure she strips him of any sign of nobility.

She withers the handsome flesh that is on his supple limbs
And thins the fair hair on his head.

She puts the skin of an old, old man over his whole body
And dims the two eyes that were once so beautiful.

Now he is at home, he has never been more at sea. But he is not at a loss. He tells lying stories about who he is and where he has come from, gradually working his way toward the confrontation that will bring him victory, slipping into his own palace much as the Trojan Horse that he devised was slipped into the citadel at Troy. Homer shapes Odysseus to be the universal man, dressed in rags, stronger for appearing weaker, but even in that disguise he consistently pretends to come not from the margins of the Homeric world—he is no northern vagabond—but from one of its centers of riches and power: Crete, the focus of the great palatial culture which Sir Arthur Evans, the English excavator of the palace complex at Knossos in the early years of the twentieth century, called the Minoan. Odysseus describes his island in the middle of the wine-dark sea as a fair, rich land, surrounded by water, with so many men in it they could not be counted and ninety cities, including "Knossos, where Minos reigned."

Odysseus has become the man who knows the world, who has been a great warrior at Troy, a great traveler to dimensions of existence few other men will ever encounter, an absorber of the Cretan civilization, now preparing to perform his great and terrifying act of revenge. He has lost nothing in all his journeying. He has become the agent of a new fused culture, the man who will establish civility in his city by bringing war into it. He looks at Ithaca with eyes rimmed red with sea-salt, the hardened eyes of the returning king. He is the agent of reduction, there to remove the fat, and the irony of Odysseus's return is that the nearer he gets to his own house, the more uncompromisingly like Achilles he becomes, wanting to strip away the muddle and complexities and return Ithaca to an essential, Iliadic condition.

Set against this powerful and threatening presence is Penelope, his incomparable queen, the greatest woman in Homer. She does not yet know that her husband has at last returned. Her halls are filled with the suitors. Everything about them reeks of luxury and abuse, but she is withdrawn and self-protective. The epithet Homer uses of her most often is *periphrōn*, meaning "wise," or more exactly that she has a mind that encompasses all sides of a question, not exactly wary or circumspect, but "understanding the whole," filled with an enveloping intelligence.

Penelope's mind is one of the most precious places in Homer, the inner citadel of virtue and value. She is deeply identified with the well-being of her house. When she appears in front of the suitors, she always stands by the columns of the beautiful hall, as if she were one of them herself, "shining among women" just as the upper chambers to which she retires shine within the palace. This is the great woman who, as she descends her stairs, looks like Artemis and Aphrodite, the greatest of the goddesses, the queens of the wildland and of love.

Her heart is of iron, and like her husband she has "a well-balanced mind." Like him, she can deceive and manipulate her enemies, but also like him, she is passionate in her love for her lost spouse and weeps bitterly over him. Like him, she lies awake at night and her troubles crowd around her throbbing heart. In one of Homer's most beautiful similes, she says that just as

> the nightingale of the greenwood sings so sweetly when the spring is
>   newly come, sitting perched in the thick and leafy trees, pouring out
>   her rich voice in quavering and bubbling notes,
> even so my heart is stirred to and fro in doubt.

Odysseus's great phrase, *entha kai entha*, to and fro, there and there, is hers too; but have midnight thoughts and the anxieties of a troubled mind in the dark ever been so beautifully described?

Like all the great women in Homer, she weaves, no cloth more famous than the one she is making as a shroud for her father-in-law, Laertes, weaving it every day, unweaving it every night, not only to keep the suitors at arm's length but as an emblem of her command in her world. She is a queen regnant, her fame reaching heaven for the way she rules over men, upholds justice, sees that the fertile earth brings forth wheat and barley, that her orchards are heavy with fruit and her flocks with young. All this, Homer says, comes from her "good command"—one word: *euēgesia*—while her people "grow in goodness under her."

This is Homer's architecture of crisis: a great woman, her husband in disguise, a gang of young men who do not realize that the beggar is their king, witnessing their abuse and their vulgarity, eating his food, drinking his drink and sleeping with his serving-women. The tension builds over four long books of the poem, an unavoidable sexual metaphor at work: the king wolf has been away, the she-wolf is under siege, the promise of blood is in the air.

Odysseus is troubled. He knows that he must bring war into his own house, but when he longs to do violence to those servant-women who have betrayed him, anxiety reverberates within him.

> Just as a bitch stands over her young puppies,
> growling at a man she does not know,
> thinking she would attack him,
> so Odysseus's heart growls inside him.

He has to punch his own chest to keep it in order. But is Odysseus the growling heart? Or the man who keeps his heart down? Is he one of the puppies that needs protection? Or the bitch doing the protecting? Or even the man who is threatening the puppies? There is no primitive simplicity here: as Homer portrays it, complexity ripples through every contour of the human heart.

When the terrifying reprise of the *Iliad* erupts into the poem, it brings with it an almost orgasmic release of destructive energy, a balloon of mesmeric violence in which Odysseus slaughters all 108 of the young men. It is a frenzy of killing, an orgy of revenge that leaves the floors of the palace swimming in blood. The most horrible moment of the *Iliad*, when Odysseus and Diomedes kill Dolōn even as he is begging for his life, and his head is still speaking as it lands in the dust—those same actions and words are repeated here with one of the more pathetic of the victims. Odysseus ends slobbered with their guts, his thighs shiny with their blood, filthy with it, "like a lion that comes from feeding on an ox at the farmstead, and all his chest and cheeks on either side are stained with blood and he is terrible to look at; even so was Odysseus dirty with their blood and filth, his feet red, his hands and arms red with it."

Any idea that this is a tale of diverting fantasy is buried under the horror. Odysseus emerges from the tumult and goes through his house, looking for any sign of life from the suitors, any stirring of a limb, so that none might escape.

> He finds them one and all, mired in blood and dust, all of them like
> fishes that the fishermen have drawn in their meshed nets from the grey

sea on to the curved beach. And all the fishes, longing for the waves of
the sea, lie upon the sand. And the sun shines forth and takes from
them their life.

Their glazed stupidity is nothing more than the measure of Odysseus's
triumph. It is a moment of ecstatic slaughter, a huge gratification, filled
with delight that he has destroyed his enemies. He has won and reclaimed
his woman, his house and land and life. There is no euphemism here.
Melanthius had been Odysseus's goatherd but had betrayed him with
the suitors.

> They lead him out through the doorway and the court
> And cut off his nose and his ears with the pitiless bronze
> And tear out his genitals for the dogs to eat raw
> And cut off his hands and his feet in the anger of their hearts.

I have read these lines on Ithaca, listening one summer night to the
nightingales in a thicket nearby, rocked back by this arrival of war in the
house; no political solution sought, no compensatory agreement arrived
at, feeling horrified that for all Odysseus's subtlety and fineness, he has
ended up as a cannibal-minded cur. Nothing in Homer is more troubling.
You might have thought you knew this poem and its hero, but these scenes
push far out into strange territory. Is this, in the end, for all our ships and
palaces, our poetry, our beautiful cloths and veils, how we are, predatory
carnivores snarling our dominance over mounds of filth-spattered corpses?

Odysseus has the place cleaned. He gets the serving-women of the
house to purify it, fumigating it, using a hoe to scrape up the horror, behav-
ing as the sanitizing angel, instructing the women to carry out the dead
bodies of the men they have been sleeping with. After the work is done,
he identifies the twelve women he considers guilty of that sexual crime,
finds "the cable of a dark-prowed ship," a piece of marine equipment, and
ties it high up outside the house, around a pillar and some rafters, just
high enough so that if someone was attached to it, their feet would not
quite reach the ground.

> Just as when in the evening long-winged thrushes or doves, trying to
>   reach their roosting place for the night,

fall into a snare set in a thicket,
finding the bed that greets them filled with hate,
even so the women hold their heads out in a row,
and nooses are placed around their necks,
so that they can die most pitiably.
They writhe a little with their feet but not for very long.

It is, in Odysseus and Telemachus, a moment of pure pitilessness and, in Homer, of pure pity. Homer loves birds. Athene has been there, just a moment before, as a swallow up in the rafters of the palace. The word Homer uses for the pitiability of the girls' death, *oiktista*, is always used to describe the mournful notes of the song of the nightingale, Penelope's own heart-bird. There can be no doubt where Homer's sympathies lie. The suffering of those poor hanged girls, strung up with their feet quivering and kicking under the noose, their toes an inch or so from the ground beneath them, summons all the ghosts of Beslan, Srebrenica and Aleppo. An air of trouble thickens around this crime, and any identity you might have felt with Odysseus is threatened by it. An unbridgeable distance seems to open between us. It is a step too far, an ancientness too far. But Homer remains on our side of the divide, and it is clear that if Odysseus thinks he can solve life's problems by the ferocious imposition of moral authority, Homer, the poem, knows you cannot.

All that remains is for Odysseus to be at one again with Penelope. She tests him, famously, with the suggestion that they should move their bed from "the well-built bridal chamber," where it had been ever since he left for Troy. She knows, and he knows, but she does not yet know that the man in front of her knows, that the bed can never be moved, because Odysseus had built it around a living, long-leafed olive tree that had been growing in the courtyard for more years than anyone could remember. Their marriage bed is no temporary construction, but built for continuity and fixity, not afloat on the world but rooted in it. Odysseus, the great storyteller, had made it from living, inherited materials, had cut it and trimmed it and had beautified it with gold, silver and ivory inlays. The bed, in other words, like the raft he made, is another version of the great epic poem, made and remade, the reshaping of an inheritance to a new and ever more beautiful purpose.

When Penelope sees that Odysseus knows what she knows, that theirs is a marriage of true minds, and that their companionship is in the knowledge of the world they share, "her knees are loosened where she sits, and her heart melts . . . and in tears she throws her arms around his neck and kisses his face."

This is what, in the most literal translation that makes sense in English, Homer says:

> As when the land appears welcome to those who are swimming, after Poseidon has smashed their strong-built ship on the open water, pounding it with the weight of wind and the heavy seas, and only a few escape the grey water by swimming to the land, with a thick scurf of salt coated on them, and happily they set foot on the shore, escaping the evil; so welcome is her husband to her as she looks at him, and she cannot let him go from the embrace of her white arms.

These verses dance around the edges of tenderness. Odysseus has returned from the sea, but Penelope recognizes him as her homeland, the shore on which she can at last set foot after too long adrift on the chaos of her life. Understanding comes in seeing things from the other side. The language is clotted with formulas, the stock phrases used in every part of the poem: the strong-built ship, the gray water, the description of the sea merely as evil, her white arms. These are the words of antiquity, a frame of inherited sobriety and seriousness for the emotion that can scarcely be contained within them. What is painfully and marvelously real lies within the embrace of what is profoundly shared and ancient.

CONCLUSION: THE BRIGHT WAKE

Homer does not provide any kind of guidance to life if the lessons derived are the usefulness of violence, the lack of regret at killing, the subjection and selling of women, the extinction of all men in a surrendering city or the sense that justice resides in personal revenge. That recipe for gang hell has always been troubling to the civilized. Pope was shocked at the "spirit of cruelty which appears too manifestly in the *Iliad*." William Blake blamed Homer for desolating Europe with wars. Joel Barlow, the American friend of Thomas Paine and advocate of Enlightenment virtues, lectured the governing classes of a misguided Europe on how Homer was satisfactory as a poet,

> but he has given to military life a charm which few men can resist, a splendor which envelopes the scenes of carnage in a cloud of glory, which dazzles the eyes of every beholder. Alexander is not the only human monster that has been formed after the model of Achilles; nor Persia and Egypt the only countries depopulated for no other reason than the desire of rivalling predecessors in military fame.

What is valuable and essential in these poems is the opposite of that: the ability to regard all aspects of life with clarity, equanimity and sympathy, with a loving heart and an unclouded eye. Homer knows more than the people in the poems can ever know. He knows more than the

Greek warriors on the Trojan beach and more than the citizens of Troy. He even knows more than Odysseus and can look down on Odysseus, despite his failings, with paternal love. Homer matters because Homer, in a godlike way, understands what mortals do not. He even understands more than the gods, who emerge from the poems as sometimes terrifying but unreliable, intemperate and eventually ridiculous beings. That is his value, a reservoir of understanding beyond the grief and turbulence of a universe in which there is no final authority.

I am aware of how twenty-first-century this sounds—Homer with no trust in the metaphysical; a multiculturalist, able to empathize with both gang and city; a fusionist, seeing in Odysseus a man who might bring together the virtues of both worlds; even a liberal and feminist, who has a deep understanding of the dignity and beauty of women, their central role in human destiny. Nevertheless, it is a picture of Homer that seems true, and it is not a sentimental vision. The depiction of wrongness is fundamental to it. In a review of the harsh, extremist essays of Simone Weil, Susan Sontag speculated on why these dark Homeric qualities are so necessary.

> There are certain ages which do not need truth as much as they need a deepening of the sense of reality, a widening of the imagination. I, for one, do not doubt that the sane view of the world is the true one. But is that what is always wanted, truth? The need for truth is not constant; no more than is the need for repose. The truth is balance, but the opposite of truth, which is unbalance, may not be a lie.

Homer's embrace of wrongness, his depiction of a world that stands at a certain angle to virtue, is the heart of why we love him. He does not give us a set of exemplars. These poems are not sermons. We do not want Achilles or even Odysseus to be our model for a man. Nor Penelope or Helen for a woman. Nor do we want to worship at the shrine of Bronze Age thuggery. What we want is Homeric wisdom, his fearless encounter with the dreadful, his love of love and hatred of death, the sheer scale of his embrace, his energy and brightness, his resistance to nostalgia or to what the American philosopher Richard Rorty described as "belatedness." Most literature and philosophers, Rorty wrote, put value only in the past.

Nietzsche, at his worst, gestured towards some narcissistic and inarticulate hunks of Bronze Age beefcake. Carlyle gestured towards some contented peasants working the lands of a kindly medieval abbot. Lots of us occasionally gesture in the direction of the lost world in which our parents or our grandparents told us they grew up.

Homer doesn't do that. There is no sense that he has come late to life. These epic poems may enshrine the past, but they exist in a radiant present and in that way are hymns to present being. The English poet Alice Oswald has described recently how Homer is infused with this glowing sense of reality. Ancient critics "praised Homer's *enargeia*," she wrote in the foreword to *Memorial*, her beautiful and stripped-down translation of the *Iliad*, "which means something like 'bright unbearable reality.' It's the word used when gods come to earth not in disguise but as themselves." *Enargeia*, a noun derived from the Greek word *argos*, meaning "bright" or "shining," is "the quality of having brightness in it," of being vividly there. For Greek rhetoricians *enargeia* was a necessary aspect of description, or *ekphrasis*, a word that literally means "a telling out." And that pair of terms encapsulates the Homeric ideal: Homer's greatness is in his telling out of the embedded vivid, the core of life made explicit. Homer is not Greek; he is the light shining in the world.

He provides no answers. Do we surrender to authority? Do we abase ourselves? Do we indulge the self? Do we nurture civility? Do we nourish violence? Do we love? Homer says nothing in reply to those questions; he merely dramatizes their reality. The air he breathes is the complexity of life, the bubbling vitality of a boat at sea, the resurgent energy, as he repeatedly says, of the bright wake starting to gleam behind you.

NOTES

FOREWORD

2   *poet of a boom:* For most of the early twentieth century, in the wake of the discoveries at Troy and Mycenae made by the romantic German businessman/archaeologist Heinrich Schliemann, Homer was thought to describe the palatial Mycenaean world of ca. 1450 to ca. 1200 BC. Sir Moses Finley, in *The World of Odysseus* (New York: Viking, 1954), demolished that idea and considered Homer a product of the ninth or tenth century BC. For a clear and comprehensive discussion of the current orthodoxy that considers Homer an eighth-century poet and his use as "an archaeological artifact," see Ian Morris, "The Use and Abuse of Homer," *Classical Antiquity* 5, no. 1 (Apr. 1986), 81–138. Gregory Nagy, in *Homeric Questions* (Austin: University of Texas Press, 1996), argued that the poems did not reach their definitive form until the sixth century BC, but the archaeologist Susan Sherratt's "Archaeological Contexts," in John Miles Foley, ed., *A Companion to Ancient Epic* (Oxford: Blackwell, 2005), 119–42, insists on the syncretism of early Mediterranean cultures. Their core characteristic was the fusion of stories and ideologies. The Homer poems, she says, are the clearest example of "the ideological bricolage" of different cultures spread across the whole of the eastern Mediterranean and over a time period that stretches from at least 1800 to 800 BC (p. 139). In the Mediterranean everything was borrowed and shared, and that meeting of cultures is both Homer's subject and his method. Sherratt's point is that no picture of Homer can be pinned to a particular moment in that long millennium, nor could it be complete without looking for a deep prehistory to the epics, back to the beginning of the second millennium BC or farther. In the "social fluidity and instability" of that deep past were stories and questions that would have appealed to the audiences of the equally troubled ninth and eighth centuries BC more than the steady bureaucratic calm of the intervening palatial period of the late Bronze Age (p. 138).

3   *Epic's purpose:* See the many essays in John Miles Foley, ed., *A Companion to Ancient Epic* (Oxford: Blackwell, 2005).

3   *a revelatory fresco:* This is the watercolor reconstruction made for Blegen by the Anglo-Dutch artist and architect Piet de Jong, first published in Carl W. Blegen, "The Palace of Nestor Excavations of 1955," *American Journal of Archaeology* 60, no. 2 (Apr. 1956), 95–101, plate 41 (b&w). Mabel L. Lang, in *The Palace of Nestor at Pylos in Western Messenia*, Vol. 2, *The Frescoes* (Princeton, N.J.: Princeton University Press, 1969), after a decade of heroic work with burned and intransigent materials, reconstructed the fragments differently and separated the bard from the bird. But there is no certainty here. Emily Vermeule, in her review of that book in *The Art Bulletin* 52, no. 4 (Dec. 1970), 428–30, was skeptical about Mabel Lang's reconstruction.

4   *leaving Homer's own:* See Casey Dué, "*Epea Pteroenta*: How We Came to Have Our *Iliad*," in *Recapturing a Homeric Legacy: Images and Insights from the Venetus A Manuscript of the* Iliad, edited by Casey Dué (Washington, D.C.: Center for Hellenic Studies, 2009), 19–30.

5   *"the neon edges":* Christopher Logue, *War Music* (London: Faber, 2001), 54.

5   *"Warm'd in the brain":* Alexander Pope, *Iliad* XX.551.

5   *"like furnace doors":* Logue, *War Music*, 193.

5   *"sometimes travels beside":* George Seferis, "Memory II," lines 5–9, from Logbook 3, in *Complete Poems*, trans. and ed. by E. Keeley and P. Sherrard (1995; reprint, Greenwich: Anvil Press, 2009), 188. Seferis may have been thinking of the cosmic power of Apollo himself, the god of truth and poetry, becoming a magical dolphin in the *Homeric Hymn to Delian Apollo*: "In the open sea Apollo sprang upon their swift ship, like a dolphin in shape, and lay there, a great and awesome monster, and none of the crew gave heed so as to understand; but they sought to cast the dolphin overboard. But he kept shaking the black ship every way and made the timbers quiver. So they sat silent in their craft for fear, and did not ease the sheets throughout the black, hollow ship, nor lowered the sail of their dark-prowed vessel, but as they had set it first of all with oxhide ropes, so they kept sailing on; for a rushing south wind hurried on the swift ship from behind." Eventually, the god-driven ship grounded on the beach at Crisa, not far from Delphi, and "like a star at noonday, the lord, far-working Apollō, leaped from the ship: flashes of fire flew from him thick and their brightness reached to heaven." As translated by H. G. Evelyn-White in *Hesiod, Homeric Hymns, Epic Cycle, Homerica* (Cambridge, Mass: Loeb/Harvard University Press, 1914), vol. 57, p. 395ff.

6   *"as the wings":* Seferis, "Memory II," line 10, p. 188.

1: MEETING HOMER

7   *Robert Fagles:* Homer, *The Odyssey*, trans. Robert Fagles, introduction and notes by Bernard Knox (New York: Penguin, 1996).

8   *"Who would want":* *Odyssey* V.100–101.

8   *what he thinks:* Ibid., X.472–74.

9   *"sea-blue":* Ibid., VIII.84.

9   *"the man of twists":* Ibid., I.1.

10   *"starred with flowers":* Ibid., XII.173. The Greek adjective *anthemoenta* means

strictly no more than "flowery," and it is Robert Fagles who has poeticized this phrase. But if Homer is, in the end, neither a pair of poems, nor the single author of them, but a living tradition, then that kind of enrichment of the inherited text seems entirely legitimate.

10   *"We know all"*: Ibid., XII.189–91, Fagles XII.205–7.

11   *That is what*: Carol Dougherty, in *The Raft of Odysseus: The Ethnographic Imagination of Homer's* Odyssey (Oxford: Oxford University Press, 2001), 71–73, has a wonderful discussion of Odysseus's "metapoetic ship" as a vehicle for the heroic life.

11   *Matthew Arnold's famous lectures*: Matthew Arnold, *On Translating Homer: Three Lectures Given at Oxford* (London: Longman, Green, Longman, Roberts, 1861), available online at http://www.victorianprose.org/.

2: GRASPING HOMER

13   *"Beauty is always"*: The following scenes are based on but expanded and adapted from *The Goncourt Journals by Edmond and Jules de Goncourt*, ed. and trans. Robert Baldick (1962; reprint, New York: *New York Review of Books*, 2007), 83–85, 118–19.

16   *"I can't remember"*: The point that Renan failed to remember may have been that the word usually translated as "unharvestable" was said by the second-century AD Graeco-Roman grammarian Herodian, in a marginal comment on Homer's text, to mean "never worn out," or "unresting," and so in several nineteenth-century translations the phrase became "the restless sea." Most modern translations prefer "barren" or "unharvestable," perhaps on the grounds that Homer doesn't do cliché.

18   *Almost at the beginning*: Odyssey II.337–70.

18   *" far from battle"*: It can also mean "fighting at a distance," like an archer, and so it was an appropriate name because archery was one of Odysseus's skills and he might have wanted to pass it on to his son.

19   *"Ah dear child"*: *Odyssey* II.363–70 (with parallel translation by A. T. Murphy, revised by G. E. Dimock [Cambridge, Mass.: Locb / Harvard University Press, 1999]).

20   *"Each time I"*: Kenneth Rexroth, *Classics Revisited* (New York: New Directions, 1968), 7.

20   *"a jumbled heap"*: John Keats, sonnet, "O Solitude," lines 2–3.

20   *"the barbarous age"*: Quoted in Andrew Motion, *Keats* (London: Faber, 1997), 10.

20   *Edmund Spenser's* Faerie Queene: Spenser, *Faerie Queene*, book 2, canto 12, line 204; Motion, *Keats*, 52.

21   *"The tide!"*: Motion, *Keats*, 93.

21   *"both a lovely"*: Ibid., 63.

21   *"a parallel universe"*: Ibid., 41.

21   *"The conscious swains"*: Pope's translation of the *Iliad*, VIII.559.

21   *the 1780s*: This point is brutally addressed by Matthew Arnold in *On Translating Homer: Three Lectures Given at Oxford* (London: Longman, Green, Longman, Roberts, 1861), available online at http://www.victorianprose.org/.

21   *"No man of true"*: *The Iliad of Homer, Translated by Alexander Pope, Esq* (London: W. Baynes and Son, 1824), 4. For an illuminating modern discussion of translation as a kind of alchemical process, see Matthew Reynolds, *The Poetry of Translation: From Chaucer and Petrarch to Homer and Logue* (Oxford: Oxford University Press, 2011).

22   *"What he writes"*: *The Iliad of Homer, Translated by Alexander Pope, Esq*, 4.

22   *"In Homer"*: Ibid.

22   *"Virgil bestows"*: Ibid., 12.

22   *"unaffected and equal"*: Ibid., 18.

23   *"In vain his youth"*: *Iliad* XX.537–46.

23   *"It is not to be doubted"*: *The Iliad of Homer, Translated by Alexander Pope, Esq*, 17.

23   *"a treasure of poetical elegances"*: Samuel Johnson, "Life of Pope" (1779), in *The Works of the English Poets, from Chaucer to Cowper* (London: J. Johnson, 1810), vol. 12, p. 112.

23   *"money-mongering"*: Sonnet to Haydon, quoted in Motion, *Keats*, 119.

24   *"the ocean"*: Keats, "Sonnet I. To My Brother George," Aug. 1816, from Margate.

24   *"the fine rough"*: Motion, *Keats*, 109.

24   *"turning to some"*: Charles Cowden Clarke, "Recollections of Keats" (1861), in *Recollections of Writers* (London: 1878), 120–57.

24   *"There did shine"*: Quoted in Andrew Laing, *The English Poets: Selections with Critical Introductions*, ed. Thomas Humphry Ward (London, 1880), vol. 1, p. 510.

24   *"loose and rambling"*: *The Iliad of Homer, Translated by Alexander Pope, Esq*, 17.

24   *"now totally neglected"*: Johnson, "Life of Pope," 112.

24   *"Chapman writes & feels"*: S. T. Coleridge, "Notes on Chapman's Homer," in *Notes and Lectures Upon Shakespeare and Some of the Old Poets and Dramatists: With Other Literary Remains of S. T. Coleridge* (London: Pickering, 1849), vol. 2, p. 231.

25   *"cool their hooves"*: A phrase later borrowed by Christopher Logue for the moment when the two armies sit down to watch the duel between Paris and Menelaus.

      Now dark, now bright, now watch—
      As aircrews watch tsunamis send
      Ripples across the Iwo Jima Deep,
      Or, as a schoolgirl makes her velveteen
      Go dark, go bright—
      The armies as they strip, and lay their bronze
      And let their horses cool their hooves
      Along the opposing slopes.

25   *"One scene I could not fail"*: Charles Cowden Clarke, "Recollection of Keats" (1861) in *Recollections of Writers* (London, 1878), 130.

25   *"Just as when"*: *Odyssey* V.328–30.

26   *"he then bends both knees"*: Ibid., V.453–57.

26   *As a hero*: See J. P. Mallory and D. Q. Adams, *The Oxford Introduction to Proto-Indo-European and the Proto-Indo-European World* (Oxford Linguistics) (Oxford: Oxford University Press, 2006), 136.

26   *"his knees no more"*: Pope, *Odyssey* V.606–10.

27   *"For the heart"*: Ibid., V.454 (Murray/Dimock, parallel text).

27   *"Odysseus bent his knees"*: Homer, *The Odyssey*, trans. E. V. Rieu, revised by
       D. C. H. Rieu (1946; reprint, London: Penguin, 1991), 83.

27   *"his very heart"*: Richmond Lattimore, *The Iliad of Homer* (Chicago: University
       of Chicago Press, 1951), V.454.

27   *"The sea had beaten"*: Homer, *The Odyssey*, trans. Robert Fagles, introduction
       and notes by Bernard Knox (New York: Viking, 1996), V.502.

27   *"beastly place"*: Quoted in Motion, *Keats*, 74.

27   *"On the first looking"*: This early draft, differing from the published version, is in
       the Houghton Library, Harvard University, MS Keats 2.4 A.MS.

29   *"The troops exulting"*: Pope's *Iliad* VIII.553–65.

30   *"the cockney Homer"*: J. G. Lockhart, "On the Cockney School of Poetry, No. V,"
       Blackwood's Edinburgh Magazine, Apr. 1819, 97.

30   *"A thing of beauty"*: Keats, *Endymion*, book 1, 1–5.

30   *Andrew Motion*: Motion, *Keats*, 162.

31   *"And such too"*: Keats, *Endymion*, book 1, 20–21.

31   *"That question has no answer"*: Lattimore, *The Iliad of Homer*, foreword, 7.

3: LOVING HOMER

32   *they don't eat bread*: *Odyssey* IX.191.

32   *Grilled meat*: Ibid., XX.25–28.

32   *no moment was happier*: Ibid., IX.10.

32   *"all professional athletes"*: Plato, *The Republic*, book 3.

32   *fish was*: The classical Greeks were baffled by Homer's dislike of fish; they
       thought fish the ultimate delicacy and couldn't understand why Homer's
       heroes ate beef when they were so often sitting next to a prime fishing spot. This
       contempt for fish was perhaps a steppeland inheritance, from the time when a
       large herd of meaty animals was one of the identifying marks of a king or hero.

33   *Mindjack*: "Mindjacking" is a term invented by the cyberpunk novelist William
       Gibson.

33   *"I am conscious"*: Plato, *Ion*, 380 BC, trans. Benjamin Jowett; see also Penelope
       Murray and T. Dorsch, *Classical Literary Criticism* (London: Penguin, 2000), 1.

33   *"The gift which you possess"*: Plato, *Ion*; see also Murray and Dorsch, *Classical
       Literary Criticism*, 5.

33   *"There is no invention"*: Plato, *Ion*; see also Murray and Dorsch, *Classical Liter-
       ary Criticism*, 5.

34   *"1 panegyrick poem"*: See Macaulay's *History* (London: Penguin, 1989), vol. 2,
       p. 32, describing the Homeric world of the late-seventeenth-century Highlands
       and islands: "Within the four seas and less than six hundred miles of London
       were many miniature courts, in each of which a petty prince, attended by guards,
       by armour bearers, by musicians, by an hereditary orator, by an hereditary poet
       laureate, kept a rude state, dispensed a rude justice, waged wars, and concluded
       treaties." Also see David Stevenson, *Highland Warrior: Alasdair Maccolla and
       the Civil Wars* (Edinburgh: John Donald, 1980), for the reemergence of a warrior

society in the power vacuum created by the failure of the Scottish crown. The warrior world emerges not at a moment in history but at repeated phases of human social and political arrangements, when there is no overarching authority in control.

34   *the people of Pylos: Odyssey* III.5–6.

34   *Odysseus weeps:* Ibid., V.151.

34   *he finds Nausicaa:* Ibid., VI.1ff.

34   *draw up their ships:* Ibid., XI.20.

34   *Odysseus lands:* Ibid., XIII.195ff.

34   *"The way they take":* Lattimore, *Iliad* IX.182, Fagles IX.217–20; a mixture of the two.

35   *"To wander in anguish":* Adapted from Fagles, *Iliad* XXIV.14–15.

36   *"on her golden throne": Odyssey* X.541.

36   *"her veil the colour": Iliad* XXIII.227.

37   *"that bellows": Odyssey* II.421.

37   *He spreads his sail:* Ibid., V.268.

37   *"and the wind":* Ibid., XI.10.

37   *"So these two":* Lattimore, *Iliad* VIII.1–8.

38   *"Back towards home":* Ibid., XXIII.229–30.

38   *"the black ship": Odyssey* XI.1–14.

39   *red-painted bows:* Lattimore, *Iliad* II.637.

39   *"The wind catches":* T. E. Shaw, *The Odyssey* (1932), quoted in Rodelle Weintraub and Stanley Weintraub, "Chapman's Homer," *Classical World* 67, no. 1 (Sept.–Oct. 1973), 16–24.

39   *"Thus with stretched sail":* Ezra Pound, "Canto 1," 9–10.

4: SEEKING HOMER

40   *"germana et sincera":* Joh. Baptista Caspar d'Ansse de Villoison, *Homeri Ilias ad Veteris Codicis Veneti Fidem Recensita* (Paris, 1788), xxxiv.

41   *"I will send":* Robert Southey, ed., *The Works of William Cowper* (London, 1836), vol. 6, p. 266.

41   *Friedrich August Wolf:* Wolf, a highly irritable man, claimed never to have had a dream in his life. See Nicholas Boyle, *Goethe: Revolution and Renunciation, 1790–1803* (Oxford: Oxford University Press, 2003), 265.

42   *"No such person":* Thomas De Quincey, "Homer and the Homeridae," *Blackwood's Edinburgh Magazine*, Oct. 1841, 411–27.

42   *"sovereign poet":* Dante, *Inferno* IV.88.

42   *"was dumb to me and I am deaf to it":* E. H. Wilkins, *Life of Petrarch* (Chicago: Chicago University Press, 1962), 136.

42   *Medieval* Odysseys: For the most illuminating account of the early texts of Homer, see M. L. West, ed. and trans., *Lives of Homer*, in *Homeric Hymns etc.* (Cambridge, Mass.: Loeb/Harvard University Press, 2003), 296ff.

43   *brought to Italy:* L. Labowsky, *Bessarion's Library and the Biblioteca Marciana— Six Early Inventories* (Rome: Sussidi Eruditi, 1979).

44   *Flinders Petrie found:* William M. Flinders Petrie, *Hawara, Biahmu, and Arsinoe* (London, 1889). Plate xix shows many of these objects.

44   *"The floating sand"*: Ibid., chapter 5, on the papyri, written by Archibald Sayce, p. 39.

44   *"The roll had belonged"*: Ibid., p. 35.

45   *This Hawara Homer*: P. Hawara 24–28 (Bodleian Libr., Gr. Class. A.1 (P)). *Iliad* I.506–10, II.1–877, with many lacunae. http://ipap.csad.ox.ac.uk/Hawara-bw /72dpi/Hawara_Homer%28viii%29.jpg.

45   *"the grandeur of the dooms"*: Keats, *Endymion*, book 1, 20–21.

47   *Phaeacians*: A mythical people, not to be confused with the Phoenicians, an ancient civilization with its origins on the eastern shore of the Mediterranean, in modern Lebanon and Syria. *Odyssey* IX.8–10.

47   *"Homer is the greatest"*: Plato, *The Republic*, 607 a 2–5.

47   *"Just as a poppy"*: *Iliad* VIII.306–8.

48   *"to a place"*: Ibid., VIII.491.

48   *In Troy itself*: The Venetus A scholia on this passage are analyzed by Graeme Bird in "Critical Signs—Drawing Attention to 'Special' Lines of Homer's *Iliad* in the Manuscript Venetus A," in *Recapturing a Homeric Legacy: Images and Insights from the Venetus A Manuscript of the Iliad*, ed. Casey Dué (Washington, D.C.: Center for Hellenic Studies, 2009), 112–14.

48   *"dogs, carried by the fates"*: *Iliad* VIII.526–40; combination of Murray/Dimock and Fagles VIII.617–28.

50   *"We go to liberate"*: BBC News, 20 March 2003: "UK Troops Told: Be Just and Strong," originally from a pooled report by Sarah Oliver, *Mail on Sunday*.

51   *Alexandrian scholars*: See Richard P. Martin, "Cretan Homers: Tradition, Politics, Fieldwork," *Classics@* 3 (Washington, D.C.: Center for Hellenic Studies, 2012).

52   *"The further back"*: Casey Dué, "Epea Pteroenta: How We Came to Have Our Iliad," in *Recapturing a Homeric Legacy*, 25.

52   *"young, headstrong"*: S. Butler, *The Authoress of the Odyssey*, 2nd ed. (London: Longmans, Green, 1922), 142.

52   *Would a man*: Ibid., 9, referring to *Odyssey* IX.483, 540. But see the footnote on pp. 350–51 of *The Odyssey*, Murray/Dimock (1999), which justifies Homer's apparent mistake by explaining that between the two mentions of the rudder on Odysseus's ship, the Greeks had turned the ship around. The ship of course only had a rudder, or steering oar, at the stern, but within the course of the story, the ship was facing in two different directions.

52   *"killed many men"*: David Garnett, ed., *The Letters of T. E. Lawrence* (London: Jonathan Cape, 1938), letter no. 431, January 31, 1931, pp. 709–10.

52   *in fact the Baltic*: Felice Vinci, *Omero nel Baltico*, with introductions by R. Calzecchi Onesti and F. Cuomo (Rome: Palombi Editori, 1998).

52   *guidebook to the stars*: Florence Wood and Kenneth Wood, *Homer's Secret Iliad: The Epic of the Night Skies Decoded* (London: John Murray, 1999).

52   *Homer was from Cambridgeshire*: Iman Wilkens, *Where Troy Once Stood*, 2nd ed. (London: Rider, 2009; a theory first developed by Théophile Cailleux, a Belgian lawyer, in *Pays atlantiques décrits par Homère. Ibérie, Gaule, Bretagne, Archipels, Amérique* (Paris, 1878) and *Théorie nouvelle sur les origines humaines. Homère en Occident. Troie en Angleterre* (Brussels, 1883).

52   *Henriette Mertz*: Henriette Mertz, *The Wine Dark Sea: Homer's Heroic Epic of the North Atlantic* (Chicago: self-published, 1964).

53   *everywhere and nowhere:* M. L. West, ed. and trans., *Lives of Homer*, 433.

53   *"The people of Ios":* Ibid., 435.

54   *"For you were born":* Ibid., 413. Pseudo-Plutarch is quoting the epigrammatist Antipater of Thessalonica, writing ca. 20 BC.

55   *He is the embodiment:* See, for example, ibid., 429.

55   "U re u re na-nam": Quoted in M. L. West, *The East Face of Helicon* (Oxford: Oxford University Press, 1999), 61.

56   *"attend to what":* J. Black, "Some Structural Features of Sumerian Narrative Poetry," in *Mesopotamian Epic Literature: Oral or Aural?*, ed. M. E. Vogelzang and H. L. J. Vanstiphout (Lampeter: Edwin Mellen Press, 1992), 71–101.

56   *One more story:* See West, *Lives of Homer*, 399, 411, 421–23, 437–39, 441–43, 447–49, for versions of this story.

57   *"Here the earth":* Ibid., 448.

5: FINDING HOMER

59   *"the purple on account":* Eustathius VI.8, quoted in M. L. West, *The Making of the* Iliad: *Disquisition and Analytical Commentary* (Oxford: Oxford University Press, 2011), 75; impossibly expensive editions of Eustathius commentaries are M. van der Valk, ed., *Eustathii Archiepiscopi Thessalonicensis Commentarii ad Homeri Iliadem Pertinentes ad Fidem Codicis Laurentiani Editi*, 4 vols. (Leiden: Brill, 1971–1987).

60   *"Remember me":* H. G. Evelyn-White, trans., *Hesiod, Homeric Hymns, Epic Cycle, Homerica* (Cambridge, Mass.: Loeb/Harvard University Press, 1914), vol. 57, pp. 165ff.

62   *"a well-girt man":* John Boardman, *Excavations in Chios, 1952–1955: Greek Emporio* (London: British School at Athens, 1967), supplementary vols., no. 6, pp. iii–xiv, 5.

62   *"wretched throughout":* Ibid., pp. iii–xiv, 4.

63   *If Homer was an ancient inheritance:* It may feel a little awkward referring to Homer as "it," but that awkwardness reflects the question at the heart of this book. Is Homer to be thought of as an author or a cultural phenomenon? A man or a society? Or a sequence of societies? The discomfort we feel is the point. If he is an ancient inheritance, then "he" must be an "it."

       "For masterpieces are not single or solitary births; they are the outcome of many years of thinking in common, of thinking by the body of the people, so that the experience of the mass is behind the single voice."—Virginia Woolf in *A Room of One's Own.*

66   *Giorgio Buchner:* Giorgio Buchner, "Recent Work at Pithekoussai (Ischia), 1965–71," *Archaeological Reports* 17 (1970–1971), 63–67; D. Ridgway, *The First Western Greeks* (Cambridge: Cambridge University Press, 1992); G. Buchner and D. Ridgway, *Pithekoussai, La necropoli: Tombe 1–723. Scavate dal 1952 al 1961* (Rome: Accademia Nazionale dei Lincei, 1993).

66   *"to monkey about":* Catherine Connors, "Monkey Business: Imitation, Authenticity, and Identity from Pithekoussai to Plautus," *Classical Antiquity* 23, no. 2 (Oct. 2004), 179–207.

67   *Much of their pottery:* For images and information on the exhibits in the Museo

Archeologico di Pithecusae in the Villa Arbusto on Ischia, see http://www
.pithecusae.it/colonia1.htm.

68   *"will lick the blood"*: Iliad XXI.122–27.

69   *voracious monsters:* In 1934, part of the scapula of a young fin whale (average
adult length sixty feet) was found in a well in the area that would later become
the Agora in Athens. The pottery alongside it was slightly earlier than the Attic
cratēr found in Ischia. Terrifyingly vast fish undoubtedly swam in the Odyssean
world. This shoulder blade was probably used as a cutting surface, perhaps by a
butcher or fishmonger. John K. Papadopoulos and Deborah Ruscillo, "A Ketos
in Early Athens: An Archaeology of Whales and Sea Monsters in the Greek
World," *American Journal of Archaeology* 106, no. 2 (Apr. 2002), 187–227.

69   *"someone whose name"*: From Kate Monk, *Onomastikon* (1997). http://tekeli.li
/onomastikon/Ancient-World/Greece/Male.html.

69   *Eighth-century inscriptions:* Rufus Bellamy, "Bellerophon's Tablet," *Classical Journal* 84, no. 4 (Apr.–May 1989), 293.

69   *but witty remarks:* Ibid., 299.

70   *the first joke:* Another scratched inscription on a mid-eighth-century wine jug
unearthed in Athens may be slightly older. It was probably given as a prize in a
dancing competition and carries the beautiful verse "*hos nun orcheston pan-
ton atalotata paizēi,*" "whoever of all these dancers now plays most delicately"
would, the implication is, receive this jug as a prize. This Greek Renaissance
writing begins with dance and delight and competition. B. Powell, "The Dipylon Oinochoe Inscription and the Spread of Literacy in 8th Century Athens,"
Kadmos 27 (1988), 65–86.

70   *during a passage:* Iliad XI.632–37.

70   *giant unliftable cups:* M. L. West, "Grated Cheese Fit for Heroes," *Journal of
Hellenic Studies* 118 (1998), 190–91.

70   *bronze cheese graters:* D. Ridgway, "Nestor's Cup and the Etruscans," *Oxford
Journal of Archaeology* 16 (1997), 325–44.

70   *the joke and invitation:* Not everyone agrees it was a joke. See Christopher A.
Faraone, "Taking the 'Nestor's Cup Inscription' Seriously: Erotic Magic and
Conditional Curses in the Earliest Inscribed Hexameters," *Classical Antiquity*
15, no. 1 (Apr. 1996), 77–112.

6: HOMER THE STRANGE

72   *essentially oral:* M. S. Edmondson, *Lore: An Introduction to the Science of Folk-
lore and Literature* (New York: Holt Rinehart and Winston, 1971), 323.

73   *"a sequel of songs"*: R. Bentley, *Remarks Upon a Late Discourse of Free Thinking*
(London, 1713).

73   *"quiet in manner"*: William C. Greene, "Milman Parry (1902–1935)," *Proceedings of the American Academy of Arts and Sciences* 71, no. 10 (Mar. 1937),
535–36.

73   *the first to develop:* Albert Lord, *The Singer of Tales* (Cambridge: Harvard University Press, 2000), vol. 1, p. x.

74   *"an aura of the Latin Quarter"*: Harry Levin, "Portrait of a Homeric Scholar,"
Classical Journal 32, no. 5 (Feb. 1937), 259–66.

75 *"How can we grasp"*: Renan's essay on *L'Avenir de Science* (Paris, 1892), 292, quoted in Adam Parry, ed., *The Making of Homeric Verse: The Collected Papers of Milman Parry* (Oxford: Oxford University Press, 1987), 2, 409.

77 *Here . . . is an English hexameter*: Henry Wadsworth Longfellow, *Evangeline: A Tale of Acadie* (1847), line 1.

77 *Just under a third:* There are 9,253 repetitive lines out of a total of 27,803.

78 *and so on through the whole cast:* Parry, *The Making of Homeric Verse*, 39.

79 *"The poetry . . . was not one"*: Ibid., 425.

79 *"Darwin of Homeric scholarship"*: Ibid., xxvi.

80 *"a machine of memory"*: James I. Porter, "Homer: The Very Idea," *Arion*, 3rd ser., 10, no. 2 (Fall 2002), 57–86.

80 *up to 494:* Steve Reece, "Some Homeric Etymologies in the Light of Oral-Formulaic Theory," *Classical World* 93, no. 2, Homer (Nov.–Dec. 1999), 185–99; M. M. Kumpf, *Four Indices of the Homeric Hapax Legomena* (Hildesheim: 1984), 206; M. W. Edwards, *The Iliad: A Commentary* (Cambridge: Cambridge University Press, 1991), vol. 5, p. 55.

80 *But for Parry:* Parry, *The Making of Homeric Verse*, 21.

80 *"The tradition is"*: Ibid., 450.

80 *"One's style should"*: Aristotle, *Rhetoric*, 1404 b 10.

80 *"genuine poetry"*: T. S. Eliot, *Selected Essays*, 3rd ed. (London: Faber, 1999), 238.

81 *not originally a written:* Parry, *The Making of Homeric Verse*, xxiii–xxiv.

81 *You have your formulas:* Ibid., 448.

82 *the overused recourse:* Ibid.

83 *almost exactly a ton:* http://chs119.chs.harvard.edu/mpc/index.html.

84 *"a tall, lean"*: From the draft of a text intended for a popular audience written in 1937 by Parry's youthful assistant Albert Lord. http://chs119.chs.harvard.edu/mpc/about/intro.html.

84 *"Finally Avdo came"*: Ibid.

85 *"It takes the full strength"*: Parry, *The Making of Homeric Verse*, 457.

85 *Each singer sang:* Ibid., 458, 460.

85 *In June 1935:* Halil Bajgoric, "The Wedding of Mustajbey's Son Bećirbey," Parry, no. 6699. www.oraltradition.org/static/zbm/zbm.pdf.

87 *"The moment he cherished"*: Harry Levin, "Portrait of a Homeric Scholar," *Classical Journal* 32, no. 5 (Feb. 1937), 259–66.

88 *"But why did you"*: From Parry, Conversation 6698, in *An eEdition of "The Wedding of Mustajbey's Son Bećirbey,"* as performed by Halil Bajgorić, ed. and trans. John Miles Foley, on www.oraltradition.org.

88 *"The verses and the themes"*: Parry, *The Making of Homeric Verse*, 449.

88 *They asked one singer:* John Miles Foley, *Traditional Oral Epic: The Odyssey, Beowulf, and the Serbo-Croatian Return Song* (Berkeley: University of California Press, 1993), 43–44.

89 *"What is, let's say"*: Ibid., 44.

89 *"Plato thought nature"*: W. B. Yeats, "Among School Children," VI. 1–2, *The Tower* (London: Macmillan, 1928).

90 *"The more I understand"*: Parry, *The Making of Homeric Verse*, 451 (written in Jan. 1934), quoted in Richard Janko, "The Homeric Poems as Oral Dictated Texts," *Classical Quarterly*, new ser., 48, no. 1 (1998), 1–13.

90   *written much later:* Lord, *The Singer of Tales.*

91   *"It was the wet spring":* A conversation I reported before, in *Sea Room* (London: HarperCollins, 2001), 292.

92   *everything in his songs:* Foley, *Traditional Oral Epic*, 44; Parry, Conversation 6598 (same conversation as the words/phrases).

92   *"making the wince":* http://www.recordingpioneers.com/RP_NOTOPOULOS1 .html; G. N. Antonakopoulos, "Mia Agnosti Seira Diskon Ellinikis Mousikis" (in *Laïko Tragoudi*, no. [2005], 16–19); see turcopolier.typepad.com/sic_semper _tyrannis/files/arion_odysseus.doc.

93   *He found Sfakia:* James A. Notopoulos, "The Genesis of an Oral Heroic Poem," *Greek, Roman and Byzantine Studies* 3 (1960), 135–44.

96   *the opposite conclusion:* Maartje Draak, "Duncan MacDonald of South Uist," *Fabula* 1 (1957), 47–58; William Lamb, "The Storyteller, the Scribe, and a Missing Man: Hidden Influences from Printed Sources in the Gaelic Tales of Duncan and Neil MacDonald," *Oral Tradition* 27, no. 1 (2012), 109–60.

96   *heir to the great traditions:* See the Calum Maclean Project, Department of Celtic and Scottish Studies, University of Edinburgh, http://www.calum-maclean-proj ect.celtscot.ed.ac.uk/home/; Lamb, "The Storyteller, the Scribe, and a Missing Man."

97   *"polished, shapely":* http://calumimaclean.blogspot.co.uk/2013_02_01_archive .html.

97   *On analysis:* Draak, "Duncan Macdonald of South Uist."

98   *ethnographers have discovered:* Douglas Young, "Never Blotted a Line? Formula and Premeditation in Homer and Hesiod," *Arion* 6, no. 3 (Fall 1967), 279–324.

98   *"had in his head":* Ibid.

7: HOMER THE REAL

100   *"the terrible noise":* Iliad VI.105.

101   *"As the generation":* From E. R. Lowry Jr., "Glaucus, the Leaves, and the Heroic Boast of *Iliad* VI.146–211," in *The Ages of Homer: A Tribute to E. Townsend Vermeule*, ed. J. B. Carter and S. P. Morris (1995; reprint, Austin: University of Texas Press, 1998), 193; combined with Fagles, *Iliad* VI.171–75.

101   *"as many as the leaves":* Iliad II.468.

102   *"Near the city":* Ibid., II.811–14 (Murray/Wyatt, slightly adapted).

102   *Epic poetry serves us:* Jonas Grethlein, "Memory and Material Objects in the *Iliad* and the *Odyssey*," *Journal of Hellenic Studies* 128 (2008), 27–51.

102   *"such as will remain":* Iliad III.287.

102   *the Muse provides:* Odyssey VIII.479–81.

102   *in the same class:* Iliad IX.364.

103   *Achilles's iron heart:* Ibid., XX.372. This is a translation of the phrase *aithōni sidērō*, which might also mean more prosaically "shining iron."

103   *a profoundly ancient world:* See Susan Sherratt, "Archaeological Contexts," in *A Companion to Ancient Epic*, ed. John Miles Foley (Oxford: Blackwell, 2005), 119–42.

104   *his team had found six hundred:* C. W. Blegen and M. Rawson, *The Palace of*

Nestor at Pylos in Western Messenia, vol. 1, *The Buildings and Their Contents* (Princeton, N.J.: Princeton University Press, 1966), 6, 95–100; C. W. Blegen and K. Kourouniotis, "Excavations of Pylos, 1939," *American Journal of Archaeology* 43 (1939), 569.

104   *No one could guess:* Ione Mylonas Shear, "Bellerophon Tablets from the Mycenaean World? A Tale of Seven Bronze Hinges," *Journal of Hellenic Studies* 118 (1998), 187–89.

104   *A piece of firewood:* Christoph Bachhuber, "Aegean Interest on the Uluburun Ship," *American Journal of Archaeology* 110, no. 3 (July 2006), 345–63.

106   *a moment from the* Iliad: *Iliad* VI.119–236.

106   *"he quickly sent":* Ibid., VI.168–70.

107   *What does this description:* T. R. Bryce, "The Nature of Mycenaean Involvement in Western Anatolia," *Historia* 38 (1989), 13–14; Rufus Bellamy, "Bellerophon's Tablet," *Classical Journal* 84 (1989), 289–307; Shear, "Bellerophon Tablets from the Mycenaean World?"; Byron Harries, "'Strange Meeting': Diomedes and Glaucus in *Iliad* 6," *Greece and Rome* 40 (1993), 133–47; T. R. Bryce, "Anatolian Scribes in Mycenaean Greece," *Historia* 48 (1999), 257–64.

107   *It is a tiny:* Not everyone agrees with this view of Homer's Greeks—or in this distinction between Greek and Trojan. From the *Odyssey* comes all kinds of evidence that the Greeks were at home in palaces: Nestor and Menelaus live with elaborate and comfortable set-ups at Pylos and Sparta, full of warmth and ritualized hospitality. Even Odysseus's home on Ithaca, while clearly not a major citadel, has *megara skioenta,* "shadowed halls," like the rich Near Eastern palace of Alcinous in Scheria. These hints and suggestions can be taken as a sign that the *Odyssey* was deeply colored by its transmission through the palace centuries of the Mycenaean period, where the cultural expectations of a great man's equipment had come to include a palace establishment.

107   *It is not the world:* The *Iliad,* perhaps because the circumstances of war did not encourage it, remained more resistant to these later influences. It is true that even in the *Iliad* Mycenae is described as *euktimenon ptoliethron,* "a well-founded citadel" (*Iliad* 2.569–70), *polychrysos,* "rich in gold" (*Iliad* 11.46) and, like Troy, *euruaguia,* "with broad streets" (*Iliad* 4.52). But these are no more than marginal suggestions. The poetic weight of warriorhood in the poem remains firmly on the Greek side, and the poetic weight of civility and urbanness firmly on the Trojan. Hector is undoubtedly a ferocious warrior, but he is nearly alone as such among the Trojans, who do not entirely admire him for it. Paris and Priam, on the other hand, represent two contrasting dimensions of urban civility—wise government and a tendency to foppishness—and they appear as they do not because of the circumstances in which they find themselves but because of their essential natures. The same is true of Achilles: he will be the unaccommodated man in whatever circumstances he finds himself. For all the surrounding realism and nuance, these are the polarities the *Iliad* dramatizes.

108   *"floats all through":* Emily Townsend Vermeule, "Jefferson and Homer," *Proceedings of the American Philosophical Society* 137, no. 4, 250th anniversary issue (Dec. 1993), 689–703.

108   *in many parts earlier:* M. L. West, "The Rise of the Greek Epic," *Journal of Hellenic Studies* 108 (1988), 151–72.

108   *but the Iliadic words:* Ibid.

109   *"There are in all":* Quoted in Ernst Meyer, "Schliemann's Letters to Max Müller in Oxford," *Journal of Hellenic Studies* 82 (1962), 24, 92.

110   *he identified the warriors:* Schliemann claimed in a telegram to a Greek newspaper that on exposing one of the jewel-encrusted kings he felt that "this corpse very much resembles the image which my imagination formed long ago of wide-ruling Agamemnon" (Cathy Gere, *The Tomb of Agamemnon: Mycenae and the Search for a Hero* [London: Profile, 2006], 76). He never said, as is usually reported, that he had "gazed on the face of Agamemnon," nor was he referring to the wonderful gold face mask now universally referred to as the Mask of Agamemnon. That handsome, mustachioed boulevardier king, the most famous face of the Bronze Age, belonged to another grave. Immediately before sending his telegram, Schliemann had looked at a dead body "whose round face, with all its flesh had been wonderfully preserved," eyes and teeth all there. That face had also been covered in a gold mask, but it is a strange thing, clean-shaven, as round as a football, fat-cheeked and pig-eyed, an image of regality that has never been explained. (See Gere, *The Tomb of Agamemnon,* 79, for an illustration of the gold mask from Shaft Grave IV of Grave Circle A, Mycenae, 1550–1500 BC.)

110   *very like the world:* Homer does not describe burials of the kind that are found in the Shaft Graves at Mycenae. The Homeric hero is always cremated on a pyre and his remains put in a container that is then buried within a large tumulus. That form of interment is found all over the Indo-European world but not in Greece, at least until the eighth century BC (see H. L. Lorimer, "Pulvis et Umbra," *Journal of Hellenic Studies* 53 [1933], 161–80). Different Indo-European peoples at different times both cremated and buried their dead. So this is a conundrum: are the burial practices in Homer evidence of their being very late poems, no earlier than the eighth century BC? Or is this evidence of some deep memory of early Indo-European traditions which also gave rise to cremation for heroes in Scandinavia, and to people in India and Iran? See J. P. Mallory and Douglas Q. Adams, eds., *Encyclopedia of Indo-European Culture* (Oxford: Routledge, 1997), 151.

111   *"the slayers and the slain":* Iliad XI.83–162.

111   *"ungentle is":* Ibid., XI.137: *ameiliktos d'op akousan.*

111   *"more loved by the vultures":* Ibid., XI.162.

111   *"And just as when":* Ibid., XI.269–72 (Murray/Wyatt, adapted).

113   *"As when the open sea":* Ibid., XIV.16–20 (Lattimore, adapted).

113   *"Philologists often dislike":* Vermeule, "Jefferson and Homer."

114   *"He speaks":* Iliad XVI.856–57, XXII.362–63.

114   *The difference:* Emily Vermeule, *Aspects of Death in Early Greek Art and Poetry* (Oakland: University of California Press, 1979), 9, 10. "Now a doctor in Düsseldorf has succeeded in quantifying the soul by placing the beds of his terminal patients on extremely sensitive scales. 'As they died and the souls left their bodies, the needles dropped twenty-one grams.'" She was quoting Dr. Nils-Olof Jacobson, "Life After Death," *Boston Globe,* December 19, 1972. The claim that the weight of the soul is twenty-one grams was first made in 1901 by a group of American doctors, most prominently Duncan MacDougall of Massachusetts, who carried out experiments reported in the *New York Times* in March 1907.

8: THE METAL HERO

116   *Parys Mountain:* For a full account of Parys Mountain, see Bryan D. Hope, *A Curious Place: The Industrial History of Amlwch (1550–1950)* (Wrexham: Bridge Books, 1994).

116   *In about 8000 BC:* B. W. Roberts, C. P. Thornton and V. C. Piggott, "Development of Metallurgy in Eurasia," *Antiquity* 83 (2009), 1012–22.

116   *Only then did someone:* Evgenii N. Chernykh, *Ancient Metallurgy in the USSR: The Early Metal Age*, trans. Sarah Wright (Cambridge: Cambridge University Press, 1992).

117   *It became a world:* Kristian Kristiansen and Thomas B. Larsson, *The Rise of Bronze Age Society: Travels, Transmissions and Transformations* (Cambridge: Cambridge University Press, 2005), 108–9, 114, 123–24.

117   *"The broad picture":* Richard J. Harrison, *Symbols and Warriors: Images of the European Bronze Age* (Bristol: Western Academic and Specialist Press, 2004).

117   *patterns that recur:* See Kristiansen and Larsson, *The Rise of Bronze Age Society*, passim.

117   *Were these movements:* Ibid., 142–250.

117   *The teeth of an early Bronze Age man:* A. P. Fitzpatrick, *The Amesbury Archer and the Boscombe Bowmen* (Salisbury: Trust for Wessex Archaeology, 2011).

118   *Chemical analysis:* See online report at www.wessexarch.co.uk/projects/kent /ramsgate.

118   *It seems inescapable:* Stephen Oppenheimer, "A Reanalysis of Multiple Prehistoric Immigrations to Britain and Ireland Aimed at Identifying Celtic Contributions," in *Celtic from the West*, ed. B. Cunliffe and J. T. Koch (Oxford: Oxbow, 2010), 142.

118   *A different, nonurban:* Philip L. Kohl, *The Making of Bronze Age Eurasia* (Oxford: Cambridge University Press, 2007), 126ff.

121   *"They clothe their bodies":* Iliad XIV.384ff.

121   *"as snug as a gun":* Seamus Heaney, "Digging," from *Death of a Naturalist* (London: Faber, 1966).

122   *"doupēsen de pesōn":* E.g., *Iliad* IV.504, XVII.50.

124   *their life dependent:* See Emily Vermeule, *Aspects of Death in Early Greek Art and Poetry* (Oakland: University of California Press, 1979), 99–101, 112–15.

125   *Adolf Schulten:* A. Schulten, *Fontes Hispaniae Antiquae* (Barcelona: Universidad de Barcelona, 1922), vol. 1, p. 90.

126   *Inner and outer landscapes:* Circe's description at *Odyssey* X.510. Odysseus comes to the shores of Hades at *Odyssey* XI.22.

126   *"flutter through his fingers":* Ibid., XI.206–8.

127   *"Never try to sweeten death":* Ibid., XI.408ff.

127   *the ghost says through his tears:* It's not certain that the hero was weeping— *olophuromai* usually means "lament, be sad"—but this is likely to be the sense.

127   *"like consuming fire":* Iliad XX.372.

128   *"But tell me":* Odyssey XI.491.

128   *murdering Priam:* This was the scene, transmitted through the *Aeneid*, when Neoptolemos was slaughtering his way through Troy, "And all his father sparkled in his eyes," which caught Hamlet's imagination; the young Greek was

total gules; horridly trick'd
With blood of fathers, mothers, daughters, sons,
Bak'd and impasted with the parching streets,
That lend a tyrannous and damned light
To their lord's murder. (*Hamlet* II.ii.457–61)

128   *"So I spoke": Odyssey* XI.538–40 Fagles, XI.613–16.

129   *"Set up your mast":* Ibid., X.506–7 (Murray/Dimock, adapted slightly).

129   *"But when in your ship":* Ibid., X.508–12 (Murray/Dimock).

129   *"There into the ocean":* Ibid., X.513–15 (Murray/Dimock).

130   *"they stowed their gear and laid the mast in the hollow hulls": Odyssey* XI. 20.

131   *there is a museum:* www.parquemineroderiotinto.com/.

132   *at a place called Chinflón:* The mine at Chinflón is at 37°40'N, 6°40'W; see B. Rothenberg and A. Blanco-Freijeiro, "Ancient Copper Mining and Smelting at Chinflón (Huelva, SW Spain)," *British Museum Occasional Paper* 20 (1980), 41–62; for bronze mining, see Ben Roberts, "Metallurgical Networks and Technological Choice: Understanding Early Metal in Western Europe," *World Archaeology* 40, issue 3 (2008), 354–72; Anthony F. Harding, *European Societies in the Bronze Age* (Cambridge: Cambridge University Press, 2000), 197–241.

133   *In Cornwall:* M. A. Courtney, "Cornish Folk-Lore," part 3, *Folk-Lore Journal* 5, no. 3 (1887), 177–220; James C. Baker, "Echoes of Tommy Knockers in Bohemia, Oregon, Mines," *Western Folklore* 30, no. 2 (Apr. 1971), 119–22.

133   *"called the little miners":* Georgius Agricola, *De Animantibus Subterraneis* (Freiburg, 1548).

133   *"represent man's inner universe":* Ronald Finucane, *Appearances of the Dead* (London: Junction Books, 1982).

134   *their ancient beliefs:* Agricola, *De Animantibus Subterraneis*; Courtney, "Cornish Folk-Lore," part 3; Finucane, *Appearances of the Dead*; Baker, "Echoes of Tommy Knockers in Bohemia, Oregon, Mines."

134   *"When it comes to":* Gaston Bachelard, *The Poetics of Space* (1958; reprint, Boston: Beacon Press, 1994), 18–20.

135   *in his catalog:* Harrison, *Symbols and Warriors.* The stelae in the Archaeological Museum in Badajoz represent perhaps the richest of all collections. Others are in Córdoba, Huelva, Seville and Madrid, and in Portugal.

135   *topped and mended with thorns: Odyssey* XIV.10.

135   *None of this is different:* Harrison, *Symbols and Warriors*, 12, 24.

137   *"red with the blood": Iliad* XVIII.538.

137   *"fruit in wicker baskets":* Ibid., XVIII.568.

137   *"the perfect circle":* Menelaus's, for example, in *Iliad* XVII.6.

137   *obsessed with male beauty:* M. Eleanor Irwin, "Odysseus's 'Hyacinthine Hair' in *Odyssey* 6.231," *Phoenix* 44, no. 3 (Fall 1990), 205–18.

138   *"who held his head": Iliad* VI.509–10.

138   *"His strength can do nothing":* Ibid., XXI.316–18.

139   *"Great Priam entered in":* Ibid., XXIV.477–79.

139   *"roused in Achilles":* Ibid., XXIV.507–8.

139   *"And they come":* Ibid., IX.185ff.

140   *Archaeologists working:* http://www.aocarchaeology.com/news/the-lyre-bridge-from-high-pasture-cave.

140   *It seems unlikely*: Harrison, *Symbols and Warriors*, 104.

141   *A huge warrior figure*: Ibid., 298–99; Catalog number C80, found at Ategua, Córdoba. Now in the Museo Arqueológico Provincial de Córdoba.

142   *"Ah Sokos"*: *Iliad* XI.450–55 (Lattimore, adapted).

142   *"He is a unique"*: Harrison, *Symbols and Warriors*, 116.

143   *"Hector . . . talk not"*: *Iliad* XXII.261–67.

143   *"There are no oaths"*: *Iliad* XXII.262–67.

143   *"the heroes gave orders"*: Harrison, *Symbols and Warriors*, 116.

9: HOMER ON THE STEPPES

144   *The origins of the Greeks*: J. P. Mallory, *In Search of the Indo-Europeans: Language, Archaeology and Myth* (London: Thames & Hudson, 1989).

145   *And before that*: N. G. L. Hammond, "Tumulus-Burial in Albania, the Grave Circles of Mycenae, and the Indo-Europeans," *Annual of the British School at Athens* 62 (1967), 77–105.

145   *Right in the middle*: *Odyssey* XI.119–37.

145   *"You must go out"*: Ibid., XI.121–30, Fagles, XI.138–49.

146   *"in the ebbing time"*: *Odyssey* XI.136.

147   *recorded from Sophocles*: R. Scott Smith and Stephen M. Trzaskoma, trans., *Apollodorus' Library and Hyginus' Fabulae: Two Handbooks of Greek Mythology* (Indianapolis: Hackett, 2007), Fabula, 95.

148   *"Our land"*: Plato, *Critias*.

148   *it is possible*: M. L. West, *The Making of the* Iliad: *Disquisition and Analytical Commentary* (Oxford: Oxford University Press, 2011), 42.

149   *"the smoke ascending"*: Lattimore, *Iliad* XXI.522–23.

149   *the speech he makes*: *Iliad* IX.308–409.

149   *"rich with fat"*: Ibid., IX.205–8.

149   *Odysseus then lists*: Ibid., IX.264–98.

150   *"Let him submit"*: Ibid., IX.160.

150   *"the greediest"*: Ibid., I.122.

150   *"As I detest the doorways"*: Lattimore, *Iliad* XI.312–14.

150   *"Hateful in my eyes"*: *Iliad* IX.378ff.

151   *"All the wealth"*: Ibid., IX.401–2.

151   *"Cattle and fat sheep"*: Lattimore, *Iliad* IX.405–9.

152   *These questions*: See: Adam Parry, "The Language of Achilles," *Transactions and Proceedings of the American Philological Association* 87 (1956), 1–7; M. D. Reeve, "The Language of Achilles," *Classical Quarterly*, new ser., 23, no. 2 (Nov. 1973), 193–95; Steve Nimis, "The Language of Achilles: Construction vs. Representation," *Classical World* 79, no. 4 (Mar.–Apr. 1986), 217–25; W. Donlan, "Duelling with Gifts in the *Iliad*: As the Audience Saw It," *Colby Quarterly* 24 (1993), 171; Dean Hammer, "Achilles as Vagabond: The Culture of Autonomy in the 'Iliad,'" *Classical World* 90, no. 5 (May–June 1997), 341–66.

152   *Those connections*: For these and many of the examples in the following pages of reconstructed and inherited words in the Indo-European family, see the outstanding J. P. Mallory and D. Q. Adams, *The Oxford Introduction to Proto-Indo-European*

and the Proto-Indo-European World (Oxford: Oxford University Press, 2006), 138, especially 220ff.

152   "phrater": This word, from the same root as the others, in fact means something like "clansman" in Greek. The usual Greek word for brother is *adelphos*, meaning "from the same womb."

153   *words that have been transmitted:* For an overview of the Indo-European world, see Benjamin W. Fortson IV, *Indo-European Language and Culture: An Introduction*, 2nd ed. (Chichester: Wiley-Blackwell, 2010).

153   *the same word at root:* See Mallory and Adams, *The Oxford Introduction to Proto-Indo-European*, 138. The reconstructed root for "otter" in PIE is *udrós*, with descendants in Latin, English, Lithuanian, Russian, Greek, Iranian and Sanskrit. That reconstructed word is itself formed from the word for water, *wódr*.

153   *A verb for the driving:* J. P. Mallory, *In Search of the Indo-Europeans* (London: Thames and Hudson, 1989), 117–18: the frozen expression "to drive cattle" is found in Celtic, Italic and Indo-Iranian. Sanskrit and Greek share a word for the special sacrifice of "one hundred cows," for which the Greek word is a hecatomb.

153   *It seems as if:* Ibid., 118: "It has long been regarded as reasonable that there was an irreversible semantic development that led from a word 'to comb' and a noun 'sheep' (the woolly animal) to livestock in general and finally to wealth, hence German *Vieh* 'cattle' and English *fee*. More recently, however, this was challenged by Emile Benveniste who argued that the semantic development should indeed be reversed and begin with the concept of 'movable possessions' which, under the influence of later cultural development, was gradually specified to sheep." The PIE root is reconstructed as *péku*. See Emile Benveniste, *Indo-European Language and Society* (Miami: University of Miami Press, 1973).

154   *The word for marry:* Mallory, *In Search of the Indo-Europeans*, 123: "Many Indo-European languages do employ the same Proto-Indo-European verb *wedh*—'To lead (home)' when expressing the act of becoming married from a groom's point of view."

154   *That original compound word:* Mallory and Adams, *The Oxford Introduction to Proto-Indo-European*, 323.

155   *In other languages:* Bernard Comrie, *Tense* (Cambridge: Cambridge University Press, 1985).

157   *It was probably domesticated:* For the transforming role of the horse in steppe-land life, see David W. Anthony, *The Horse, the Wheel, and Language: How Bronze-Age Riders from the Eurasian Steppes Shaped the Modern World* (Princeton, N.J.: Princeton University Press, 2007).

157   *both descended from:* Mallory and Adams, *The Oxford Introduction to Proto-Indo-European*, 134.

157   *or in hill figures:* The White Horse at Uffington (illustrated), not merely scratched into the turf but deliberately constructed with chalk rammed into deep trenches, nearly in the form it still maintains, has been dated to the Bronze Age, perhaps as early as 1400 BC, and has been regularly maintained ever since. David Miles and Simon Palmer, "White Horse Hill," *Current Archaeology* 142 (1995), 372–78. Images of horses on Celtic Iron Age coinage (the illustration is of a gold *stater* coined by the Gaulish Parisii ca. 70–60 BC) draw as much on that tradition as on Mediterranean examples.

158   *a place called Sintashta:* Anthony, *The Horse, the Wheel and Language,* 371–411.
159   *they might have been:* Ibid., 371–411, 452–57.
160   *it is possible for one man: Iliad* X.505.
160   *at the funeral games:* The chariot race at Patroclus's funeral games is at ibid., XXIII.286–534.
160   *camp build for many days:* They took nine days bringing in the timber for Hector's funeral pyre. Ibid., XXIV.783–84.
160   *both Poseidon and Athene:* M. Detienne and A. B. Werth, "Athena and the Mastery of the Horse," *History of Religions* 11, no. 2 (Nov. 1971), 161–84.
161   *"a prize-winning horse": Iliad* XXII.22.
161   *whiter than snow:* Ibid., X.436, 547.
161   *"like a horse":* Ibid., XV.263ff.
161   *The Trojans sacrifice:* Ibid., XXI.132.
161   *the horse dominates the names:* Grace H. Macurdy, "The Horse-Taming Trojans," *Classical Quarterly* 17, no. 1 (Jan. 1923), 50–52.
162   *tells Telemachus: Odyssey* IV.271ff.
162   *"dear, steadfast heart":* Ibid., IV.240.
162   *The second time:* Ibid., VIII.499ff.
162   *"his whole body": Aeneid* VI.497–99.
163   *"As a woman weeps": Odyssey* VIII.523–32 (Lattimore, fundamentally).
164   *"Those who had dreamed":* Simone Weil, *L'Iliade ou le poème de la force.* See Simone Weil and Rachel Bespaloff, *War and the* Iliad, trans. Mary McCarthy (New York: New York Review of Books, 2005), 3.
164   *the word Homer uses: Iliad* XIII.393.
166   *"We did not dare":* Edwin Muir, "The Horses," from *One Foot in Eden* (London: Faber, 1956).
166   *Sleep sits: Iliad* XIV.290.
166   *beautiful as a star:* Ibid., VI.399–403.
166   *like cattle stepping:* Ibid., XX.495.
167   *"a snowy mountain":* Ibid., XIII.754.
168   *Usatovo, near Odessa:* D. Ya. Telegin and David W. Anthony, "On the Yamna Culture," *Current Anthropology* 28, no. 3 (June 1987), 357–58.
169   *a world not of palaces:* Katarzyna Ślusarska, "Funeral Rites of the Catacomb Community: 2800–1900 BC: Ritual, Thanatology and Geographical Origins," *Baltic-Pontic Studies* (Poznań) 13 (2006).
169   *Scholars have pursued:* For many of these references, see M. L. West, "The Rise of the Greek Epic," *Journal of Hellenic Studies* 108 (1988), 151–72.
170   *as Nestor tells: Iliad* II.362.
171   *phrase that recurs repeatedly: Iliad* II. 159, *Odyssey* III.142.
171   *ep' eurea nota thalasses:* Ibid., XX.228, et cetera.
171   *"He harnessed to the chariot":* Ibid., XIII.23ff.
171   *When Aeneas is remembering:* Ibid., XX.217.
172   *"They would play":* Ibid., XX.225.
172   *"It is by cunning":* Ibid., XXIII.316–18, 325.
172   *fast-running ships: Odyssey* IV.707–8.
172   *"Just as in a field":* Ibid., XIII.81ff.

172   *beautiful metal dogs:* Ibid., VII.91–94.

173   *robotic golden girls: Iliad* XVIII.372ff.

173   *"and the spearhead":* Ibid., V.65ff (Lattimore and Fagles combined/altered).

173   *"Who understands how": Iliad* V.60ff (Lattimore and Fagles combined/altered).

174   *At this most fundamental level:* For these transitions, see Mallory and Adams, *The Oxford Introduction to Proto-Indo-European and the Proto-Indo-European World;* and Anthony, *The Horse, the Wheel and Language,* 371–411, 452–57.

174   *They can only have arrived:* Thomas F. Strasser et al., "Stone Age Seafaring in the Mediterranean, Plakias Region for Lower Palaeolithic and Mesolithic Habitation of Crete," *Hesperia* 79 (2010), 145–90.

174   *"the colossal vortex":* For the transforming arrival of the sailing ship, see the concluding chapter of Cyprian Broodbank, *An Island Archaeology of the Early Cyclades* (Cambridge: Cambridge University Press, 2000).

174   *And above all:* Ibid., 345.

175   *Topsail, Riptide:* Fagles, *Odyssey* VIII.130–39.

175   *"Our ships can sail": Odyssey* VIII.556–63.

176   *"drastically shrunk":* Broodbank, *An Island Archaeology of the Early Cyclades,* 345.

176   *Menelaus remembers: Odyssey* III.158.

176   *It was fast ships: Iliad* VII.467–75.

176   *It is the ships:* Ibid., XV.502ff.

10: THE GANG AND THE CITY

178   *"the abandoned weapons": Iliad* X.469.

178   *dog-eyed:* Ibid., I.159.

178   *"the most savage man alive":* Ibid., I.146.

178   *"shaggy breasts":* Ibid., I.189.

178   *"black blood":* Ibid., I.303.

179   *"the wives and daughters":* Ibid., VI.237–38 (adapted from Murray/Dimock, Loeb).

179   *"that most beautiful house".* Ibid., VI.242–49 (adapted from Fagles).

180   *"Let no man":* Ibid., II.354–55 (adapted from Fagles).

180   *formulaic adjectives:* Ibid., II.540; rocky Aulis is at II.496, Eteonus has many ridges at II.479 and Orchomenos is very sheepy at II.605.

180   *They love their land:* Ibid., XIV.120.

180   *phrase that is repeated:* See, for example, *Iliad* XII.243, XXIV.500.

181   *"And now sweeter":* Ibid., II.450–54.

181   *"Beware the toils":* Ibid., V.487–88, Fagles V.559–60.

182   *264 people:* C. B. Armstrong, "The Casualty Lists in the Trojan War," *Greece and Rome* 16 (1969), 30–31, gives 238 named casualties and twenty-six unnamed, sixty-one of whom are Greek and 208 Trojan.

182   *"they limp and halt":* Fagles, *Iliad* IX.502–6.

182   *"Of all that breathe": Iliad* XVII.441–47, Fagles, XVII.509–15.

183   *"Patroclus keeps on sweeping": Iliad* XVI.397–98.

183   *"Hah! look at you!":* Ibid., XVI.745–50.

183   *"Erymas and Amphoterus":* Ibid., XVI.414–18.

183   *"Next he goes": Iliad* XVI.401ff, Fagles, XVI.472ff; see Fagles, *Odyssey* XII.271–75.

184   *"Ahead, Patroclus":* Christopher Logue, "The *Iliad*: Book XVI. An English Version," *Arion* 1, no. 2 (Summer 1962), 3–26.

184   *The first fighting: Iliad* IV.446.

184   *a cause for rejoicing:* Ibid., VII.189.

184   *"Now the sun":* Ibid., VII.421–29.

185   *Bruce Jacobs and Richard Wright:* Bruce A. Jacobs and Richard Wright, *Street Justice: Retaliation in the Criminal Underworld*, Cambridge Studies in Criminology (Cambridge: Cambridge University Press, 2006).

186   *"This desire for payback":* Ibid., 25.

186   *"urban nomads":* Ibid., 12.

186   *"maintaining a reputation":* Ibid., 32.

186   *"Everyone was watching":* Ibid., 76.

186   *"two lions": Iliad* X.279.

186   *"like two rip-fanged hounds":* Ibid., X.360.

187   *The two Greeks:* Ibid., X.400.

187   *"strikes the middle":* Ibid., X.454.

187   *Odysseus laughs aloud:* Ibid., X.565.

187   *calling them fools:* Ibid., II.870, XI.450–55, XVI.833.

187   *"I got your punk ass":* Jacobs and Wright, *Street Justice*, 35.

187   *"I felt like I was":* Ibid., 36.

188   *"When he smiles":* Colton Simpson with Ann Pearlman, *Inside the Crips* (New York: St. Martin's Press, 2005), 14.

188   *"No one forgets":* Martín Sánchez-Jankowski, *Islands in the Street: Gangs and American Urban Society* (Berkeley: University of California Press, 1991), 140–41.

189   *Neither rape nor fighting:* Ibid., 79.

190   *"Troy must have been":* D. F. Easton, J. D. Hawkins, A. G. Sherratt and E. S. Sherratt, "Troy in Recent Perspective," *Anatolian Studies* 52 (2002), 75–109.

190   *It sat at one:* A city at Troy, at the southern end of the narrows between the Aegean and the Black Sea, might be seen as a strategic alternative to a city on the site of Istanbul, at the other end. Byzantium was founded as a colony by the Greek city of Megara only in 667 BC, by which time the ruined site of Troy was also occupied by a small number of Greek colonists, probably from Lesbos.

190   *The great Trojan treasures:* D. F. Easton, "Priam's Gold: The Full Story," *Anatolian Studies* 44 (1994), 221–43.

190   *The silver and gold vessels:* Christoph Bachhuber, "The Treasure Deposits of Troy: Rethinking Crisis and Agency on the Early Bronze Age Citadel," *Anatolian Studies* 59 (2009), 1–18; Mikhail Treister, "The Trojan Treasures: Description, Chronology, Historical Context," in *The Gold of Troy*, ed. Vladimir Tolstikov and Mikhail Treister (New York: Harry N. Abrams, 1996), 225–29.

190   *from the very beginning:* Susan Heuck Allen, "A Personal Sacrifice in the Interest of Science: Calvert, Schliemann, and the Troy Treasures," *Classical World* 91, no. 5, *The World of Troy* (May–June 1998), 345–54.

190   *"the ruins and red ashes":* E. Meyer, "Schliemann's Letters to Max Müller in Oxford," *Journal of Hellenic Studies* 82 (1962), 75–105.

190   *"three different sets":* D. F. Easton, "Heinrich Schliemann: Hero or Fraud?," *Classical World* 91, no. 5, *The World of Troy* (May–June 1998), 335–43.

191   *Schliemann's suggestion:* J. B. Carter and S. P Morris, eds., *The Ages of Homer: A Tribute to E. Townsend Vermeule* (1995; reprint, Austin: University of Texas Press, 1998), 5. Burkert: "The Greeks knew no date for the Trojan war. This makes modern attempts to match ancient Greek dates with archaeological remains an exercise in illusion."

192   *The Boston treasure:* MFA Boston, Inv 68116–68139, Centennial Gift of Landon T. Clay. The museum bought it in 1968 from George Zacos, a Greek dealer in antiquities, based in Basel, who could not say where he had gotten it from. It may have been looted from an otherwise unknown tomb in Turkey.

192   *four Trojan hammer-axes:* James C. Wright, "The Place of Troy Among the Civilizations of the Bronze Age," *Classical World* 91, no. 5, *The World of Troy* (May–June 1998), 356–68.

193   *stolen by Schliemann:* Susan Heuck Allen, "A Personal Sacrifice in the Interest of Science: Calvert, Schliemann, and the Troy Treasures," *Classical World* 91, no. 5, *The World of Troy* (May–June, 1998), 345–54.

193   *his son Agamemnon:* He became a member of the Greek Chamber of Deputies and briefly the Greek minister in Washington, D.C.

193   *a linen fabric:* Elizabeth Wayland Butler, *Women's Work: The First 20,000 Years: Women, Cloth and Society in Early Times* (New York: Norton, 1994), 212.

193   *tiny gold beads:* Ibid., 213.

194   *"a great cloth":* Iliad III.125ff. The word for cloth can mean "web," "loom-beam" or even "mast."

194   *shimmering linen:* Ibid., III.140.

194   *"how terribly like":* Ibid., III.158.

194   *"Come over here":* Ibid., III.160.

195   *"The queen herself":* Ibid., VI.287ff.

195   *women and womanliness:* See ibid., XVI.100, where the Greek warriors refer to the battlements of Troy as its "veil."

195   *A woman and a tripod:* Ibid., XXII.262–64.

195   *twelve oxen:* Ibid., XXIII.702–5.

195   *Hera . . . prepares herself for love:* Ibid., XIV.165ff.

196   *"the whispered words":* Ibid., XIV.217.

196   *"He goes down":* Ibid., II.870.

196   *kill Trojan babies:* Ibid., VI.57–60.

196   *Zeus accused Hera:* Ibid., IV.35.

197   *"Idomeneus stabs":* Ibid., XVI.345–50.

197   *"like wolves":* Ibid., XVI.156–62.

197   *"Patroclus, you have thought":* Ibid., XVI.825ff.

197   *soaked and clotted:* Ibid., XVII.51.

198   *"mauling the kill":* Ibid., XVII.64.

198   *"and give the rest":* Ibid., XVII.125–27, 241.

198   *He promises:* Ibid., XVII.241.

198   *the straps of his shield:* Ibid., XVII.290.

198   *"oozes out from the wound":* Ibid., XVII.297–98.

198   *under the collarbone:* Ibid., XVII.309.

198   *"so that he claws":* Ibid., XVII.315.

198   *a spear in the liver:* Ibid., XVII.349.

198   *"with so many pulling"*: Ibid., XVII.389–97.

198   *"as on some lion"*: Ibid., XVII.540–42.

198   *"who though it is"*: Ibid., XVII.570.

198   *"a tawny lion"*: Ibid., XVIII.162.

198   *"cut the head"*: Ibid., XVIII.175.

199   *wants more than anything*: Ibid., V.863. See Tamara Neal, "Blood and Hunger in the *Iliad*," *Classical Philology* 101, no. 1 (Jan. 2006), 15–33.

199   *wants to feast on the body*: Iliad XIX.305.

199   *he pops out death*: Ibid., XX.386ff.

199   *"These bewildered boys"*: Ibid., XXI.29–32 (Lattimore cum Fagles).

199   *"an unlooked for evil"*: Iliad XXI.39.

199   *"Now there is not one"*: Ibid., XXI.125.

200   *"Die on"*: Ibid., XXI.128–29.

200   *"I will not leave off"*: Ibid., XXI.225.

200   *"The aged Priam"*: Ibid., XXI.525.

200   *"fierce with the spear"*: Ibid., XXI.540.

200   *"For they dare"*: Ibid., XXI.608.

200   *"shackled by destiny"*: Ibid., XXII.5.

201   *"Come into the walls"*: Ibid., XXII.57.

201   *"I have looked upon evils"*: Lattimore, *Iliad* XXII.61–76.

201   *"Sweet branch"*: Ibid., XXII.87, 82.

202   *like a dream*: Ibid., XXII.199.

202   *"and forces him"*: Ibid., XXII.198.

202   *"to hack your meat"*: Ibid., XXII.346–48.

202   *"and clean out"*: Ibid., XXII.327.

202   *"gasping the life breath"*: Ibid., XXII.440.

203   *"All of these"*: Ibid., XXII.510.

203   *robes, mantles, blankets*: Ibid., XXIV.228, 580.

203   *"kisses his hands"*: Ibid., XXIV.478ff.

204   *"Priam weeps freely"*: Ibid., XXIV.509ff (Fagles, XXIV.594ff).

204   *"They reach down"*: Iliad XXIV.630ff.

11: HOMER'S MIRROR

205   *the Egyptian city of Thebes*: A place, incidentally, known to Achilles for its riches: *Iliad* IX.381–84.

205   *fragments of papyrus*: For an illustration from Papyrus Chester Beatty IV, see A. H. Gardiner, *Hierat Papyri in the British Museum, Third Series: Chester Beatty Gift* (London: British Museum, 1935), 41.

206   *Sinuhe's story*: R. B. Parkinson, ed. and trans., *The Tale of Sinuhe and Other Egyptian Poems, 1940–1640 BC* (1997; reprint, Oxford: Oxford University Press, 2009), 1.

206   *"Be a scribe"*: Quoted in Barry Kemp, *Ancient Egypt: Anatomy of a Civilisation* (London: Routledge, 2007), 163.

206   *Peace had prevailed*: Ibid., 62.

206   *"makes those born"*: Parkinson, *Sinuhe*, 31.

207   *It is Indo-European*: Carleton T. Hodge, "Indo-Europeans in the Near East,"

Anthropological Linguistics 35, no. 1/4, *A Retrospective of the Journal Anthropological Linguistics: Selected Papers, 1959–1985* (1993), 90–108.

207   *"numberless are its cattle"*: Parkinson, *Sinuhe*, 31.

207   *"rushy place"*: Ibid., 46.

208   *"This is the taste"*: Ibid., 29.

208   *"milk in every cooked dish"*: Ibid., 32.

208   *"each man subjugating"*: Kemp, 32.

209   *"What can establish"*: Parkinson, *Sinuhe*, 33.

209   *"What matters"*: Ibid., 34.

209   *"the enduring security"*: Kemp, *Ancient Egypt*, 24.

209   *"I was appointed"*: Parkinson, *Sinuhe*, 42–43.

211   Timē *and* Aretē: See Margalit Finkelberg, "*Timē* and *Aretē* in Homer," *Classical Quarterly*, new ser., 48, no. 1 (1998), 14–28, for a long and elegant discussion of this core Homeric tension.

211   *the bath is always beautiful:* J. M. Cook, "Bath-Tubs in Ancient Greece," *Greece and Rome*, 2nd ser., 6, no. 1 (Mar. 1959), 31–41; Steve Reece, "The Homeric *asaminthos:* Stirring the Waters of the Mycenaean Bath," *Mnemosyne*, 4th ser., 55, fasc. 6 (2002), 703–8.

212   *"washing his long hair"*: Gilgamesh, Epic XI.239–55, trans. in Gary A. Rendsburg, "Notes on Genesis XXXV," *Vetus Testamentum* 34, fasc. 3 (July 1984), 361–66.

212   *"wash yourselves"*: Genesis XXXV.2.

212   *"daughters of the springs"*: Odyssey X.350.

212   *"brought in the water"*: Odyssey X.357–67 (Lattimore/Murray/Dimock).

213   *"mind wandering"*: Ibid., X.374.

213   *The Hittites were:* See J. P. Mallory and D. Q. Adams, *The Oxford Introduction to Proto-Indo-European and the Proto-Indo-European World* (Oxford: Oxford University Press, 2006).

214   *"in the city of Urikina"*: Gary Beckman, ed., *Hittite Diplomatic Texts,* 2nd ed., SBL Writings from the Ancient World series (Atlanta: Society of Biblical Literature, 1999), 113.

214   *"never suffer strangers gladly"*: Odyssey VII.32.

214   ptoliporthos Odysseus: Ibid., VIII.3.

214   prēktēres: Ibid., VIII.162.

215   *"Strangers, who are you?"*: Ibid., IX.252–54.

215   *"much-wandering pirates"*: Ibid., XVII.425.

215   *"From Ilium the wind"*: Ibid., IX.39–42.

216   *In about 1350 BC:* Beckman, *Hittite Diplomatic Texts*, 26.

216   *"a low-born"*: Ibid., 31.

217   *"Furthermore this sister"*: Ibid., 32.

217   *"When you see a palace woman"*: Ibid.

218   *"If the King"*: Ibid., 106.

218   *it is now generally accepted:* Hans G. Güterbock, "Hittites and Akhaeans: A New Look," *Proceedings of the American Philosophical Society* 128, no. 2 (June 1984), 114–22.

218   *"The father of My Majesty"*: Beckman, *Hittite Diplomatic Texts*, 154.

219   *"the untrembling"*: Martin L. West, "Atreus and Attarissiyas," *Glotta* 77 (2001), 262–66.

219   *A letter also survived:* Adrian Kelly, "Homer and History: 'Iliad' 9.381–4," *Mne-mosyne*, 4th ser., 59, fasc. 3 (2006), 321–33.

219   *Hittite scholars:* Güterbock, "Hittites and Akhaeans: A New Look," 128 (1984), 114–22.

219   *"People are treacherous":* Beckman, *Hittite Diplomatic Texts*, 90.

220   *it is clear:* T. Dothan, *The Philistines and Their Material Culture* (New Haven, Conn.: Yale University Press, 1982); T. Dothan and M. Dothan, *People of the Sea: The Search for the Philistines* (Upper Saddle River, N.J.: Prentice Hall, 1992); L. E. Stager, "The Impact of the Sea Peoples in Canaan (1185–1050 BCE)" in *The Archaeology of Society in the Holy Land*, ed. T. E. Levy (Leicester: Leicester University Press, 1995), 332–48; Seymour Gitin, Amihai Mazar and Ephraim Stern, eds., *Mediterranean Peoples in Transition, Thirteenth to Early Tenth Centuries B.C.E.* (Jerusalem: Israel Exploration Society, 1998).

220   *at its symbolic climax:* The David and Goliath story is in 1 Samuel, chapter XVII. For a brilliant discussion of it, see Azzan Yadin, "Goliath's Armor and Israelite Collective Memory," *Vetus Testamentum* 54, fasc. 3 (July 2004), 373–95.

221   *six feet nine inches tall:* See J. Daniel Hays, "Reconsidering the Height of Goliath," *Journal of the Evangelical Theological Society* 48, no. 4 (Dec. 2005), 701–14. In the Septuagint manuscripts and in the Dead Sea Scrolls, Goliath's height is given as "four cubits and a span," which is six feet nine inches. Later versions make it six cubits and a span, which is nine feet nine inches. The average height of Semites in the ancient Near East was about five feet. One warrior in the Shaft Graves at Mycenae was measured at five feet five inches. See A. J. N. W. Prag, Lena Papazoglou-Manioudaki, R. A. H. Neave, Denise Smith, J. H. Musgrave and A. Nafplioti, "Mycenae Revisited: Part 1. The Human Remains from a Grave Circle," *Annual of the British School at Athens* 104 (2009), 233–77.

221   *"Why do you":* 1 Samuel XVII.8–10 (New English Bible).

221   *Shouted aggression:* For the continuing emotional power of the battle shout, in attack or mourning, see the New Zealanders grieving the death of their companions in Afghanistan, http://www.nzherald.co.nz/nz/news/article.cfm?c_id=1&objectid=10829992.

221   *"When Saul and the Israelites":* 1 Samuel XVII:11.

221   *"Morning and evening":* Ibid., XVII.16 (New English Bible/King James Bible).

221   *"Who is he":* Ibid., XVII:26.

222   *"I cannot go":* Ibid., XVII.39–40 (New English Bible/King James Bible).

222   *"And the Philistine came on":* Ibid., XVII. 42–44 (New English Bible/King James Bible).

222   *"and all the world":* Ibid., XVII.46–47 (New English Bible).

223   *"And David put":* Ibid., XVII. 49 (King James Bible).

12: HOMER'S ODYSSEY

224   *"fall like winter snowflakes":* Odyssey XII.187.

224   *"tossing backwards and forwards":* Ibid., XX.25.

225   *"at which any immortal god":* Ibid., V.72–73.

225   *but was called Thapsos:* For Thapsos in the Bronze Age, see Anthony Russell, "In the Middle of the Corrupting Sea: Cultural Encounters in Sicily and Sardinia

between 1450–900 BC," PhD thesis, University of Glasgow, 2011, online at http:// theses.gla.ac.uk/2670/; David Abulafia, *The Great Sea: A Human History of the Mediterranean* (Oxford: Oxford University Press, 2011), 34–35.

226   *"at a loss"*: P. Leigh Fermor, letters to D. Devonshire; Diodorus Siculus, *Library of History*, 5.3.2, online at http://penelope.uchicago.edu/Thayer/E/Roman/Texts /Diodorus_Siculus/5A*.html.

227   *"swooping down"*: *Odyssey* V.50–53 (combination of Fagles, Lattimore).

227   *Hermes does everything*: Mary W. Helms, *Ulysses' Sail: An Ethnographic Odyssey of Power, Knowledge and Geographical Distance* (Princeton, N.J.: Princeton University Press, 1988), 111ff.

228   *"Sleep never falls on his eyelids"*: *Odyssey* V.271.

228   *"the axis always fixed"*: Ibid., V.274.

229   *"reaching towards him"*: Ibid., V.281.

230   *"death's decision"*: Ibid., V.326.

231   *Seabirds are too beautifully present*: For birds in Homer, see J. MacLair Boraston, "The Birds of Homer," *Journal of Hellenic Studies* 31 (1911), 216–50; Sylvia Benton, "Note on Sea-Birds," *Journal of Hellenic Studies* 92 (1972), 172–73; Paul Friedrich, "An Avian and Aphrodisian Reading of Homer's Odyssey," *American Anthropologist*, new ser., 99, no. 2 (June 1997), 306–20.

231   *"the most beautiful ankles"*: *Odyssey* V.33.3.

232   *"like a diving tern"*. *Odyssey* V.353.

232   *The earth shaker*: Ibid., V.367.

232   *"Just like the kind of joy"*: Ibid., V.394–99.

233   kai dē doupon akouse: *Odyssey* V. 401–3.

233   *"Spent to all use"*: George Chapman's translation of *Odyssey*, V.454–55.

234   *"heartsick on the open sea"*: *Odyssey* I.4.

234   *"from his thigh"*: *Odyssey* X.321.

234   *"her surpassingly beautiful"*: Ibid., X.347.

235   *"lay in the sea-Lord's loving waves"*: *Odyssey* XI.306.

235   *"his story held them"*: Ibid., XI.334 (Fagles translation, XI.379).

236   *"Many were the people"*: *Odyssey* I.3.

236   *"for his return"*: Ibid., I.13.

236   *"the fascinating imaginative realm"*: Quoted by Richard Rorty in "Trotsky and the Wild Orchids" (1992), from *Philosophy and Social Hope* (London: Penguin, 1999).

236   *"the sweetest place"*: *Odyssey* IX.34 (Fagles translation, IX.38).

236   *"rocky Ithaca"*: *Odyssey* XXI.346.

236   *the kind of island*: This point, in connection with the Iron Age, is made by Helen Waterhouse in "From Ithaca to the *Odyssey*," *Annual of the British School at Athens* 91 (1996), 301–17.

237   *"bends to kiss"*: *Odyssey* XIII.354.

237   *an Assyrian relief*: See, e.g., Julian Reade, *Assyrian Sculpture* (1983; reprint, London: British Museum, 1998), fig. 57, p. 54.

237   *"there is nothing sweeter"*: *Odyssey* IX.28.

237   *"She withers"*: Ibid., XIII.430–33.

238   *"Knossos, where Minos reigned"*: Ibid., XIX.172–78.

239   *When she appears*: Ibid., XVI.415 for Penelope standing by column; XX.42 for her shining among women.

239   *Artemis and Aphrodite:* Ibid., XVII.37, XIX.54.

239   *"the nightingale":* Ibid., XIX.518–24.

239   *Like all the great women in Homer:* Penelope with well-balanced mind, ibid., XVIII.249; weeping, XIX.209; weaving, XVII.97, XIX.128; with cloths, XIX.232, 255; and veil, XX.65.

239   *a queen regnant:* Penelope as governor, ibid., XIX.106ff.

239   *"grow in goodness":* Ibid., XIX.114.

240   *"Just as a bitch":* Ibid., XX.14–16.

240   *swimming in blood:* Ibid., XXII.307.

240   *are repeated here:* Ibid., XXII.325.

240   *"like a lion":* Ibid., XXII.401–3.

240   *"He finds them":* Ibid., XXII.383–88.

241   *"They lead him out":* Ibid., XXII.474–77.

241   *"the cable of a dark-prowed ship":* Ibid., XXII.465.

241   *"Just as when":* Ibid., XXII.468–73.

242   *"the well-built bridal chamber":* Ibid., XXIII.178.

243   *"her knees are loosened":* Ibid., XXIII.205–8.

243   *"As when the land":* Ibid., XXIII.233–40.

CONCLUSION: THE BRIGHT WAKE

244   *"spirit of cruelty":* Note to *Iliad* IV.75 in Pope's translation; see, for this and the following valuable references to William Blake and Joel Barlow, Michael Ferber, "Shelley and 'The Disastrous Fame of Conquerors,'" *Keats-Shelley Journal* 51 (2002), 145–73.

244   *Blake blamed Homer:* David V. Erdman, ed., *The Complete Poetry and Prose of William Blake*, rev. ed. (Berkeley: University of California Press, 1982), 270.

244   *"but he has given":* From David B. Davis, ed., *Advice to the Privileged Orders in the Several States of Europe*, in a chapter on "The Military System" (Ithaca, N.Y.: Cornell University Press, 1956), 39.

245   *"There are certain ages":* Susan Sontag, review of Simone Weil, *Selected Essays* (1962), trans. Richard Rees, *New York Review of Books*, Feb. 1, 1963.

246   *"Nietzsche, at his worst":* Richard Rorty, "Against Belatedness," *London Review of Books*, June 16, 1983, 3–5, a review of Hans Blumenberg, *The Legitimacy of the Modern Age*, trans. Robert Wallace (1983).

246   *"praised Homer's* enargeia": Alice Oswald, *Memorial: An Excavation of the* Iliad (London: Faber, 2011), 1.

246   *"a telling out":* See Heinrich F. Plett, Enargeia *in Classical Antiquity and the Early Modern Age: The Aesthetics of Evidence* (Leiden: Brill, 2012), 27.

BIBLIOGRAPHY

GREEK TEXTS

Hesiod, Homeric Hymns, Epic Cycle, Homerica. With parallel translation by H. G. Evelyn-White. Cambridge, Mass.: Loeb/Harvard University Press, 1914.

The Iliad. With parallel translation by A. T. Murray. Cambridge, Mass.: Loeb/Harvard University Press, 1925.

The Iliad. With parallel translation by W. F. Wyatt. Cambridge, Mass.: Loeb/Harvard University Press, 1999.

Lives of Homer. In *Homeric Hymns,* etc., with parallel translation by M. L. West. Cambridge, Mass.: Loeb/Harvard University Press, 2003.

The Odyssey. With parallel translation by A. T. Murray, revised by G. E. Dimock. Cambridge, Mass.: Loeb/Harvard University Press, 1999.

TRANSLATIONS

Fagles, Robert. *The Iliad.* New York: Penguin, 1990.
———. *The Odyssey.* New York, Penguin, 1996.
Lattimore, Richmond. *The Iliad of Homer.* Chicago: University of Chicago Press, 1951.
———. *The Odyssey.* New York: Harper, 1967.
Nicoll, Allardyce, ed. *Chapman's Homer: The Iliad.* 1956., Reprint, Princeton, N.J.: Princeton University Press 1984.
Pope, Alexander. *The Iliad.* London, 1715–1720.
Pope, Alexander, with W. Broome and E. Fenton. *The Odyssey.* London, 1726.
Rieu, E. V., revised by D. C. H. Rieu. *The Odyssey.* London: Penguin, 1946.
Shaw, T. E. *The Odyssey.* London: Oxford University Press, 1932.

ADAPTATIONS

Logue, Christopher. *War Music.* London: Faber, 2001.
Oswald, Alice. *Memorial: An Excavation of the* Iliad. London: Faber, 2011.

ON THE DATE OF HOMER

Finley, Sir Moses. *The World of Odysseus*. New York: Viking, 1954.

Foley, John Miles, ed. *A Companion to Ancient Epic*. Oxford: Blackwell, 2005.

Morris, Ian. "The Use and Abuse of Homer." *Classical Antiquity* 5, no. 1 (Apr. 1986), 81–138.

Nagy, Gregory. *Homeric Questions*. Austin: University of Texas Press, 1996.

Sherratt, Susan. "Archaeological Contexts." In *A Companion to Ancient Epic*, edited by John Miles Foley, 119–42. Oxford: Blackwell, 2005.

THE PYLOS FRESCO

Blegen, Carl W. "The Palace of Nestor Excavations of 1955." *American Journal of Archaeology* 60, no. 2 (Apr. 1956), 95–101.

Dué, Casey. "*Epea Pteroenta*: How We Came to Have Our Iliad." In *Recapturing a Homeric Legacy: Images and Insights from the Venetus A Manuscript of the Iliad*, edited by Casey Dué, 19–30. Washington, D.C.: Center for Hellenic Studies, 2009.

Lang, Mabel L. *The Palace of Nestor at Pylos in Western Messenia*, vol. 2, *The Frescoes*. Princeton, N.J.: Princeton University Press, 1969.

Vermeule, Emily. Review of Lang in *Art Bulletin* 52, no. 4 (Dec. 1970), 428–30.

SEFERIS

Seferis, George. *Complete Poems*. Translated and edited by E. Keeley and P. Sherrard. 1995. Reprint, Greenwich: Anvil Press, 2009.

ANTHROPOLOGY OF HOMER

Dougherty, Carol. *The Raft of Odysseus: The Ethnographic Imagination of Homer's Odyssey*. Oxford: Oxford University Press, 2001.

Helms, Mary W. *Ulysses' Sail: An Ethnographic Odyssey of Power, Knowledge and Geographical Distance*. Princeton, N.J.: Princeton University Press, 1988.

CRITICISM AND RECEPTION

Arnold, Matthew. *On Translating Homer: Three Lectures Given at Oxford*. London: Longman, Green, Longman, Roberts, 1861. Online at http://www.victorianprose.org/.

Baldick, Robert, ed. and trans. *The Goncourt Journals by Edmond and Jules de Goncourt*. 1962. Reprint, New York: New York Review of Books, 2007.

Boyle, Nicholas. *Goethe: Revolution and Renunciation, 1790–1803*. Oxford: Oxford University Press, 2003.

Johnson, Samuel. "Life of Pope" (1779). In *The Works of the English Poets, from Chaucer to Cowper*, vol. 12, 112. London: J. Johnson, 1810.

Murray, Penelope, and T. Dorsch. *Classical Literary Criticism*. London: Penguin, 2000.

Rexroth, Kenneth. *Classics Revisited*. New York: New Directions, 1968.

Reynolds, Matthew. *The Poetry of Translation: From Chaucer and Petrarch to Homer and Logue*. Oxford: Oxford University Press, 2011.

Weintraub, Rodelle, and Stanley Weintraub. "Chapman's Homer." *Classical World* 67, no. 1 (Sept.–Oct. 1973), 16–24. (An article on T. E. Lawrence.)

KEATS

Clarke, Charles Cowden. "Recollections of Keats" (1861). In *Recollections of Writers*, 120–57. London, 1878.

Coleridge, S. T. "Notes on Chapman's Homer." In *Notes and Lectures Upon Shakespeare and Some of the Old Poets and Dramatists: With Other Literary Remains of S. T. Coleridge*, vol. 2, 231. London, 1849.

Laing, Andrew. *The English Poets: Selections with Critical Introductions.* Edited by Thomas Humphry Ward. Vol. 1, 510. London, 1880.

Lockhart, J. G. "On the Cockney School of Poetry, No. V." *Blackwood's Edinburgh Magazine*, Apr. 1819.

Mallory, J. P., and D. Q. Adams. *The Oxford Introduction to Proto-Indo-European and the Proto-Indo-European World (Oxford Linguistics)*, 136. Oxford: Oxford University Press, 2006.

Motion, Andrew. *Keats.* London: Faber, 1997.

TRANSMISSION OF THE TEXT

Bird, Graeme. "Critical Signs—Drawing Attention to 'Special' Lines of Homer's Iliad in the Manuscript Venetus A." In *Recapturing a Homeric Legacy: Images and Insights from the Venetus A Manuscript of the Iliad*, edited by Casey Dué, 112–14. Washington, D.C.: Center for Hellenic Studies, 2009.

Boyle, Nicholas. *Goethe: Revolution and Renunciation, 1790–1803.* Oxford: Oxford University Press, 2003.

Dante. *Inferno.* London: Penguin, 2013, tr. by Robin Kirkpatrick.

Labowsky, L. *Bessarion's Library and the Biblioteca Marciana—Six Early Inventories.* Rome: Sussidi Erudite, 1979.

Martin, Richard P. "Cretan Homers: Tradition, Politics, Fieldwork." *Classics@* 3. Washington, D.C.: Center for Hellenic Studies, 2012.

Petrie, William M. Flinders. *Hawara, Biahmu, and Arsinoe.* London, 1889.

Quincey, Thomas de. "Homer and the Homeridae." *Blackwood's Edinburgh Magazine*, Oct. 1841, 411–27.

Southey, Robert, ed. *The Works of William Cowper.* Vol. 6. London, 1836.

Villoison, Joh. Baptista Caspar d'Ansse de. *Homeri Ilias ad Veteris Codicis Veneti Fidem Recensita.* Paris, 1788.

IDEAS OF HOMER

Black, J. "Some Structural Features of Sumerian Narrative Poetry." In *Mesopotamian Epic Literature: Oral or Aural?*, edited by M. E. Vogelzang and H. L. J. Vanstiphout, 71–101. Lampeter: Edwin Mellen Press, 1992.

Butler, S. *The Authoress of the Odyssey.* 2nd ed. London: Longmans, Green, 1922.

Cailleux, Théophile. *Pays atlantiques décrits par Homère. Ibérie, Gaule, Bretagne, Archipels, Amérique.* Paris, 1878.

———. *Théorie nouvelle sur les origines humaines. Homère en Occident. Troie en Angleterre.* Brussels, 1883.

Garnett, David, ed. *The Letters of T. E. Lawrence.* London, 1938.

Mertz, Henriette. *The Wine Dark Sea: Homer's Heroic Epic of the North Atlantic.* Chicago: self-published, 1964.

van der Valk, M., ed. *Commentarii ad Homeri Iliadem Pertinentes ad Fidem Codicis Laurentiani Editi.* 4 vols. Leiden: Brill, 1971–1987.

Vinci, Felice. *Omero nel Baltico.* With introductions by R. Calzecchi Onesti and F. Cuomo. Rome: Palombi Editori, 1998.

West, M. L. *The East Face of Helicon.* Oxford: Oxford University Press, 1999.

———, ed. and trans. *Lives of Homer.* In *Homeric Hymns*, etc. Cambridge, Mass.: Loeb/Harvard University Press, 2003.

———. *The Making of the* Iliad: *Disquisition and Analytical Commentary.* Oxford: Oxford University Press, 2011.

Wilkens, Iman. *Where Troy Once Stood.* 2nd ed. London: Rider, 2009.

Wood, Florence, and Kenneth Wood. *Homer's Secret Iliad: The Epic of the Night Skies Decoded.* London: John Morris, 1999.

EMPORIO AND PITHEKOUSSAI

Boardman, John. *Excavations in Chios, 1952–1955: Greek Emporio.* Supplementary volumes, no. 6, iii–xiv. Athens: British School at Athens, 1967.

Buchner, Giorgio. "Recent Work at Pithekoussai (Ischia)." *Archaeological Reports* 17 (1970–1971), 63–67.

Buchner, G., and D. Ridgway. *Pithekoussai, La necropoli: Tombe 1–723. Scavate dal 1952 al 1961.* Rome: Accademia Nazionale dei Lincei, 1993.

Connors, Catherine. "Monkey Business: Imitation, Authenticity, and Identity from Pithekoussai to Plautus." *Classical Antiquity* 23, no. 2 (Oct. 2004), 179–207.

Faraone, Christopher A. "Taking the 'Nestor's Cup Inscription' Seriously: Erotic Magic and Conditional Curses in the Earliest Inscribed Hexameters." *Classical Antiquity* 15, no. 1 (Apr. 1996), 77–112.

Monk, Kate. *Onomastikon.* 1997. http://tekeli.li/onomastikon/Ancient-World/Greece/Male.html.

Papadopoulos, John K., and Deborah Ruscillo. "A Ketos in Early Athens: An Archaeology of Whales and Sea Monsters in the Greek World." *American Journal of Archaeology* 106, no. 2 (Apr. 2002), 187–227.

Powell, B. "The Dipylon Oinochoe Inscription and the Spread of Literacy in 8th Century Athens." *Kadmos* 27 (1988), 65–86.

———. "Nestor's Cup and the Etruscans." *Oxford Journal of Archaeology* 16 (1997), 325–44.

Ridgway, D. *The First Western Greeks.* Cambridge: Cambridge University Press, 1992.

West, M. L. "Grated Cheese Fit for Heroes." *Journal of Hellenic Studies* 118 (1998), 190–91.

MILMAN PARRY AND THE ORAL HOMER

Bajgorić, Halil. The Wedding of Mustajbey's Son Bećirbey, Parry no. 6699, www.oraltradition.org/static/zbm/zbm.pdf. (For the eEdition performed by Halil Bajgorić and edited and translated by John Miles Foley, see www.oraltradition.org.)

Bentley, R. *Remarks upon a Late Discourse of Free Thinking*. London, 1713.

The Calum Maclean Project. Department of Celtic and Scottish Studies, University of Edinburgh,   http://www.calum-maclean-project.celtscot.ed.ac.uk/home/;http://calumimaclean.blogspot.co.uk/2013_02_01_archive.html.

Draak, Maartje. "Duncan MacDonald of South Uist." *Fabula* 1 (1957), 47–58.

Edmondson, M. S., *Lore: An Introduction to the Science of Folklore and Literature*. New York: Holt Rinehart and Winston, 1971, 323.

Edwards, M. W. *The Iliad: A Commentary*. Vol. 5. Cambridge: Cambridge University Press, 1991.

Eliot, T. S. *Selected Essays*. 3rd ed. London: Faber, 1999.

Foley, John Miles. *Traditional Oral Epic: The Odyssey, Beowulf, and the Serbo-Croatian Return Song*. Oakland: University of California Press, 1993.

Greene, William C. "Milman Parry (1902–1935)." *Proceedings of the American Academy of Arts and Sciences* 71, no. 10 (Mar. 1937), 535–36.

Janko, Richard. "The Homeric Poems as Oral Dictated Texts." *Classical Quarterly*, new ser., 48, no. 1 (1998), 1–13.

Kumpf, M. M. *Four Indices of the Homeric Hapax Legomena*. Hildesheim: Georg Olms, 1984.

Lamb, William. "The Storyteller, the Scribe, and a Missing Man: Hidden Influences from Printed Sources in the Gaelic Tales of Duncan and Neil MacDonald." *Oral Tradition* 27.1 (2012), 109–60.

Levin, Harry. "Portrait of a Homeric Scholar." *Classical Journal* 32, no. 5 (Feb. 1937), 259–66.

Lord, Albert. *The Singer of Tales*. Cambridge, Mass.: Harvard University Press, 1960.

Notopoulos, James A. "The Genesis of an Oral Heroic Poem." *Greek, Roman and Byzantine Studies* 3 (1960), 135–44.

Parry, Adam. *The Making of Homeric Verse: The Collected Papers of Milman Parry*. Oxford: Oxford University Press, 1987.

Porter, James I. "Homer: The Very Idea." *Arion*, 3rd ser., 10, no. 2 (Fall 2002), 57–86.

Reece, Steve. "Some Homeric Etymologies in the Light of Oral-Formulaic Theory." *Classical World* 93, no. 2, *Homer* (Nov.–Dec. 1999), 185–99.

Renan, Ernest. Essay on *L'Avenir de Science*, p. 292. Paris, 1892. Quoted in Adam Parry, *The Making of Homeric Verse: The Collected Papers of Milman Parry*. Oxford: Oxford University Press, 1987.

Young, Douglas. "Never Blotted a Line? Formula and Premeditation in Homer and Hesiod." *Arion* 6, no. 3 (Fall 1967), 279–324.

EPIC AND MEMORY

Bachhuber, Christoph. "Aegean Interest on the Uluburun Ship." *American Journal of Archaeology* 110, no. 3 (July 2006), 345–63.

Bellamy, Rufus. "Bellerophon's Tablet." *Classical Journal* 84 (1989), 289–307.

Blegen, C. W., and K. Kourouniotis. "Excavations of Pylos, 1939." *American Journal of Archaeology* 43 (1939), 569.

Blegen, C. W., and M. Rawson. *The Palace of Nestor at Pylos in Western Messenia*. Vol. 1, *The Buildings and Their Contents*. Princeton, N.J.: Princeton University Press, 1966.

Bryce, T. R. "Anatolian Scribes in Mycenaean Greece." *Historia* 48 (1999), 257–64.

———. "The Nature of Mycenaean Involvement in Western Anatolia." *Historia* 38 (1989), 13–14.

Carter, J. B., and S. P. Morris. *The Ages of Homer. A Tribute to E. Townsend Vermeule.* 1995; reprint, Austin: University of Texas Press, 1998.

Gere, Cathy. *The Tomb of Agamemnon: Mycenae and the Search for a Hero.* London: Profile, 2006.

Grethlein, Jonas. "Memory and Material Objects in the *Iliad* and the *Odyssey*." *Journal of Hellenic Studies* 128 (2008), 27–51.

Harries, Byron. "'Strange Meeting': Diomedes and Glaucus in *Iliad* 6." *Greece and Rome* 40 (1993), 133–47.

Lowry, E. R., Jr. "Glaucus, the Leaves, and the Heroic Boast of *Iliad* 6.146–211." In *The Ages of Homer. A Tribute to E. Townsend Vermeule*, edited by J. B. Carter and S. P. Morris, 193. 1995; reprint, Austin: University of Texas Press, 1998.

Shear, Ione Mylonas. "Bellerophon Tablets from the Mycenaean World? A Tale of Seven Bronze Hinges." *Journal of Hellenic Studies* 118 (1998), 187–89.

Vermeule, Emily Townsend. *Aspects of Death in Early Greek Art and Poetry.* Oakland: University of California Press, 1979.

———. "Jefferson and Homer." *Proceedings of the American Philosophical Society* 137, no. 4, 250th anniversary issue (Dec. 1993), 689–703.

West, M. L. "The Rise of the Greek Epic." *Journal of Hellenic Studies* 108 (1988), 151–72.

BRONZE AND THE MINE

Agricola, Georgius. *De Animantibus Subterraneis.* Freiburg, 1548.

Bachelard, Gaston. *The Poetics of Space.* 1958; reprint, Boston: Beacon Press, 1994.

Baker, James C. "Echoes of Tommy Knockers in Bohemia, Oregon, Mines." *Western Folklore* 30, no. 2 (Apr. 1971), 119–22.

Bradley, Pippa. "Death Pits at Cliffs End." *British Archaeology* 131 (July–Aug. 2013).

Chernykh, Evgenii N. *Ancient Metallurgy in the USSR: The Early Metal Age.* Translated by Sarah Wright. Cambridge: Cambridge University Press, 1992.

Courtney, M. A. "Cornish Folk-Lore," part 3. *Folk-Lore Journal* 5, no. 3 (1887), 177–220.

Finucane, Ronald. *Appearances of the Dead.* London: Junction Books, 1982.

Fitzpatrick, A. P. *The Amesbury Archer and the Boscombe Bowmen.* Salisbury: Trust for Wessex Archaeology, 2011.

Harding, Anthony F. *European Societies in the Bronze Age.* Cambridge: Cambridge University Press, 2000.

Harrison, Richard J. *Symbols and Warriors: Images of the European Bronze Age.* Bristol: Western Academic and Specialist Press, 2004.

Heaney, Seamus. *Death of a Naturalist.* London: Faber, 1966.

Hope, Bryan D. *A Curious Place: The Industrial History of Amlwch (1550–1950).* Wrexham: Bridge Books, 1994.

Irwin, M. Eleanor. "Odysseus's 'Hyacinthine Hair' in *Odyssey* 6.231." *Phoenix* 44, no. 3 (Fall 1990), 205–18.

Kohl, Philip L. *The Making of Bronze Age Eurasia.* Cambridge: Cambridge University Press, 2007.

Kristiansen, Kristian, and Thomas B. Larsson. *The Rise of Bronze Age Society: Travels, Transmissions and Transformations.* Cambridge: Cambridge University Press, 2005.

Oppenheimer, Stephen. "A Reanalysis of Multiple Prehistoric Immigrations to Britain and Ireland Aimed at Identifying Celtic Contributions." In *Celtic from the West*, edited by B. Cunliffe and J. T. Koch. Oxford: Oxbow Books, 2010.

Roberts, Ben. "Metallurgical Networks and Technological Choice: Understanding Early Metal in Western Europe." *World Archaeology* 40, no. 3 (2008), 354–72.

Roberts, B. W., C. P. Thornton and V. C. Piggott. "Development of Metallurgy in Eurasia." *Antiquity* 83 (2009), 1012–22.

Rothenberg, B., and A. Blanco-Freijeiro. "Ancient Copper Mining and Smelting at Chinflon (Huelva, SW Spain)." *British Museum Occasional Paper* 20 (1980), 41–62.

Schulten, A. *Fontes Hispaniae Antiquae.* Vol. 1. Barcelona: Universidad de Barcelona, 1922.

Vermeule, Emily Townsend. *Aspects of Death in Early Greek Art and Poetry.* Oakland: University of California Press, 1979.

THE BACKGROUND ON THE STEPPE

Anthony, David W. *The Horse, the Wheel, and Language: How Bronze-Age Riders from the Eurasian Steppes Shaped the Modern World*, Princeton, N.J.: Princeton University Press, 2007.

Detienne, M., and A. B. Werth. "Athena and the Mastery of the Horse." *History of Religions* 11, no. 2 (Nov. 1971), 161–84.

Donlan, W. "Duelling with Gifts in the *Iliad*: As the Audience Saw It." *Colby Quarterly* 24 (1993), 171.

Fortson IV, Benjamin W. *Indo-European Language and Culture: An Introduction.* 2nd ed. Chichester: Wiley-Blackwell, 2010.

Hammer, Dean. "Achilles as Vagabond: The Culture of Autonomy in the 'Iliad.'" *Classical World* 90, no. 5 (May–June 1997), 341–66.

Hammond, N. G. L. "Tumulus-Burial in Albania, the Grave Circles of Mycenae, and the Indo-Europeans." *Annual of the British School at Athens* 62 (1967), 77–105.

Macurdy, Grace H. "The Horse-Taming Trojans." *Classical Quarterly* 17, no. 1 (Jan. 1923), 50–52.

Mallory, J. P. *In Search of the Indo-Europeans: Language, Archaeology and Myth.* London: Thames and Hudson, 1989.

Mallory, J. P., and D. Q. Adams. *The Oxford Introduction to Proto-Indo-European and the Proto-Indo-European World.* Oxford: Oxford University Press, 2006.

Miles, David, and Simon Palmer. "White Horse Hill." *Current Archaeology* 142 (1995), 372–78.

Muir, Edwin. *One Foot in Eden.* London: Faber, 1956.

Nimis, Steve. "The Language of Achilles: Construction vs. Representation." *Classical World* 79, no. 4 (Mar.–Apr. 1986), 217–25.

Parry, Adam. "The Language of Achilles." *Transactions and Proceedings of the American Philological Association* 87 (1956), 1–7.

Reeve, M. D. "The Language of Achilles." *Classical Quarterly,* new ser., 23, no. 2 (Nov. 1973), 193–95.

Ślusarska, Katarzyna. "Funeral Rites of the Catacomb Community: 2800–1900 BC: Ritual, Thanatology and Geographical Origins." *Baltic-Pontic Studies* (Poznań) 13 (2006).

Smith, R. Scott, and Stephen M. Trzaskoma, trans. *Apollodorus' Library and Hyginus'*

Fabulae: *Two Handbooks of Greek Mythology*. Fabula 95. Indianapolis: Hackett, 2007.

Telegin, D. Ya., and David W. Anthony. "On the Yamna Culture." *Current Anthropology* 28, no. 3 (June 1987), 357–58.

Weil, Simone. *L'Iliade ou le poème de la force*. See Simone Weil and Rachel Bespaloff. *War and the* Iliad. Translated by Mary McCarthy. New York: New York Review of Books, 2005.

West, M. L. "The Rise of the Greek Epic." *Journal of Hellenic Studies* 108 (1988), 151–72.

THE IMPACT OF THE SAIL

Broodbank, Cyprian. *An Island Archaeology of the Early Cyclades*. Cambridge: Cambridge University Press, 2000.

Strasser, Thomas F., et al. "Stone Age Seafaring in the Mediterranean, Plakias Region for Lower Palaeolithic and Mesolithic Habitation of Crete." *Hesperia* 79 (2010), 145–90.

THE GANG AND THE CITY

Allen, Susan Heuck. "A Personal Sacrifice in the Interest of Science: Calvert, Schliemann, and the Troy Treasures." *Classical World* 91, no. 5, *The World of Troy* (May–June 1998), 345–54.

Armstrong, C. B. "The Casualty Lists in the Trojan War." *Greece and Rome* 16 (1969), 30–31.

Bachhuber, Christoph. "The Treasure Deposits of Troy: Rethinking Crisis and Agency on the Early Bronze Age Citadel." *Anatolian Studies* 59 (2009), 1–18.

Butler, Elizabeth Wayland. *Women's Work: The First 20,000 Years: Women, Cloth and Society in Early Times*. New York: Norton, 1994.

Carter, J. B., and S. P. Morris. *The Ages of Homer. A Tribute to E. Townsend Vermeule*. 1995; reprint, Austin: University of Texas Press, 1998.

Easton, D. F. "Heinrich Schliemann: Hero or Fraud?" *Classical World* 91, no. 5, *The World of Troy* (May–June 1998), 335–43.

——. "Priam's Gold: The Full Story." *Anatolian Studies* 44 (1994), 221–43.

Easton, D. F., J. D. Hawkins, A. G. Sherratt and E. S. Sherratt. "Troy in Recent Perspective." *Anatolian Studies* 52 (2002), 75–109.

Jacobs, Bruce A., and Richard Wright. *Street Justice: Retaliation in the Criminal Underworld*. Cambridge Studies in Criminology. Cambridge: Cambridge University Press, 2006.

Meyer, E. "Schliemann's Letters to Max Müller in Oxford." *Journal of Hellenic Studies* 82 (1962), 75–105.

Neal, Tamara. "Blood and Hunger in the *Iliad*." *Classical Philology* 101, no. 1 (Jan. 2006), 15–33.

Sánchez-Jankowski, Martín. *Islands in the Street: Gangs and American Urban Society*. Oakland: University of California Press, 1991.

Simpson, Colton, with Ann Pearlman. *Inside the Crips*. Cambridge: St. Martin's Press, 2005.

Treister, Mikhail. "The Trojan Treasures: Description, Chronology, Historical Context." In *The Gold of Troy*, edited by Vladimir Tolstikov and Mikhail Treister. New York: Harry N. Abrams, 1996, 225–29.

Wright, James C. "The Place of Troy among the Civilizations of the Bronze Age." *Classical World* 91, no. 5, *The World of Troy* (May–June 1998), 356–68.

THE VIEW IN THE MIRROR

Beckman, Gary, ed. *Hittite Diplomatic Texts*. 2nd ed. SBL Writings from the Ancient World series. Atlanta: Society of Biblical Literature, 1999.

Cook, J. M. "Bath-Tubs in Ancient Greece." *Greece and Rome*, 2nd ser., 6, no. 1 (Mar. 1959), 31–41.

Dothan, T. *The Philistines and Their Material Culture*. New Haven, Conn.: Yale University Press, 1982.

Dothan, T., and M. Dothan. *People of the Sea: The Search for the Philistines*. Upper Saddle River, N.J.: Prentice Hall, 1992.

Finkelberg, Margalit. "*Timē* and *Aretē* in Homer." *Classical Quarterly*, new ser., 48, no. 1 (1998), 14–28.

Gardiner, A. H. *Hieratic Papyri in the British Museum*, Third Series: Chester Beatty Gift. I, 41. London: British Museum, 1935.

Gilgamesh. Epic XI.239–55. Translated in Gary A. Rendsburg, "Notes on Genesis XXXV." *Vetus Testamentum* 34, fasc. 3 (July 1984), 361–66.

Gitin, Seymour, Amihai Mazar, and Ephraim Stern, eds. *Mediterranean Peoples in Transition, Thirteenth to Early Tenth Centuries B.C.E.* Jerusalem: Israel Exploration Society, 1998.

Güterbock, Hans G. "Hittites and Akhaeans: A New Look." *Proceedings of the American Philosophical Society* 128, no. 2 (June 1984), 114–22.

Hays, J. Daniel. "Reconsidering the Height of Goliath." *Journal of the Evangelical Theological Society* 48, no. 4 (Dec. 2005), 701–14.

Hodge, Carleton T. "Indo-Europeans in the Near East." *Anthropological Linguistics* 35, no. 1/4, *A Retrospective of the Journal Anthropological Linguistics: Selected Papers, 1959–1985* (1993), 90–108.

Kelly, Adrian. "Homer and History: 'Iliad' 9.381–4." *Mnemosyne*, 4th ser., 59, fasc. 3 (2006), 321–33.

Kemp, Barry. *Ancient Egypt: Anatomy of a Civilisation*. Oxford: Routledge, 2007.

Mallory, J. P., and D. Q. Adams. *The Oxford Introduction to Proto-Indo-European and the Proto Indo-European World (Oxford Linguistics)*. Oxford: Oxford University Press, 2006.

Parkinson, R. B., ed. and trans. *The Tale of Sinuhe and Other Egyptian Poems, 1940–1640 BC*. 1997; reprint, Oxford University Press, 2009.

Prag, A. J. N. W., Lena Papazoglou-Manioudaki, R. A. H. Neave, Denise Smith, J. H. Musgrave and A. Nafplioti. "Mycenae Revisited: Part 1. The Human Remains from a Grave Circle." *Annual of the British School at Athens* 104 (2009), 233–77.

Reece, Steve. "The Homeric *asaminthos*: Stirring the Waters of the Mycenaean Bath." *Mnemosyne*, 4th ser., 55, fasc. 6 (2002), 703–8.

Stager, L. E. "The Impact of the Sea Peoples in Canaan (1185–1050 BCE)." in *The Archaeology of Society in the Holy Land*, edited by T. E. Levy, 332–48. Leicester: Leicester University Press, 1995.

West, Martin L. "Atreus and Attarissiyas." *Glotta* 77 (2001), 262–66.

Yadin, Azzan. "Goliath's Armor and Israelite Collective Memory." *Vetus Testamentum* 54, fasc. 3 (July 2004), 373–95.

ODYSSEUS'S JOURNEYS

Abulafia, David. *The Great Sea: A Human History of the Mediterranean.* Oxford: Oxford University Press, 2011.
Benton, Sylvia. "Note on Sea-Birds." *Journal of Hellenic Studies* 92 (1972), 172–73.
Boraston, J. MacLair. "The Birds of Homer." *Journal of Hellenic Studies* 31 (1911), 216–50.
Diodorus Siculus. *Library of History*, 5.3.2. Online at http://penelope.uchicago.edu/Thayer /E/Roman/Texts/Diodorus_Siculus/5A*.html.
Friedrich, Paul. "An Avian and Aphrodisian Reading of Homer's *Odyssey.*" *American Anthropologist*, new ser., 99, no. 2 (June 1997), 306–20.
Helms, Mary W. *Ulysses' Sail: An Ethnographic Odyssey of Power, Knowledge and Geographical Distance.* Princeton, N.J.: Princeton University Press, 1988.
Reade, Julian. *Assyrian Sculpture.* 1983; reprint, London: British Museum, 1988.
Rorty, Richard. "Trotsky and the Wild Orchids" (1992). In *Philosophy and Social Hope.* London: Penguin, 1999.
Russell, Anthony. "In the Middle of the Corrupting Sea: Cultural Encounters in Sicily and Sardinia between 1450–900 BC." PhD thesis, University of Glasgow, 2011, online at http://theses.gla.ac.uk/2670/.
Waterhouse, Helen. "From Ithaca to the Odyssey." *Annual of the British School at Athens* 91 (1996), 301–17.

HOMER'S MEANING

Davis, David B., ed. *Advice to the Privileged Orders in the Several States of Europe.* Ithaca, N.Y.: Cornell University Press, 1956.
Erdman, David V., ed. *The Complete Poetry and Prose of William Blake*, revised edition. Berkeley: University of California Press, 1982.
Ferber, Michael. "Shelley and 'The Disastrous Fame of Conquerors.'" *Keats-Shelley Journal* 51 (2002), 145–73.
Oswald, Alice. *Memorial: An Excavation of the* Iliad. London: Faber, 2011.
Plett, Heinrich F. Enargeia *in Classical Antiquity and the Early Modern Age: The Aesthetics of Evidence.* Leiden: Brill, 2012.
Rorty, Richard. "Against Belatedness." *London Review of Books*, June 16, 1983, 3–5.
Sontag, Susan. Review of *Selected Essays*, by Simone Weil (1962), translated by Richard Rees. *New York Review of Books*, Feb. 1, 1963.

ACKNOWLEDGMENTS

This is to thank everyone who, over many years, knowingly or not, has helped me along Homer's tangled paths.

George Fairhurst; Vassilis Papadimitriou; Gavin Francis; Robert Macfarlane; Ali Serle; Juliet Nicolson; Rebecca Nicolson; Aurea Carpenter; Andrew Palmer; Paul Johnston; Alexandra Chaldecott; Ivan Samarine; Jim Richardson; Oliver Payne; Claire Whalley; Koenraad Kuiper; Liz Broomfield; Mary Keen; Laura Beatty; Martin Thomas; Matthew Reynolds; Matthew Rice; Nicholas Purcell; Philip Marsden; Robert Sackville-West; Richard Klein; Sarah Longley; Sigrid Rausing; Stephen Romer; Thomas Pennybacker; Casey Dué; David Sansone; Garry Fabian Miller; Charlie Burrell; Issy Burrell.

Sofka Zinovieff is the best friend, guide and companion anyone could wish for. Tim Dee took me to all sorts of Homeric places in a way that transformed my understanding of Homer. Caroline Alexander came and talked about my Homeric ideas for many vigorous and illuminating hours. David Anthony provided supremely helpful signposts to the world of the steppe.

I would particularly like to thank Kylie Richardson of Trinity Hall, Cambridge, and Matt Hosty of Jesus College, Oxford, for the care and trouble they took in saving me from the worst of mistakes. Needless to say, they bear no responsibility for those that remain.

At Henry Holt, Courtney Reed has been efficiency itself and Jack Macrae nothing short of an inspiration. I would particularly like to thank

Zoë Pagnamenta, my agent, for encouragement and brilliance over many years.

Above all I want to thank my wife, Sarah, and the children for co-habiting with Homer, who is not the easiest of houseguests, for quite so long. This book is dedicated to them.

Sarah Raven
Molly Nicolson
Rosie Nicolson
Benedict Nicolson
William Nicolson
Thomas Nicolson

INDEX

Page numbers in *italics* refer to illustrations.

ABOUT THE AUTHOR

ADAM NICOLSON's books include *Sissinghurst, God's Secretaries, Sea Room* and the acclaimed *Gentry*. He is winner of the Somerset Maugham Award and the W. H. Heinemann and Ondaatje Prizes, both awarded by the Royal Society of Literature. He lives on a farm in Sussex with his wife, Sarah Raven.